Vietnam Tax Guide

Lorenzo Riccardi

Vietnam Tax Guide

Domestic Fiscal System and International Treaties

Lorenzo Riccardi
Bergamo
Italy

ISBN 978-3-319-02137-9   ISBN 978-3-319-02138-6 (eBook)
DOI 10.1007/978-3-319-02138-6
Springer Cham Heidelberg New York Dordrecht London

© Springer International Publishing Switzerland 2014
This work is subject to copyright. All rights are reserved by the Publisher, whether the whole or part of the material is concerned, specifically the rights of translation, reprinting, reuse of illustrations, recitation, broadcasting, reproduction on microfilms or in any other physical way, and transmission or information storage and retrieval, electronic adaptation, computer software, or by similar or dissimilar methodology now known or hereafter developed. Exempted from this legal reservation are brief excerpts in connection with reviews or scholarly analysis or material supplied specifically for the purpose of being entered and executed on a computer system, for exclusive use by the purchaser of the work. Duplication of this publication or parts thereof is permitted only under the provisions of the Copyright Law of the Publisher's location, in its current version, and permission for use must always be obtained from Springer. Permissions for use may be obtained through RightsLink at the Copyright Clearance Center. Violations are liable to prosecution under the respective Copyright Law.
The use of general descriptive names, registered names, trademarks, service marks, etc. in this publication does not imply, even in the absence of a specific statement, that such names are exempt from the relevant protective laws and regulations and therefore free for general use.
While the advice and information in this book are believed to be true and accurate at the date of publication, neither the authors nor the editors nor the publisher can accept any legal responsibility for any errors or omissions that may be made. The publisher makes no warranty, express or implied, with respect to the material contained herein.

Printed on acid-free paper

Springer is part of Springer Science+Business Media (www.springer.com)

For my mother.

Contents

Part I Vietnamese Tax System

1 Introduction to the Vietnamese Tax System 3
   1.1 Legislative Background and Tax Reform 3
   1.2 VAT Changes 4
   1.3 Types of Taxes 4

2 Personal Income Tax 7
   2.1 General Principles 7
   2.2 Tax for Residents and Non-Residents 7
         2.2.1 Tax Year 8
   2.3 Taxable Income 8
   2.4 Exempt Income 9
   2.5 Deductions and Tax Breaks 9
   2.6 Tax Rates 10
         2.6.1 Resident Persons 10
   2.7 Tax Administration 10
         2.7.1 Tax Registration 10
   2.8 Declaration and Payment of Taxes 10
   2.9 Social Contributions 11

3 Income Tax on Enterprises 13
   3.1 Rates and Tax Incentives 13
   3.2 Determination of Taxable Income 14
         3.2.1 Calculation Formula 14
         3.2.2 Tax Administration 15
         3.2.3 Deductible Expenses 15
         3.2.4 Depreciation 16
         3.2.5 Losses Carry Forward 16
   3.3 Taxes on Income from the Sale of Shares 16

	3.4	Withholding Tax	17
		3.4.1 Methods of Payment	17
		3.4.2 Agreements Against Double Taxation	19
		3.4.3 Dividends	19
	3.5	Anti-Avoidance Rules	19
		3.5.1 Thin Capitalization and Anti-Avoidance Rules	19
		3.5.2 Transfer Pricing	19
4	**Turnover Taxes and Other Taxes**		**21**
	4.1	Value Added Tax	21
		4.1.1 Scope of VAT	21
		4.1.2 Goods and Services Exempted from VAT	21
		4.1.3 VAT Rates	22
		4.1.4 Calculation of VAT	22
	4.2	Tax Administration	23
	4.3	Special Sales Tax	23
		4.3.1 Tax Rates	24
	4.4	Capital Duty and Stamp Duty	24
	4.5	Duties on Imports and Exports	24
		4.5.1 Tax Rates	24
		4.5.2 Calculation of Import Tariffs	25
		4.5.3 Exemption from Duties on Imports	26
		4.5.4 Reimbursement of Duties on Imports	26
		4.5.5 Duties on Exports	26
5	**Audit and Transfer Pricing Policies**		**27**
	5.1	Background of Tax Audits	27
	5.2	Background of Accounting and Auditing	29
	5.3	Definitions and Application in Vietnam	30
	5.4	OECD Guidelines	31
		5.4.1 Advance Pricing Arrangement ("APA")	32
		5.4.2 Arm's Length Principle	32
		5.4.3 Arm's Length Range	32
		5.4.4 Associated Enterprises	32
		5.4.5 Balancing Payment	32
		5.4.6 Buy-in Payment	33
		5.4.7 Buy-Out Payment	33
		5.4.8 Commercial Intangible	33
		5.4.9 Comparability Analysis	33
		5.4.10 Comparable Uncontrolled Transaction	33
		5.4.11 Comparable Uncontrolled Price (CUP) Method	34
		5.4.12 Compensating Adjustment	34
		5.4.13 Contribution Analysis	34
		5.4.14 Controlled Transactions	34
		5.4.15 Corresponding Adjustment	34

	5.4.16	Cost Contribution Arrangement ("CCA")	35
	5.4.17	Cost Plus Mark Up	35
	5.4.18	Cost Plus Method	35
	5.4.19	Direct-Charge Method	35
	5.4.20	Direct Costs	35
	5.4.21	Functional Analysis	35
	5.4.22	Global Formulary Apportionment	36
	5.4.23	Gross Profits	36
	5.4.24	Independent Enterprises	36
	5.4.25	Intra-Group Service	36
	5.4.26	Intentional Set-Off	36
	5.4.27	Marketing Intangible	36
	5.4.28	Multinational Enterprise Group (MNE Group)	37
	5.4.29	Multinational Enterprise (MNE)	37
	5.4.30	Mutual Agreement Procedure	37
	5.4.31	Net Profit Indicator	37
	5.4.32	"On Call" Services	37
	5.4.33	Primary Adjustment	37
	5.4.34	Profit Potential	38
	5.4.35	Profit Split Method	38
	5.4.36	Resale Price Margin	38
	5.4.37	Resale Price Method	38
	5.4.38	Residual Analysis	38
	5.4.39	Secondary Adjustment	39
	5.4.40	Secondary Transaction	39
	5.4.41	Shareholder Activity	39
	5.4.42	Simultaneous Tax Examinations	39
	5.4.43	Trade Intangible	39
	5.4.44	Traditional Transaction Method	40
	5.4.45	Transactional Net Margin Method	40
	5.4.46	Transactional Profit Method	40
	5.4.47	Uncontrolled Transactions	40
5.5	Transfer Pricing in Vietnam		40
5.6	Related Party Transactions		41
5.7	Documentation and Disclosure Requirements		41
5.8	Penalties		42
5.9	Transfer Pricing Methods		43
	5.9.1	Comparable Uncontrolled Price Method (CUP)	43
	5.9.2	Resale Price Method (Table 5.5)	44
	5.9.3	Cost Plus Method (Table 5.5)	44
	5.9.4	Profit Split Method	44
	5.9.5	Note on Deductions	44
5.10	Transfer Pricing Audit and Adjustments		45
5.11	Advance Pricing Arrangements (APA)		46

Part II International Treaties

6 Introduction to International Taxation and Treaties 49
    6.1   Conventions Against Double Taxation 49

7 American Area Treaties 51
    7.1   Vietnam–American Area Bilateral Agreements' History 51
        7.1.1   Vietnam–USA Bilateral Agreement's History
                    and Evolution 51
        7.1.2   Vietnam–Canada Bilateral Agreement's History 52
    7.2   Canada–Vietnam Treaty 55

8 Asian Area Treaties 71
    8.1   Vietnam–Asian Area Bilateral Agreements' History 71
        8.1.1   Vietnam–India Bilateral Agreement's History
                    and Evolution 71
        8.1.2   Vietnam–Singapore Bilateral Agreement's History
                    and Evolution 72
        8.1.3   Vietnam–Korea Bilateral Agreement's History and
                    Evolution 73
        8.1.4   Vietnam–Japan Bilateral Agreement's History and
                    Evolution 75
        8.1.5   Vietnam–China Bilateral Agreement's History and
                    Evolution 76
        8.1.6   Vietnam–Thailand Bilateral Agreement's History and
                    Evolution 77
        8.1.7   Vietnam–Taiwan Bilateral Agreement's History and
                    Evolution 78
        8.1.8   Vietnam–Hong Kong Bilateral Agreement's History 80
    8.2   Thailand–Vietnam Treaty 81
    8.3   Korea–Vietnam Treaty 94
    8.4   China–Vietnam Treaty 108
    8.5   Hong Kong–Vietnam Treaty 122

9 European Area Treaties 139
    9.1   Vietnam–European Union Bilateral Agreement's History
            and Evolution 139
    9.2   Italy–Vietnam Treaty 141
    9.3   Sweden–Vietnam Treaty 156
    9.4   Denmark–Vietnam Treaty 170
    9.5   Germany–Vietnam Treaty 188

Bibliography 205

Part I
Vietnamese Tax System

Chapter 1
Introduction to the Vietnamese Tax System

1.1 Legislative Background and Tax Reform

In recent years, Vietnam has established itself as one of the most popular investment destinations in East Asia. Some of the characteristics of Vietnam that make it attractive to investors include a well-educated population, a strong potential labor market, mineral resources, proximity to other key markets in Southeast Asia, continued support from foreign aid, a strong potential consumer goods industry, a government committed to economic progress, and economic incentives for investment in certain types of businesses.

Vietnam, which started as a one-party state run by the collective leadership of the Communist Party General Secretary, Prime Minister, and President, has committed significant resources to promote its transition towards a market economy. It has also experimented with more flexible strategies and market-oriented policies aimed at promoting the growing private sector, as well as the achievement of macroeconomic stability.

However, despite Vietnam's economic progress, its banking system remains poorly developed—to combat this problem, the Vietnamese government has launched several reforms aimed at improving its financial system and strengthening the stability of its national banks, and those measures have allowed the country to guarantee loans made by lenders—thus, significantly enhancing the financial stability and transparency of the country.

Vietnam has also recently reformed its tax system in order to adapt its regulatory system to the country's economic development. The new *Enterprise Income Tax Law*, which replaced the previous legislation on the taxation of business income, has been in effect since January 1st, 2009. The Personal Income Tax *Law* was also introduced on January 1st, 2009—this law introduced major changes in the system of taxation on individual income and eliminated previously existing tax-treatment disparities between citizens and foreigners in Vietnam.

Several sources of law govern different types of taxes: the *Enterprise Income Tax Law* regulates taxation on business income, the *Personal Income Tax Law* sets the framework for the taxation of individuals, and the VAT is governed by the *Law on Value Added Tax*. The General Department of Taxation, under the Ministry of Finance, constitutes the tax authorities in Vietnam. Circulars, rulings, and regulations further specify the implementation of the laws to which they refer.

1.2 VAT Changes

A VAT Decree was issued on December 27th, 2011, expanding the definition of VAT exempt supplies. Effective from March 1st, 2012, VAT exemptions include the following supplies:

- Export of goods and services with special conditions for international transportation,
- Certain financial transactions,
- Goods and services provided outside of Vietnam,
- Assets disposed of for liquidation purposes,
- Additional goods and services such as financing services, reinsurance, debt factoring, foreign currency trading, and securities trading services.

The new regulation included a change to the VAT taxable value of goods and services, subject to special sales tax (SST) and environment tax and certain land transfer transactions.

Such Decree introduced a disallowance of deduction of the input VAT incurred on the purchase of machinery and equipment by credit institutions and enterprises involved in reinsurance, life insurance, and securities trading.

1.3 Types of Taxes

Most foreign investments and foreign investors will be subject to the following taxes:

- Corporate Income Tax,
- Various withholding taxes,
- Capital Assignment Profits Tax,
- Value Added Tax,
- Import duties,
- Personal Income Tax of Vietnamese and expatriate employees, and
- Social insurance, unemployment insurance, and health insurance contributions.

There are various other taxes that may affect only certain investors:

- Special Sales Tax,
- Natural Resources Tax,

1.3 Types of Taxes

- Property taxes,
- Export duties, and
- Environment Protection Tax.

All these taxes are imposed at the national level; there are no local, state, or provincial taxes.

Chapter 2
Personal Income Tax

2.1 General Principles

The new law on personal income taxes (Personal Income Tax Law, or PIT Law) replaced Ordinance 35, which only taxed the income of individuals in the high-income sectors. This new tax law has features that represent a significant departure from the older system, including the extension of the scope of the Personal Income Tax to nearly all the income earned by individuals, as well as to income previously exempt from income tax. The new system also taxes residents and foreigners on similar criteria, in place of the older two-tier system that taxed them separately. Furthermore, the reform introduced deductions and allowances for individuals and families and implemented new administrative procedures and data storage useful to the monitoring, calculation, and payment of tribute.

2.2 Tax for Residents and Non-Residents

Personal Income Tax is applied based on the residence principle. Residents are taxed on their total income, while non-residents are taxed only on income earned in Vietnam. The existing law uses different tax rates for residents and non-residents, as well as for different types of income.

Taxpayers who are considered residents:

- Those who have lived in Vietnam for more than 183 consecutive days or for 12 months from first entry into the country,
- Those who have a domicile in Vietnam, which implies a place of permanent residence or a real estate lease for a period exceeding 90 days in a fiscal year.

Resident taxpayers are subject to progressive tax rates (Tables 2.1 and 2.2) based on their global income, meaning income earned regardless of its source. Non-resident taxpayers who do not meet the above conditions are subject to a

Table 2.1 Personal income tax rates in Vietnam, employment and service income for residents

Annual taxable income (million VND)	Monthly taxable income (million VND)	Tax rate (%)
0–60	0–5	5
60–120	5–10	10
120–216	10–18	15
216–384	18–32	20
384–624	32–52	25
624–960	52–80	30
>960	>80	35

fixed tax rate of 20 % on their income derived from work carried out in Vietnam and are subject to other various tax rates in reference to income not derived from work-related activities (Table 2.3).

2.2.1 Tax Year

The Vietnamese tax year is the calendar year. However, where in the first year of arrival, if an individual is present in Vietnam for less than 183 days, his/her first tax year is the first 12 consecutive months from the first month of arrival. Subsequently, the tax year is the calendar year.

2.3 Taxable Income

Taxable income includes income arising from conducting business activities and other sources of income. Compensation of employees comprises all income paid by the employer to the employee, either in cash or in kind, and includes:

- Wages, salaries, bonuses, allowances, and subsidies;
- Income earned from participation in professional and trade associations, boards of directors, and management of companies, etc.;
- Benefits in kind paid by the employer, including but not limited to rents, the cost of water and other services, non-compulsory insurance premiums, membership fees, and certain other benefits provided in accordance with current legislation.

Certain categories of income, not previously taxed, were recently included within the scope of the tax law—for example, investment income, transfers of real property, royalties, commercial franchises, inheritances, and gifts.

Table 2.2 Personal income tax rates in Vietnam, non-employment income for residents

Taxable income	Tax rate
Interests	5 %
Dividends	5 %
Royalties	5 %
Gain on sale of securities	20 %
Capital gain	20 %
Sale of real estate	25 % on gain, 2 % on proceed
Inheritances/prizes	10 %

Table 2.3 Personal income tax rates in Vietnam for non-residents

Taxable income	Tax rate
Interests	5 %
Dividends	5 %
Royalties	5 %
Business income	1–5 %
Gain on sale of securities	20 %
Capital gain	0.1 % on proceeds
Sale of real estate	2 % on proceed
Inheritances/prizes	10 %

2.4 Exempt Income

The following income is exempt from personal income tax:

- Interest on money deposited in banks and credit institutions in Vietnam, as well as interest on life insurance policies;
- Contribution payments on life insurance policies;
- Payments of social security contributions on pensions of individuals in accordance with the provisions contained in the applicable laws on social security;
- Income from certain officially approved charitable institutions;
- Expenditures on stationery, telephone calls, daily allowances, and clothing;
- Income from real estate transfers between spouses, parents, and children;
- Income from inheritance/gifts between spouses, parents, and children;
- Scholarships and other allowances recognized by colleges and training institutions in Vietnam and abroad.

2.5 Deductions and Tax Breaks

Certain fees and charges are deductible from business income and income from employment based on the following criteria:

- A personal deduction is granted amounting to VND 4 million/month or VND 48 million/year.

- Tax relief is granted with respect to dependents, amounting to VND 1.6 million/month or VND 19.2 million/year, for each dependent (appropriate documentation is required to substantiate this request).
- Compulsory contributions and health insurance benefits in accordance with regulations are deductible.
- Contributions to certain funds for the promotion of charitable, humanitarian, and educational causes are deductible.

2.6 Tax Rates

2.6.1 Resident Persons

The progressive tax rates for foreign residents and Vietnamese citizens are shown in Table 2.4.

Effective January 1st, 2009, the following income tax rates also apply (Table 2.5).

With regard to income from non-employment activities, see Table 2.6.

2.7 Tax Administration

2.7.1 Tax Registration

Tax registration is mandatory for all institutions and individuals whose taxable income is subject to the PIT Law. The entity designated to receive the registration form of the tax code is represented by the tax office directly and is also responsible for the receipt of the income from tax of entities and individual taxpayers.

2.8 Declaration and Payment of Taxes

Declaration of the Personal Income Tax must be submitted on a monthly basis by the 20th day of the month following the reporting period. The employer acts as a withholding agent of taxes by the 20th of the following month. Business income is declared on a quarterly basis, and the related tax returns must be submitted by the 30th of the month following the quarter of competence. Other income is taxed on a separate basis for each single transaction. In the event that the tax payment is made in excess, a tax credit will be recognized to offset the future periodic payments.

Table 2.4 Progressive tax rates for foreign residents and Vietnamese citizens

Bracket	Personal income (VND)	Tax rate (%)
1	0–5,000,000	5
2	5,000,001–10,000,000	10
3	10,000,001–18,000,000	15
4	18,000,001–32,000,000	20
5	32,000,001–52,000,000	25
6	52,000,001–80,000,000	30
7	>80,000,000	35

Table 2.5 Other income tax rates

Categories	Tax rate (%)
Income from capital gains	5
Income from commercials and royalties	5
Compensation from awards, winnings, inheritances, and gifts	10
Income from transfer of shares	0.1
Income from real estate transfers	25
Income from real estate transfers in the case that value cannot be determined	2

Table 2.6 Tax rates for income from non-employment activities

Categories	Tax rate (%)
Sale of goods	1
Provision of services	5
Manufacturing, construction, transportation, and other business activities	2

2.9 Social Contributions

The related contributions to social security (social insurance) and unemployment (unemployment insurance) are applicable only to Vietnamese employees, while the related contributions to health insurance (health insurance) are provided to both Vietnamese and foreigners.

Social security contributions are summarized in Table 2.7.

Such contributions by the employer do not constitute a taxable benefit to the employee and shall be regarded as deductible in calculating the Personal Income Tax.

Remuneration subject to social security contributions is considered on the basis of the salary indicated in the employment contract, limited to 20 times the minimum wage (Table 2.8), which varies by zones in the country.

Table 2.7 Social security contributions

Contributions and welfare			
	Social insurance (%)	Unemployment insurance (%)	Health insurance (%)
Employee	6	1	1.5
Employer	16	1	3

Table 2.8 Minimum wage in Vietnam (VND) for local and foreign companies by zone

Minimum wage in Vietnam (VND)		
Zone	Vietnamese company	Foreign company
1	980,000	1,340,000
2	880,000	1,190,000
3	810,000	1,040,000
4	730,000	1,000,000

Chapter 3
Income Tax on Enterprises

3.1 Rates and Tax Incentives

The Enterprise Income Tax Law (hereinafter EITL), approved in May 2008, changed the tax rate of legal persons (local and foreign) from 28 to 25 % starting from January 1st, 2009. This reform is similar to the situation in China a year earlier (January 1st, 2008), in which an equal level of tax was established for local and foreign companies via the definitive abolishment of the "tax holiday." For oil and gas companies, as well as companies involved in the use of precious metals, varying rates are enforced—ranging from 32 to 50 %. The law grants tax incentives based on the location of investments, such as in areas with poor socioeconomic conditions, special economic zones, or areas affected by high-technology projects, and other specially regulated sectors.

The Vietnamese government has encouraged investment in a number of areas, including new technology, water plants, power plants, water supply systems, airports, seaports, and rivers, as well as other major infrastructure such as bridges, roads, and railways. This effort has stimulated culture, sport, education, scientific research, vocational training, medical care, and environmental protection. The incentives take the form of a preferential tax rate or a tax exemption period.

1. The preferential tax rate is 10 % for a term of 15 years or 20 % for a term of 10 years starting with the first profitable year.
2. The tax exemption is granted from the application of EIT for a period of 2–4 years starting from the first profitable year. It is then to grant a reduction of 50 % for a period ranging between 4 and 9 years. If the enterprise has been profitable for the first 3 years of its operations, the tax exemption will begin from the fourth year of operation.

The eligibility criteria for these incentives and the tax exemptions are set by the EIT regulations. Additional tax relief may be granted to those firms operating in manufacturing, construction, or transportation activities and employing a higher percentage of females and/or ethnic minorities. The duration of the preferential tax

Table 3.1 EIT law incentives

Incentives	Further incentives	Beneficiaries of the incentives
Tax rate of 10 % applies for 15 years	– Exemption from EIT for up to 4 years – 50 % reduction in EIT for up to 9 years	New companies incorporated in a region on the list of geographical areas, extremely difficult economic zones, and areas of high technology
		New companies that invest in the high-tech fields of software production, scientific research, and technological development or in infrastructure development considered important by the State
		New companies operating in sectors such as education, vocational training, health, culture, sports, and environment
Tax rate of 20 % applies for 10 years	– Exemption from EIT for up to 2 years – 50 % reduction in EIT for a maximum of 4 years	New companies created in a region on the list of geographical areas with difficult socioeconomic conditions

rates can be extended for projects that require the attraction of new investments but cannot exceed the period indicated above.

Table 3.1 shows the main incentives applicable to the new Enterprise Income Tax Law.

There are also other cases in which projects are eligible for tax cuts:

- Companies that produce, manufacture, or transport, and which employ a large number of female employees, are entitled to a reduction of corporate income tax equal to the amount of additional expenses incurred by the employees themselves.
- Businesses that have favored the employment of individuals belonging to ethnic minorities are entitled to a reduction of income tax equal to the amount of additional expenses incurred for the employees themselves.

3.2 Determination of Taxable Income

3.2.1 Calculation Formula

Taxable income is calculated on the basis of the difference between total revenues, whether domestic or foreign in origin, and deductible expenses, to which is added additional taxable income, including income produced outside of Vietnam:

3.2 Determination of Taxable Income

Taxable income = [(revenues − expenses deductible) + other income] − (exempt income + losses carried forward).

The Enterprise Income Tax is calculated using the following formula:

EIT payable = taxable income × tax rate.

3.2.2 Tax Administration

The standard tax year usually coincides with the calendar year (January 1st to December 31st). However, a different accounting and tax year could be used with express authorization from the Ministry of Finance. The quarterly income statements must be filed on the basis of revenues and costs recorded in the reference quarter. The annual statement must be made available before March 30th of the year following the tax period. The Enterprise Income Tax for the fiscal year always coincides with the calendar year. Finally, expect quarterly payments along with the corresponding interim financial statements to be filed every 3 months; a net cash payment to the authority will be effected following the submission of the annual filing. The deadline for the submission of tax returns is between 30 days after the reference quarter and the last date for any adjustment to year-end for the period after March 30th. There are penalties for late payments, including a daily fine of 0.05 % of the total amount owed, while tax evasion is subject to more severe penalties (up to three times the amount evaded). A taxpayer who owns subsidiaries located in different provinces should use a single annual tax return except in the case of manufacturing companies, which are required to allocate the payment of taxes to various tax authorities at the provincial level in the place where business is conducted. This allocation is calculated using the percentage of costs (of the company's total costs) borne by each separate branch.

3.2.3 Deductible Expenses

In general, costs are considered deductible if they are related to business activity, supported by invoices or other relevant documents, and not specifically identified as non-deductible items in calculating EIT. Some examples of non-deductible costs include the following:

- Depreciation of fixed assets not complying with regulations;
- Salaries of employees who are not actually paid or are not specified in a collective or individual employment contract;
- Insurance premiums on life insurance for employees;

- Interest on loans made by organizations that are not banks or interest rates greater than 1.5 times the base interest rate set by the State Bank of Vietnam (SBV);
- Provisions for inventory obsolescence, uncollectible receivables, loss of financial investments, product warranties, or construction that does not conform to the norms set by the Ministry of Finance (MOF);
- Advertising expenses exceeding 10 % of the total of the other deductible expenses (this roof has been increased to 15 % for new firms with respect to the first 3 years of activity);
- Donations, except those made for education, health, natural disaster relief or for the construction of houses for the poor;
- Administrative penalties;
- VAT, EIT, and PIT.

3.2.4 Depreciation

Depreciation for tax purposes must comply with the regulations set by the MOF. The depreciation rates, which are set by Circular 203/2009 (issued by the Ministry of Finance), regulate lifespan minimums and maximums for each category of tangible and intangible assets. The companies' foreign capital should be used in the calculation of depreciation. Depreciation occurs on a linear basis and uses the value of the purchase (i.e. plant) minus the estimated residual value of the asset over its estimated useful life. Different criteria are applied only in certain cases governed by the MOF. Accelerated depreciation may be allowed in some cases, but with a depreciation ratio greater than two times the value set by the MOF. The main depreciation rates are shown in Table 3.2.

3.2.5 Losses Carry Forward

Taxpayers are allowed to carry forward losses that are incurred in the performance of business activities for a maximum period of 5 consecutive years. Currently, in Vietnam, the tax law does not contain any provisions related to any loss of a consolidated group.

3.3 Taxes on Income from the Sale of Shares

EIT law taxes 25 % of the profits arising from the transfer of shares or sale of securities (including stocks, bonds, certificates of funds, and other regulated securities). The taxable capital gains are determined as the excess of sales revenues

Table 3.2 Depreciation rates for various assets

Depreciation rates	
Category	Amortization period
Intangible assets	Not more than 30 years
Industrial and commercial buildings	From 25 to 50 years
Real estate	From 6 to 25 years
Machinery	From 5 to 15 years
Vehicles	From 6 to 30 years
Office equipment	From 3 to 10 years

Table 3.3 Taxes subject to EIT

Seller	Subject to EIT
Local organization	Income arising from the transfer of shares or sale of securities
Foreign organization that does not have its registered office in Vietnam	The transferee has the obligation to withhold tax from payment due to the seller

The tax return and payment must be made within 10 days from the date that the sale is approved by tax authorities. The date of the sale agreement does not require any specific authorization

over the purchase cost of the transferred capital and the associated transfer costs. Depending on the nature of the transaction, the transferor may also be subject to EIT as shown in Table 3.3.

3.4 Withholding Tax

The withholding tax known as the Foreign Contractor Withholding Tax (FCWT)—with respect to payment of interest, royalties, dividends, license fees, chargebacks for costs incurred by foreign entities, cross-border leases, insurance and reinsurance—requires the related buyer to pay a different amount for shipping and air transport. A withholding tax of 10 % is applied to interest paid on loans from foreign entities, with a possible exemption for those granted before 1999. A withholding tax of 10 % applies to royalty payments made to a foreign entity with respect to transfers of technology, defined in general terms. The Transport/Freight Tax was repealed as of January 1st, 2009, so since then foreign companies engaged in transport services have also been subject to the FCWT.

3.4.1 Methods of Payment

There are three methods for foreign entities to pay withholding taxes: the method of compensation, the direct method, and the hybrid method.

3.4.1.1 Method of Compensation

Foreign entities may register for VAT and EIT if they meet the following requirements:

- Possession of a permanent establishment in Vietnam or possession of a tax residence in Vietnam,
- A project to be executed in Vietnam that has a duration equal to or greater than 183 days,
- Adoption of the system of accounting in accordance with Vietnamese regulations.

The contractor is required to notify the Vietnamese tax office that the foreign entity will pay tax according to the method of compensation within 20 working days from the date at which the contract is signed. If the foreign entity carries out numerous projects and is qualified to apply the method of compensation to a single project, it will be required to apply this method to the other projects, subject to an EIT rate of 25 % on the profits. According to this method of tax payment, declarations and payments are made directly by the foreign entity. This method also allows the foreign company to charge VAT to customers in Vietnam and to offset VAT on purchases (up to the amount of VAT on sales).

3.4.1.2 Direct Method

If the foreign entity does not meet the above requirements, it must resort to the direct method. Taxes (VAT and EIT) will be withheld by the Vietnamese contracting party while applying the percentage in reference to the turnover tax and rates categorized according to the nature of the services provided. The VAT withheld by the Vietnamese contractor is generally regarded as a tax credit eligible for the VAT declaration.

3.4.1.3 Hybrid Method

This method allows foreign entities to register for VAT and make payments according to the method of compensation while remaining to be subject to payment of the EIT on the basis of prediction. Foreign entrepreneurs who wish to adopt the hybrid method must meet the following requirements:

- Be a tax resident of Vietnam or possess a permanent establishment there,
- Operate in Vietnam under a contract with a term of not less than 183 days,
- Manage the accounts in accordance with accounting regulations and guidelines provided by the MOF tax.

3.4.2 Agreements Against Double Taxation

The previously mentioned withholding tax can vary with respect to the application of the provisions contained in agreements against double taxation, resulting, for example, in a reduction or total exemption of EIT. To date, Vietnam has already signed about 60 agreements on tax matters, and many other agreements appear to be under implementation or negotiation.

3.4.3 Dividends

Dividends paid to foreign corporate investors are not taxed in accordance with national legislation (Table 3.4).

3.5 Anti-Avoidance Rules

3.5.1 Thin Capitalization and Anti-Avoidance Rules

To date, Vietnam has not implemented a general anti-avoidance standard in tax matters, though there are specific restrictions in respect to thin-capitalization companies. In order to maintain a fair balance between capital and debt, the legislation does not have anti-avoidance measures that affect the deductibility of interest by financial institutions or related parties.

3.5.2 Transfer Pricing

The Ministry of Finance issued the first legislative guideline on transfer pricing on December 19th, 2005 (Circular 117/2005) (Circular 177). Circular 177, which came into force on January 28th, 2006, introduces the basic principles related to transfer pricing between related parties, adopting regulations in line with the OECD Transfer Pricing Guidelines. On April 22nd, 2010, the MOF issued Circular 66/2010, replacing Circular 117, which came into force on June 6th, 2010, and is considered the most comprehensive regulation. Retaining the main compliance requirements, Circular 66 also introduced several changes in tightening the requirements on transfer pricing. The methods covered by the local rules for calculating transfer prices are shown in Table 3.5.

The legislation does not prefer any method specifically but requires that companies make an annual declaration related to transactions between related parties to be submitted with the annual tax return on the Enterprise Income Tax.

Table 3.4 Taxes on dividend payments to foreign investors

Entity	Income tax (%)
Company with a permanent establishment in Vietnam	0
Company without a permanent establishment in Vietnam (i.e. dividends that are remitted abroad)	0
Foreign resident of Vietnam	5

Table 3.5 Transfer pricing methods

Methods for calculating transfer prices	
Transfer Pricing methods:	Comparable uncontrolled price method
	Resale price method
	Cost-plus method
	Comparable profit method
	Profit split method

Taxpayers are also required to document ongoing transactions between related parties in order to demonstrate the appropriateness of the transfer prices. The authorities may make adjustments if the transfer prices are not considered to be at market price; however, the local law does not regulate any arrangement between the companies and tax authorities regarding the prices of transactions between related companies (Advanced Pricing Agreement).

Chapter 4
Turnover Taxes and Other Taxes

4.1 Value Added Tax

4.1.1 Scope of VAT

VAT is applied to goods and services used for activities involving production, trade, and/or consumption within the Vietnamese territory, including goods and services purchased abroad. In addition, VAT is also applicable to the value of customs duty paid on imported goods. The payment of VAT is calculated based on the difference between the output VAT calculated on income and the VAT credit on purchases of goods and services.

4.1.2 Goods and Services Exempted from VAT

The categories of products and services exempted from the scope of VAT include the following:

- Certain agricultural products;
- Transfer of land use rights;
- Financial and credit services;
- Certain insurance services (including life insurance and non-commercial);
- Health services;
- Education and training;
- Printing and publication of newspapers, magazines, and certain types of books;
- Transfers of technology and software services;
- Products exported with unprocessed minerals such as crude oil, rocks, sand, earth, and rare stones;

- Imports of machinery, equipment, and special means of transport to be used directly in research and technological development (which cannot be performed in Vietnam);
- Equipment, machinery, spare parts, special means of transport used, and materials necessary for the prospecting, exploration, and development of oil and gas (which cannot be produced in Vietnam).

4.1.3 VAT Rates

There are three VAT rates as outlined below:

- *Zero percent*—This rate is applied to exported goods, including property sold to companies without a permanent establishment in Vietnam (and companies operating in free trade zones), processed goods for export, goods sold in commercial duty-free export services, construction and installation works carried out abroad, and the international aviation and maritime transport.
- *Five percent*—This rate is generally applied to certain economic sectors involved in the supply of essential goods and services, such as drinking water, fertilizer production, teaching aids, books, food, medicine, medical equipment, various agricultural products and services, scientific and technical services, etc.
- *Ten percent*—This standard rate is applied to activities not specified as exempt or subject to the previous rates of 0 or 5 %.

4.1.4 Calculation of VAT

The output VAT is calculated by multiplying the taxable value by the applicable VAT rate. With respect to imported goods, VAT is calculated on the import price plus import duty and sales tax. With respect to goods sold as installment sales (excluding real estate), VAT is calculated on the total price rather than on the installment payments actually received.

4.1.4.1 Tax Credits

The VAT credits can be used from the month in which the purchase invoice is issued, while imports are calculated as of the date of payment at the customs office. The VAT credit can be compensated only in cases where payments are made through the banking system, with the exception of purchases of less than VND 20 million. When a company sells goods or services exempt from VAT, it cannot recover the tax paid on their purchases, but the company can claim a tax credit in relation to sales tax in the amount paid for the year's taxable activity.

4.1.4.2 Methods of Calculating VAT

The Vietnamese tax law provides two methods of calculating VAT:

(a) Method of compensation
   Under this method, the VAT liability is calculated by subtracting the VAT charged to customers from the VAT paid on purchases of products and services. For the purposes of applying the method of compensation to calculate VAT, it is necessary to ensure proper bookkeeping and preservation of invoices and supporting documents.
(b) Direct method
   Under this method, the value at which the VAT tax rate will be applied must have been previously calculated in order to calculate the VAT payable.

4.1.4.3 VAT Refund

The refund of VAT credit is provided only in some cases, such as when the VAT credit is greater than the VAT payable for a period of 3 consecutive months. The refund can be made monthly, quarterly, or yearly, depending on the conditions of individual taxpayers.

4.2 Tax Administration

Any organization or individual engaged in the primary production or trade of goods and taxable services in Vietnam must make a special registration for VAT. In some cases, the branches of a company must register separately, making the declaration on VAT proportional to their business activities. The VAT returns must be filed monthly by the taxpayer before the 20th day of the following month.

4.3 Special Sales Tax

The Special Sales Tax, also referred to as the Special Consumption Tax, represents a form of excise duty that is applied in reference to the production or importation of certain goods or the provision of certain services, which are also subject to the imposition of VAT.
   The Law on Special Sales recognizes two distinct categories:
- Goods: cigarettes, liquor, vehicles with less than 24 seats, motorbikes, airplanes, ships, and gasoline;
- Services: discos, massage centers, karaoke, casinos, gambling activities, golf clubs, betting shops, and lotteries.

Table 4.1 Applicable tax rates on various goods/services

Goods/services	Tax rate (%)
Cigarettes	65
Liquor	25–45
Vehicles with less than 24 seats	10–60
Motorcycles with a cylinder capacity exceeding 125 cc	20
Airplanes	30
Ships	30
Gasoline	10
Discos	40
Massage centers	30
Casino and gambling activities	30
Golf clubs	20
Betting shops	30
Lotteries	15

4.3.1 Tax Rates

In the following Table 4.1 are resumed the principal tax rates for goods and services under the Special Sales Tax Law.

4.4 Capital Duty and Stamp Duty

The Vietnamese tax system does not include stamp duty, although there exists the administrative burden of registration and renewal of licenses corresponding to the nature of the company's activities. Companies are required to pay the Business Tax Registration (Table 4.2) annually at the beginning of the calendar year according to the following tax rates parameterized according to the value of social capital as indicated in the documents of incorporation.

4.5 Duties on Imports and Exports

4.5.1 Tax Rates

The duty rates on imports are classified into three different categories:

- Ordinary rates,
- Preferential rates,
- Special preferential rates.

Table 4.2 Level of tax regulation by business size

Level of business tax registration	Registered capital (VND)	Business license tax payable annually (VND)
Level 1	Over 10 billion	3 million
Level 2	From 5 to 10 billion	2 million
Level 3	From 2 to 5 billion	1.5 million
Level 4	Under 2 billion	1 million

4.5.1.1 Ordinary Rates

The ordinary rates are applied to goods imported from countries, groups of countries, or territories that do not apply the most favored nation (MFN) treatment or special preferences on import tax to Vietnam. The ordinary tax rates shall not be 70 % higher than the preferential tax rates of the same goods items specified by the Government.

4.5.1.2 Preferential Rates

The preferential rates are applied to goods imported from any country that has been deemed a MFN in its trade relations with Vietnam. MFN rates are consistent with commitments from Vietnam following its entry into the WTO and are applied in relation to goods imported from other WTO member countries.

4.5.1.3 Special Preferential Rates

The special preferential tax rates, however, apply in relation to goods imported from countries such as Japan and ASEAN member states (China, Korea, Australia, New Zealand, and India), with which Vietnam has signed a special preferential trade agreement. In order to be eligible for preferential tariffs or special preferential pricing, imported goods must be accompanied by a valid Certificate of Origin ("C/O"), in the absence of which the goods will be tariffed at the ordinary rate.

4.5.2 Calculation of Import Tariffs

Vietnam will apply the duty of the Rating Agreement created by the WTO, from which it has made some changes. Under this agreement, the calculated value of imported goods must be linked to the value of the transaction. This parameter must also be used for alternative methods of calculation.

4.5.3 Exemption from Duties on Imports

Duty exemptions on imports are granted to projects that are specifically listed in the encouraged categories of industries and for certain goods imported under certain circumstances. There are 20 categories of exemptions from duties on imports, including:

- Machinery, equipment, special means of transportation, and materials (which cannot be produced in Vietnam);
- Raw materials, spare parts, accessories, certain supplies, samples, as well as machinery and equipment imported for the processing of goods for export.

Currently, companies are not required to pay duty on the import of raw materials used for the manufacture of goods for export. However, if the company fails to export the finished product within 275 days (even if it still intends to do so), the Customs Department will charge a local temporary duty on the import of the raw materials and could also apply penalties if the payment of duties is delayed. When the company finally performs the export of the finished product, there will be a refund in proportion to the raw materials contained in the exported product.

4.5.4 Reimbursement of Duties on Imports

Refunds of duties paid on imports can be obtained for the following:

- Assets that were not imported but on which import tariffs have already been paid;
- Imported raw materials that have not yet been used in production and are to be reexported to foreign owners, to a third country, or within a free trade zone;
- Raw materials that were imported for the production of goods for the domestic market, which are then used in the manufacture of goods for export under special contracts signed with foreign parties.

4.5.5 Duties on Exports

Export duties are paid only on certain items like natural resources, for example sand, plaster, marble, granite, minerals, crude oil, forest products, scrap metal, and the like, with tax rates ranging from 0 to 33 %. The price for the calculation of duties on exports will be free on board (i.e. the selling price of goods at the port of departure as indicated in the contract, excluding the costs of freight and insurance).

Chapter 5
Audit and Transfer Pricing Policies

5.1 Background of Tax Audits

Fiscal controls are carried out regularly and often cover several tax periods. Before carrying out an audit, tax authorities send the taxpayer a written notice regarding the timing and the specific purpose of the audit. Detailed regulations exist on the penalties to various types of illegal tax, which can range from relatively minor administrative penalties to tax penalties equal to several times the amount of additional consideration. Existing law has established that tax penalties should be prescribed within 5 years. Since the authorities may levy declared and unpaid taxes at any time, the imposition of sanctions and collection of taxes are often conducted arbitrarily. In recent times, though, the tax authorities have increased their control on foreign investment, implementing a more methodical monitoring system.

The various departments within the GDT that presently handle Tax Policy matters are the Tax Policy Department and Tax Reform and Modernization Department, Inspectorate (i.e. Inspections Department), and International Cooperation (i.e. the International Taxation Department).

Tax Policy audits were initiated in 2007 as a part of general tax audits. However, very few (fewer than five) Tax Policy audits have been conducted each year. Issues have, however, been raised and dealt with as part of general tax audits. This has mainly been due to the lack of resources within the General Department of Taxes, as well as provincial tax departments (and lack of Tax Policy expertise).

The GDT/provincial tax authorities for selecting cases/companies for Tax Policy audits adopt no specific methodology. Companies are selected based on information submitted together with tax returns (i.e. statutory accounts and forms GCN-01/QLT), as well as specific industries where the Tax Policy risk is perceived to be high.

Moreover, Vietnam Accounting Standard (VAS) no. 26 on "related party disclosures" sets out general guidelines on the accounting principles and their effects and specifies required disclosures with regard to related party transactions. However, the accounting standard does not have any materiality concept as regards

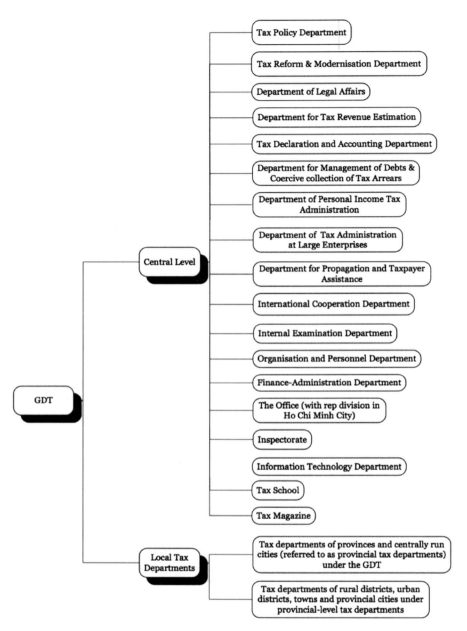

Fig. 5.1 Structure of the Vietnamese Tax Regime (*Source*: Europa, EU: Transfer Pricing and Developing Countries—Vietnam 2012)

the disclosure of related party transactions in audited financial statements. The decision to disclose the information lies with the company and its statutory auditors. Accordingly, there is no system to capture data on related party transactions other than the TP declaration form.

The current structure of the various departments within the General Department of Tax (GDT) is shown in Fig. 5.1.

5.2 Background of Accounting and Auditing

Business enterprises with foreign participation must adopt a system of records in accordance with the Vietnamese Accounting System (VAS). Enterprises must obtain written approval from the Ministry of Finance before making changes to their accounting systems. Furthermore, the accounting records must be kept in local currency (VND). Though commercial enterprises with foreign investment may choose to use a foreign currency for the relevant accounting and financial records, they must first notify the local tax authorities. The records must be kept in Vietnamese but can still be used in conjunction with an additional foreign language. The annual financial statements of each company with foreign participation must be certified by an independent audit firm operating in Vietnam, which should complete its evaluation within 90 days of the end of the year. At the end of the audit, in order to renew the appropriate licenses, the business enterprise must submit its financial statements to the competent authorities at the MOF, the local tax authority, the Department of Statistics, and other local authorities provided by law. To date, Vietnam has promulgated 26 accounting and 37 auditing standards based primarily on international principles, although with provisions for some changes at the local level.

There has been an internal restructuring of the GDT with a change from an official assessment system to a self-assessment system. The various departments under the restructured setup involved with TP and their relevant responsibilities are given in Table 5.1.

One of the steps taken by the General Department of Tax (GDT), though not specifically Tax Policy related, was setting up the Large Taxpayers Office (LTO) within the GDT for the administration of large taxpayers in Vietnam. With the increased focus on Tax Policy, the LTO's role is perceived to be important for efficient administration of tax matters, including Tax Policy issues relating to large taxpayers. The GDT is planning to have a central LTO at the GDT and subdepartments in the main provinces where there are significant multinational corporation operations.

The GDT is also receiving assistance from some donor agencies on matters relating to training, IT infrastructure, and others. Table 5.2 shows a list of donor agencies and the support provided by each of them.

Table 5.1 Functions of the GDT's departments

Department	Responsibility
Tax reforms and modernization	Formulation of the TP Law and reforms
Tax audits/inspections	Undertake TP audits along with general tax audits—actual execution of the audits will remain a responsibility of the provincial tax departments
International taxation	Formulation and implementation of DTAAs as well as dealing with bilateral issues

Source: Europa, EU: Transfer Pricing and Developing Countries—Vietnam 2012

Table 5.2 Support from donor agencies

Donor agency	Support provided to GDT
World Bank	Tax administration and modernization project comprising setting up a tax database and developing the IT infrastructure
International Monetary Fund	Developing and modernizing the administrative infrastructure including the IT infrastructure
JICA	Ongoing TP training to tax officials, assistance in developing manuals for TP audits, assistance in improving taxpayer service, funding study tours for tax officials to Japan for on-the-job training etc.
ADB	TP training to tax officials during the introduction of Circular 117
International Finance Corporation	Developing models/techniques for ratio analysis of unincorporated businesses; risk-based auditing techniques for tax audits
US Embassy	Assistance in areas of improving collections and auditing; banking money supervision and anti-money laundering

Source: Europa, EU: Transfer Pricing and Developing Countries—Vietnam 2012
JICA Japanese International Cooperation Agency, *ADB* Asian Development Bank

5.3 Definitions and Application in Vietnam

Transfer pricing is the common term for the pricing charged for intra-group, cross-border transactions of related enterprises established in different tax jurisdictions. Rapid advances in technology, communication, and transportation have given rise to a large number of multinational enterprises that have integrated global operations. The fact is that a significant volume of global trade nowadays consists of international transfer of large quantities of goods and services among operating subsidiaries in different countries, as well as capital and intangibles.

The pricing system for such intra-group and across borders transactions entails extensive tax and managerial troubles due to its direct effects on the profits of the parties and the taxable revenue of the whole countries involved in the transactions. The structure of these international transactions is a combination of market and group conditions, which can be driven by the common interests of the parties of the group. In such cases, tax authorities need to protect their revenue base and control "on an arm's length principle" (ALP) the runaway transactions between companies.

This principle refers to (article 9 of) the Organization for Economic Cooperation and Development (OECD) Model Tax Convention, which ensures that the transfer prices between multinational enterprises are established on a market value basis. The OECD Transfer Pricing Guidelines required a comparison between what the taxpayer has done and what an independent party would have done under similar circumstances. The arm's length principle (ALP) is applied by comparing controlled transactions with transaction between independent enterprises. The prices of transactions should be the same as they would have been if the parties were not related. If the prices of transaction are different, the tax authority can make adjustments to eliminate their effect.

This principle uses the comparison with independent parties as a guide to determine the allocation of income and expenses between related parties. The aim of transfer prices is to calculate the income of the parties of the group involved in the cross-border transaction. In this scenario, three parties are involved: the multinational group and the taxing authorities of the two countries involved in the transaction. The increasing prominence in the international economy and, in particular, the phenomenal spread of foreign-invested enterprises have made Vietnam's tax system more rigorous in transferring prices issued—in particular, from 2005 with new regulation in 2010. This means that the detailed transfer pricing documentation is required and that the companies have to disclose related party information on tax returns, as well as consider a possible audit.

5.4 OECD Guidelines

The new Vietnamese Regulations are generally consistent with the OECD guidelines. This section describes the OECD criteria that are followed by the Vietnamese legislation. Paragraph 1 of Article 9 of the Model Tax Convention defines the statement of the arm's length principle:

> [Where] conditions are made or imposed between the two [related] enterprises in their commercial or financial relations which differ from those which would be made between independent enterprises, then profits which would, but for those conditions, have accrued to one of the enterprises, but, by reason of those conditions, have not so accrued, may be included in the profits of that enterprise and taxed accordingly.

The arm's length principle expresses the approach of treating the members of a cross-border group as separate entities and not as independent. The reason of the adoption of this principle is to avoid the creation of tax advantages or disadvantages between same entity enterprises. The focus of this principle is promoting the growth of international trade and investment. The practical difficulty connected with the application of the arm's length principle is that it is not always easy to make a comparison between the companies. Sometimes, members of a same group face different commercial circumstances that independent enterprises would not undertake. Guidelines of the transfer pricing are summed up in the glossary of the OECD transfer pricing guidelines for multinational enterprises and tax administration as follows:

5.4.1 Advance Pricing Arrangement ("APA")

An arrangement that determines, in advance of controlled transactions, an appropriate set of criteria (e.g. method, comparable and appropriate adjustments thereto, critical assumptions as to future events) for the determination of the transfer pricing for those transactions over a fixed period of time. An advance pricing arrangement may be unilateral involving one tax administration and a taxpayer or multilateral involving the agreement of two or more tax administrations.

5.4.2 Arm's Length Principle

The international standard that OECD member countries have agreed should be used for determining transfer prices for tax purposes. It is set forth in Article 9 of the OECD Model Tax Convention as follows: where "conditions are made or imposed between the two enterprises in their commercial or financial relations which differ from those which would be made between independent enterprises, then any profits which would, but for those conditions, have accrued to one of the enterprises, but, by reason of those conditions, have not so accrued, may be included in the profits of that enterprise and taxed accordingly."

5.4.3 Arm's Length Range

A range of figures that are acceptable for establishing whether the conditions of a controlled transaction are arm's length and that are derived either from applying the same transfer pricing method to multiple comparable data or from applying different transfer pricing methods.

5.4.4 Associated Enterprises

Two enterprises are related enterprises with respect to each other if one of the enterprises meets the conditions of Article 9, sub-paragraphs 1a) or 1b) of the OECD Model Tax Convention with respect to the other enterprise.

5.4.5 Balancing Payment

A payment, normally from one or more participants to another, to adjust participants' proportionate shares of contributions, that increases the value of the contributions of the payer and decreases the value of the contributions of the payee by the amount of the payment.

5.4.6 Buy-in Payment

A payment made by a new entrant to an already active CCA for obtaining an interest in any results of prior CCA activity.

5.4.7 Buy-Out Payment

Compensation that a participant who withdraws from an already active CCA may receive from the remaining participants for an effective transfer of its interests in the results of past CCA activities.

5.4.8 Commercial Intangible

An intangible that is used in commercial activities such as the production of a good or the provision of a service, as well as an intangible right that is itself a business asset transferred to customers or used in the operation of business.

5.4.9 Comparability Analysis

A comparison of a controlled transaction with an uncontrolled transaction or transactions. Controlled and uncontrolled transactions are comparable if none of the differences between the transactions could materially affect the factor being examined in the methodology (e.g. price or margin), or if reasonably accurate adjustments can be made to eliminate the material effects of any such differences.

5.4.10 Comparable Uncontrolled Transaction

A comparable uncontrolled transaction is a transaction between two independent parties that is comparable to the controlled transaction under examination. It can be either a comparable transaction between one party to the controlled transaction and an independent party ("internal comparable") or between two independent parties, neither of which is a party to the controlled transaction ("external comparable").

5.4.11 Comparable Uncontrolled Price (CUP) Method

A transfer pricing method that compares the price for property or services transferred in a controlled transaction to the price charged for property or services transferred in a comparable uncontrolled transaction in comparable circumstances.

5.4.12 Compensating Adjustment

An adjustment in which the taxpayer reports a transfer price for tax purposes that is, in the taxpayer's opinion, an arm's length price for a controlled transaction, even though this price differs from the amount actually charged between the associated enterprises. This adjustment would be made before the tax return is filed.

5.4.13 Contribution Analysis

An analysis used in the profit split method under which the combined profits from controlled transactions are divided between the associated enterprises based upon the relative value of the functions performed (taking into account assets used and risks assumed) by each of the associated enterprises participating in those transactions, supplemented as much as possible by external market data that indicate how independent enterprises would have divided profits in similar circumstances.

5.4.14 Controlled Transactions

Transactions between two enterprises that are associated enterprises with respect to each other.

5.4.15 Corresponding Adjustment

An adjustment to the tax liability of the associated enterprise in a second tax jurisdiction made by the tax administration of that jurisdiction, corresponding to a primary adjustment made by the tax administration in a first tax jurisdiction, so that the allocation of profits by the two jurisdictions is consistent.

5.4.16 Cost Contribution Arrangement ("CCA")

A CCA is a framework agreed among enterprises to share the costs and risks of developing, producing, or obtaining assets, services, or rights, and to determine the nature and extent of the interests of each participant in the results of the activity of developing, producing, or obtaining those assets, services, or rights.

5.4.17 Cost Plus Mark Up

A mark up that is measured by reference to margins computed after the direct and indirect costs incurred by a supplier of property or services in a transaction.

5.4.18 Cost Plus Method

A transfer pricing method using the costs incurred by the supplier of property (or services) in a controlled transaction. An appropriate cost plus mark up is added to this cost, to make an appropriate profit in light of the functions performed (taking into account assets used and risks assumed) and the market conditions. What is arrived at after adding the cost plus mark up to the above costs may be regarded as an arm's length price of the original controlled transaction.

5.4.19 Direct-Charge Method

A method of charging directly for specific intra-group services on a clearly identified basis.

5.4.20 Direct Costs

Costs that incurred specifically for producing a product or rendering service, such as the cost of raw materials.

5.4.21 Functional Analysis

An analysis of the functions performed (taking into account assets used and risks assumed) by associated enterprises in controlled transactions and by independent enterprises in comparable uncontrolled transactions.

5.4.22 Global Formulary Apportionment

An approach to allocate the global profits of an MNE group on a consolidated basis among the associated enterprises in different countries on the basis of a predetermined formula.

5.4.23 Gross Profits

The gross profits from a business transaction are the amount computed by deducting from the gross receipts of the transaction the allocable purchases or production costs of sales, with due adjustment for increases or decreases in inventory or stock-in-trade, but without taking account of other expenses.

5.4.24 Independent Enterprises

Two enterprises are independent enterprises with respect to each other if they are not associated enterprises with respect to each other.

5.4.25 Intra-Group Service

An activity (e.g. administrative, technical, financial, commercial, etc.) for which an independent enterprise would have been willing to pay or perform for itself.

5.4.26 Intentional Set-Off

A benefit provided by one associated enterprise to another associated enterprise within the group that is deliberately balanced to some degree by different benefits received from that enterprise in return.

5.4.27 Marketing Intangible

An intangible that is concerned with marketing activities, which aids in the commercial exploitation of a product or service and/or has an important promotional value for the product concerned.

5.4 OECD Guidelines   37

5.4.28 Multinational Enterprise Group (MNE Group)

A group of associated companies with business establishments in two or more countries.

5.4.29 Multinational Enterprise (MNE)

A company that is part of an MNE group.

5.4.30 Mutual Agreement Procedure

A means through which tax administrations consult to resolve disputes regarding the application of double tax conventions. This procedure, described and authorized by Article 25 of the OECD Model Tax Convention, can be used to eliminate double taxation that could arise from a transfer pricing adjustment.

5.4.31 Net Profit Indicator

The ratio of net profit to an appropriate base (e.g. costs, sales, assets).
The transactional net margin method relies on a comparison of an appropriate net profit indicator for the controlled transaction with the same net profit indicator in comparable uncontrolled transactions.

5.4.32 "On Call" Services

Services provided by a parent company or a group service center, which are available at any time for members of an MNE group.

5.4.33 Primary Adjustment

An adjustment that a tax administration in a first jurisdiction makes to a company's taxable profits as a result of applying the arm's length principle to transactions involving an associated enterprise in a second tax jurisdiction.

5.4.34 Profit Potential

The expected future profits. In some cases it may encompass losses. The notion of "profit potential" is often used for valuation purposes, in the determination of an arm's length compensation for a transfer of intangibles or of an ongoing concern, or in the determination of an arm's length indemnification for the termination or substantial renegotiation of existing arrangements, once it is found that such compensation or indemnification would have taken place between independent parties in comparable circumstances.

5.4.35 Profit Split Method

A transactional profit method that identifies the combined profit to be split for the associated enterprises from a controlled transaction and then splits those profits between the associated enterprises based upon an economically valid basis that approximates the division of profits that would have been anticipated and reflected in an agreement made at arm's length.

5.4.36 Resale Price Margin

A margin representing the amount out of which a reseller would seek to cover its selling and other operating expenses and, in the light of the functions performed (taking into account assets used and risks assumed), make an appropriate profit.

5.4.37 Resale Price Method

A transfer pricing method based on the price at which a product that has been purchased from an associated enterprise is resold to an independent enterprise. The resale price is reduced by the resale price margin. What is left after subtracting the resale price margin can be regarded, after adjustment for other costs associated with the purchase of the product (e.g. custom duties), as an arm's length price of the original transfer of property between the associated enterprises.

5.4.38 Residual Analysis

An analysis used in the profit split method, which divides the combined profit from the controlled transactions under examination in two stages. In the first stage, each participant is allocated sufficient profit to provide it with a basic return appropriate for the type of transactions in which it is engaged.
Ordinarily this basic return would be determined by reference to the market returns achieved for similar types of transactions by independent enterprises.

Thus, the basic return would generally not account for the return that would be generated by any unique and valuable assets possessed by the participants. In the second stage, any residual profit (or loss) remaining after the first stage division would be allocated among the parties based on an analysis of the facts and circumstances that might indicate how this residual would have been divided between independent enterprises.

5.4.39 Secondary Adjustment

An adjustment that arises from imposing tax on a secondary transaction.

5.4.40 Secondary Transaction

A constructive transaction that some countries will assert under their domestic legislation after having proposed a primary adjustment in order to make the actual allocation of profits consistent with the primary adjustment. Secondary transactions may take the form of constructive dividends, constructive equity contributions, or constructive loans.

5.4.41 Shareholder Activity

An activity which is performed by a member of an MNE group (usually the parent company or a regional holding company) solely because of its ownership interest in one or more other group members, i.e. in its capacity as shareholder.

5.4.42 Simultaneous Tax Examinations

A simultaneous tax examination, as defined in Part A of the OECD Model Agreement for the Undertaking of Simultaneous Tax Examinations, means an "arrangement between two or more parties to examine simultaneously and independently, each on its own territory, the tax affairs of (a) taxpayer(s) in which they have a common or related interest with a view to exchanging any relevant information which they so obtain."

5.4.43 Trade Intangible

A commercial intangible other than a marketing intangible.

5.4.44 Traditional Transaction Method

The comparable uncontrolled price method, the resale price method, and the cost plus method.

5.4.45 Transactional Net Margin Method

A transactional profit method that examines the net profit margin relative to an appropriate base (e.g. costs, sales, assets) that a taxpayer realises form a controlled transaction.

5.4.46 Transactional Profit Method

A transfer pricing method that examines the profits that arise from particular transactions of one or more of the associated enterprises participating in those transactions.

5.4.47 Uncontrolled Transactions

Transactions between enterprises that are independent enterprises with respect to each other.

5.5 Transfer Pricing in Vietnam

Though the Vietnamese tax authorities do not formally refer to the OECD transfer pricing guidelines since Vietnam is not a member of OECD, the Vietnamese tax authorities issued Circular 117 in December 2005, providing the basic framework of Vietnam's transfer pricing rules. It required taxpayers to submit an Annual Transfer Pricing Declaration form, together with their corporate income tax returns, within 90 days after the year-end and maintain contemporaneous transfer pricing documentation. Circular 66, effective from 2010, required companies to take proactive steps to document their transfer pricing arrangements and documentation requirements.

Circular 66 is the only official guideline relating to transfer pricing along with some official letters issued by local departments of taxation. It defines related parties more clearly than previous circulars or regulations. The additional criteria to determine related parties are set out below:

- Two enterprises that directly or indirectly hold at least 20 % of the capital of a third party are considered related.
- An enterprise that guarantees or grants a loan constituting more than 20 % of the receiving enterprise's capital or more than 50 % of the total value of the long- and medium-term loans of another enterprise will be considered related.

The Ministry of Finance (MOF) issued Decision 1250 in May 2012, which approved an Action Program on Transfer Pricing from 2012 to 2015.

5.6 Related Party Transactions

Vietnam's local and national tax authorities can adjust taxpayers' transfer prices to an arm's length level. Taxpayers are obliged to support with prepared evidence that their transfer prices are at arm's length. The Vietnam Transfer Pricing regulations have application to all the corporations that fall within the definition of "related parties":

- One party is directly or indirectly engaged in the management, control, contribution of capital to or investment in the other party;
- The parties are directly or indirectly subject to the management, control, capital contribution, or investment in all forms by another party;
- The parties directly or indirectly participate in the management, control, capital contribution, or investment in another party;
- Over 50 % of any single product of one party is purchased by the other party, or over 50 % of the production materials of any single product of a party are provided by the other party; and
- Two parties have entered into a business cooperation agreement on a contractual basis.

The Vietnamese Transfer Pricing regulations further detail the definition of "related parties" in Circular 66 by adding the following criteria:

- Two enterprises that directly or indirectly hold at least 20 % of the capital of a third party are considered affiliated.
- An enterprise that guarantees or grants a loan constituting more than 20 % of the receiving enterprise's investment capital or more than 50 % of the total value of the long- and medium-term loans of another enterprise will be considered related.

5.7 Documentation and Disclosure Requirements

From 2010, Circular 66 has made the documentation process more rigorous. While there is no clear guidance on template of documentation, taxpayers are required to maintain "contemporaneous" documentation: several things such as transactional

Table 5.3 Documentation requirements

Organizational structure and specific information	– Organizational structure – Information of related parties and relationship – Preferential tax treatment of related parties – Effective tax rates of related parties
Business operation	– Overview of principal business operation – Market position and environment – Consolidated financial statement – Assets, functions, and risks profile
Related party transactions	– Descriptions of the related party transactions – Copy of relevant contracts – Factor influencing pricing
Comparability analysis	– Description of comparable transaction – Comparable analysis – Adjustments
Selection and application of TP methods	– Pricing methods selected – Result of comparability analysis – Other assumptions and judgments

description, including the related party, product specifications, contractual terms, and the adopted pricing method. Usually, the taxpayer is required to provide any paperwork to the tax authority within 30 working days from the date of request. After expiration of this initial period, it may be extended for 30 additional working days if a legitimate reason is provided to and approved by the tax authorities.

The Corporate Income Tax Finalization Declaration must be filed within 90 days after the end of the fiscal year, and all the documentation must be in Vietnamese (documentation in other languages must be translated into Vietnamese for filing purposes).

All the documentation requirements and the disclosure forms are listed in Tables 5.3 and 5.4.

5.8 Penalties

Vietnam imposes penalties for noncompliance with their local transfer pricing regulations and any transfer pricing adjustments that may arise in a tax audit. More than 40,000 enterprises were inspected in 2011, of which around 3 % were suspected of transfer pricing noncompliance, and penalties totalling more than US $350 million were imposed.

While Circular 66 does not provide guidelines on specific transfer pricing penalties or administrative fines, the effective Law on Tax Management governs the penalty. If an enterprise makes voluntary adjustments, the undeclared amount treated as a late payment is subject to late payment interest of 0.05 % per day. In case of an incorrect declaration, a fine of 10 % will be imposed on the undeclared tax, in addition to any late payment interest. In case of tax evasion (late filing of

Table 5.4 Disclosure forms

Related parties	– Background information of relationship – Type of association – Information about the parties
Summary of RP transactions	– Type and amount of related party transactions, domestic and cross-border
Purchase and sales	– Financial information about sales between the related parties and third parties – Name and location of the parties
Services	– Service revenue and expenses from transactions with cross-border and domestic-related parties
Intangible assets	– Information on acquisition and disposal of intangible assets between the parties
Tangible assets	– Information on acquisition and disposal of tangible assets between the parties
Financing	– Information on debt financing of the parties
Foreign investment	– Information of investment in foreign enterprises – Financial information on the invested company – Profit and dividend distribution, shareholding, and income tax status
Foreign payments	– Information about outbound payments – Any beneficial treatment under tax

90 days or more) or tax fraud, the fine is one to three times the undeclared tax. Interest is payable whenever a refund is due to the taxpayer and there is no provision for reduction in transfer pricing penalties.

5.9 Transfer Pricing Methods

While the Vietnamese Ministry of Finance has not established a priority of methods, the taxpayer is required to use the "best" (subject to interpretation) method applicable (the reliability of the supporting documentation is important to consider when choosing a method). The acceptable methods are CUP, CPM, cost plus pricing, resale price, and profit split. Circular 66 requests that data, documents, and vouchers used for comparability analysis must be of clear sources to aid the tax authority to verify them. Foreign company comparables are often accepted, though ASEAN or pan-Asian comparables are preferable to the Vietnamese tax authorities.

5.9.1 Comparable Uncontrolled Price Method (CUP)

The CUP method could be applied to all types of related party transactions, and it provides best benchmark of an arm's length price for a related party transaction. It

Table 5.5 Main transfer pricing method formula

Resale price method	Arm's length purchased price = resale price to nonrelated parties × (1 − gross margin of comparable uncontrolled transaction)
Cost plus method	Arm's length price = reasonable cost × (1 + cost plus margin of comparable uncontrolled transaction)

may be possible to reliably adjust CUPs where services, goods, or property is identical but the sales terms are different.

5.9.2 Resale Price Method (Table 5.5)

This method is more used in service transactions than in transactions involving goods. The arm's length price is determined by deducting the gross profit of an uncontrolled transaction from the resale price to nonrelated party for goods purchased.

5.9.3 Cost Plus Method (Table 5.5)

This method is usually applied to the related party transaction of manufactories. In this case, the arm's length price is the full cost of the good or service plus a gross profit markup.

5.9.4 Profit Split Method

This method is usually applied when the related party transaction is highly integrated. The methods are two:

- General profit split method,
- Residual profit split method.

In general, it refers to the methodology where the total profit of a transaction is allocated to each enterprise according to its respective contributions.

5.9.5 Note on Deductions

While the tax regime allows deduction of management fees charged to local Vietnamese subsidiaries for specific services rendered by foreign parties, many services fail to meet the specificity criteria and do not get to the question of whether or not they are at arm's length. Foreign Contractor Withholding Tax (FCWT) is applicable to such payments—it is composed of VAT and Corporate Income Tax and has various withholding rates.

Overhead expenses to permanent establishments may be allocated and must be calculated using a formula apportionment based on revenue. The tax legislation does not have provisions prohibiting stock option costs from inclusion in the cost base for intercompany services charges.

5.10 Transfer Pricing Audit and Adjustments

Potential audit targets include taxpayers that:

- Have large amounts of related party transactions or have multiple types of related party transactions;
- Have long-term losses, marginal or fluctuating profits;
- Have profit levels lower than the industry;
- Have profit levels that do not match with the functions they perform and the risks they assume;
- Have transactions with related parties registered in tax havens;
- Fail to submit annual related party transaction disclosure forms or fail to prepare contemporaneous transfer pricing documentation; or
- Do not comply with the arm's length principle.

When an entity has been selected for TP audit, the tax authorities can request any relevant information about the pricing of related party transactions (thus the requirement for contemporaneous documentation).

The documents required could be the enterprise's foundation approval documents, including articles of association, business and tax registration certificates, investment and operational contracts, feasibility studies, annual financial statements, internal audit reports, account books and vouchers, commercial contracts and other relevant documents, financial information, including profits/losses on sales of assets, rates of return on investments, sales revenues, cost of sales and operating expenses, interest rates, and prices paid for the acquisition or use of tangible and intangible property.

Once this information is reviewed, the tax officer will determine if it will be necessary to have further documents. Target enterprises will have a limited amount of time to submit the required information to tax bureaus upon request.

5.11 Advance Pricing Arrangements (APA)

A proactive instrument to reduce transfer pricing risks is an APA, which is an arrangement between tax authorities and the taxpayer in respect of the pricing of transactions for a number of years in the future. An APA ensures taxpayers that their transfer pricing policies and procedures meet the arm's length standard.

Along with the Decree and the Circular guiding the application of law, the Annual Transfer Pricing Declaration form has been revised, though the amendments also place a 5-year limitation on APAs (stating basis for tax calculation and transfer pricing methods applied prior to submitting the Corporate Income Tax Declaration and the Custom Declaration).

Part II
International Treaties

Chapter 6
Introduction to International Taxation and Treaties

6.1 Conventions Against Double Taxation

Vietnam has more than 60 agreements signed, and numerous others at various stages of implementation and negotiation. The agreements in force include those with Australia, France, Germany, Japan, Korea, Malaysia, the Netherlands, Singapore, Thailand, Hong Kong, the United Kingdom, etc. Notably absent is a DTA with the United States of America. A summary of the provisions of some key DTAs is given in Table 6.1.

Table 6.1 Withholding tax rates for cross-border transactions

Country	Dividends (%)	Interests (%)	Royalties (%)
Algeria	15	15	15
Australia	10	10	10
Bangladesh	15	15	15
Belarus	15	10	15
Belgium	5/7/10/15	10	5/10/15
Bulgaria	15	10	15
Canada	5/10/15	10	7,5/10
China	10	10	10
Cuba	5/10/15	10	10
Czech Republic	10	10	10
Denmark	5/10/15	10	10/15
Finland	5/10/15	10	10
France	7/10/15	–	10
Germany	5/10/15	10	7,5/10
Hong Kong	10	10	7/10
Hungary	10	10	10
Iceland	10/15	10	10
India	10	10	10
Indonesia	15	15	15
Italy	5/10/15	10	7,5/10
Japan	10	10	10
Laos	10	10	10
Luxembourg	5/10/15	10	10
Malaysia	10	10	10
Mongolia	10	10	10
Myanmar	10	10	10
Netherlands	5/7/10/15	7/10	5/10/15
North Korea	10	10	10
Norway	5/10/15	10	10
Pakistan	15	15	15
Philippines	10/15	15	15
Poland	10/15	10	1/10/15
Romania	15	10	15
Russia	10/15	10	15
Seychelles	10	10	10
Singapore	5/7/12,5	10	5/15
South Korea	10	10	5/15
Spain	7/10/15	10	10
Sri Lanka	10/10/15	10	15
Sweden	5/10/15	10	5/15
Switzerland	7/10/15	10	10
Thailand	15	10/15	15
Ukraine	10	10	10
United Kingdom	7/10/15	10	10
Uzbekistan	15	10	15

Chapter 7
American Area Treaties

7.1 Vietnam–American Area Bilateral Agreements' History

7.1.1 Vietnam–USA Bilateral Agreement's History and Evolution

North Vietnam's victory over US-backed South Vietnam in 1975 led to a freeze in bilateral relations between USA and Vietnam for over a decade and a half. However, overlapping economic and security interests over a wide range of issues have led to strategic alliances between the two nations since the establishment of diplomatic relations in 1995 (Manyin 2013). The possibility of such an establishment was first signaled by President Clinton's visit to Saigon (now known as Ho Chi Minh City) in 1993 to end U.S. opposition to Vietnam's receipt of international financial aid. President Clinton also ended economic sanctions against Vietnam in February 1994. The U.S. Senate's support for harmonizing relations with Vietnam was soon once again demonstrated when, 2 months after the end of trade embargo, the U.S. Congress passed the Foreign Relations Authorization Act (Manyin 2013).

Furthermore, President Clinton (who was also the first President to visit Vietnam after Nixon) appointed the first postwar U.S. Ambassador to Vietnam in 1997. The nations' entry into force of the U.S.–Vietnam Bilateral Trade Agreement (BTA), a landmark agreement in 2001 (this agreement, which was originally drafted in 2000, was not ratified by the U.S. Congress till 2001 due to concerns regarding human rights violations in Vietnam), accelerated the momentum of the commercial alliances between the nations while also accelerating Vietnam's entry into global markets through membership in the World Trade Organization (WTO) since 2007.

The BTA led to an increase in bilateral trade from $2.9 billion in 2002 to $21.8 in 2011. As of 2011, $17.4 billion or about 18 % of Vietnam's exports were to the U.S., resulting in a bilateral trade deficit of over $13 billion. In the same year, over

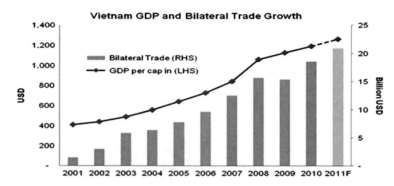

Fig. 7.1 The effect of bilateral trade growth on Vietnam's GDP. *Source*: U.S. Department of State (U.S. Embassy in Hanoi, Vietnam)

40 % of U.S. exports to Vietnam were agricultural products, though exports of other product segments in the industrial sector are steadily growing.

In 2007, the two nations signed the Trade and Investment Framework Agreement (TIFA) to advance the BTA and strengthen Vietnam's commitment to the WTO. Though Vietnam has significantly reduced tariffs on several products to be on par with the WTO's standards, there continue to exist several types of products whose inflow into Vietnam could substantially increase if tariffs were reduced further (U.S. and Foreign Commercial Service and U.S. Department of State 2012).

In addition to strengthening WTO commitment, Vietnam joined Chile, Peru, Malaysia, Brunei, Singapore, Australia, and New Zealand to participate in the Trans-Pacific Economic Partnership (TPP) negotiations as a full-time member in November 2010. The conclusion of the TPP negotiations is bound to create a more responsive and favorable environment for American businesses looking to penetrate the Vietnamese market. This is good news for Vietnam as its GDP per capita has steadily risen as bilateral trade with the U.S. has increased, as shown in Fig. 7.1.

Thus far, after continued support of normalization of bilateral relations between the U.S. and Vietnam by the Bush Administration, the Obama Administration's (which has publicly expressed concerns regarding human rights incidents in Vietnam) policy towards Vietnam is largely influenced by the United States' strategic concerns towards China, as signaled by Hillary Clinton and Robert Gates' visits to Hanoi in 2010.

In Fig. 7.2 are shown the main macro indicators of the U.S. economy.

7.1.2 Vietnam–Canada Bilateral Agreement's History

Though Canada and Vietnam established diplomatic ties in 1973, it was not until 1994 that a Canadian embassy opened up in Ho Chi Minh City (and a Consulate General in 1997), after Canada restored development assistance to Vietnam in

7.1 Vietnam–American Area Bilateral Agreements' History

UNITED STATES	
Area	9,372,610 km^2
Population (2012)	313.9 m
THE ECONOMY	
GDP (2012)	$15.68 tn
GDP growth (annual %)	2.2%
GDP per head	$45,990
COMPONENTS OF GDP	
	% of total (2011)
Private consumption	71
Public consumption	17
Industry, value added (% of GDP)	20
Exports of goods and services (% of GDP)	14
Imports of goods and services (% of GDP)	18
STATES AND MARKETS	
Time required to start a business (days)	6
Market capitalization of listed companies (% of GDP)	119.0
Military expenditure (% of GDP)	4.0
Mobile cellular subscriptions (per 100 people)	93
Internet users (per 100 people)	77.9
MAIN EXPORT DESTINATIONS	
	% of total
Canada	19
Mexico	12.2
China	6.6
Japan	4.8
United Kingdom	4.3
Germany	4.2
EU 27	20.9
GLOBAL LINKS	
Merchandise trade (% of GDP)	25.0
Foreign direct investment, net inflows (BoP, current US$)	205,790
Net migration (thousands) (2011)	4,955

Fig. 7.2 USA economic indicators. *Source*: World Bank Data (2013)

1990. After 40 years of bilateral ties, the nations' relations are expanding—largely due to the Canadian International Development Agency's (CIDA) assistance. Over the past decade, Canadian exports to Vietnam have grown by over 400 %, while imports from Vietnam have increased by over 300 % (Consulate General of Canada in Ho Chi Minh City 2011) (Fig. 7.3 and Table 7.1).

Fig. 7.3 Economic snapshot of Vietnam and Canada. *Source*: Government of Canada

Economic Information (2011)

Type	Vietnam	Canada
GDP: ($ billion)	121.38	1,719.95
GDP per capita: ($)	1,358.99	49,944.08
GDP growth rate: (%)	5.88	2.41
Inflation: (%)	18.68	2.89
Unemployment: (%)	4.51	7.47

Table 7.1 Vietnam–Canada bilateral trade (in C$)

Canada's trade with Vietnam (C$)				
	January–December		January–September	
	2010	2011	2011	2012
Exports	247,593,853	317,374,706	216,755,424	257,050,506
Imports	1,173,393,940	1,332,127,093	958,743,113	1,195,987,217
Trade balance	925,800,087	1,014,752,387	741,987,689	938,936,71

Canada's Merchandise Trade with Vietnam, 2011

	Canadian imports from Vietnam		Canadian exports to Vietnam	
	Merchandise classification	%	Merchandise classification	%
1	Woven clothing and apparel articles	12.77	Fertilizers	28.08
2	Furniture and stuffed furnishings	12.51	Oil seeds and misc. fruit, grain, etc.	15.17
3	Knitted or crocheted apparel	12.50	Fish, crustaceans, mollusks	10.72
4	Footwear	12.40	Boilers, mechanical appliances, etc.	6.18
5	Fish, crustaceans, mollusks	7.93	Iron and steel	3.64
6	Electrical machinery and equipment	7.69	Pearls, precious stones, or metals	3.45
7	Boilers, mechanical appliances, etc.	4.97	Raw hides, skins, and leather	2.97
8	Edible fruits and nuts	3.61	Meat and edible meat offal	2.65
9	Leather articles	2.53	Plastic and plastic articles	2.41
10	Prepared food: meat, fish, seafood	2.00	Cereals	2.10
	Top 10 as % of total from Vietnam	78.92	Top 10 as % of total to Vietnam	77.36
	Vietnamese imports as % of Cdn total	0.30	Vietnamese exports as % of Cdn total	0.08

Source: Trade Data Online, Industry Canada

Vietnam was declared one of CIDA's "countries of focus" in 2009, and Vietnamese Prime Minister Dung attended the G20 meeting in Toronto as Chair of the Association of Southeast Asian Nations (ASEAN) (Government of Canada 2012). Both countries, in order to create a more stable environment for Canadian investors in Vietnam, are negotiating a Foreign Investment Promotion and Protection Agreement (FIPA) similar to one Canada recently signed with China. Canada is also in the process of negotiating FIPAs with Ghana, Indonesia, and Zambia, amongst others. Apart from the fact that there are over 180,000 Vietnamese-Canadian people in Canada, Canada and Vietnam also share membership in several important

Table 7.2 Canadian FDI toward Asia (1980–2011)

Canadian outward Foreign Direct Investment to Asia (C$ millions)						
	1980	1990	2008	2009	2010	2011
China	–	6	3,519	3,471	4,789	4,463
India	61	94	782	617	492	587
Vietnam	–	–	95	99	89	–
Total Asia	1,605	7,370	33,049	39,340	49,708	54,874

Source: Trade Data Online, Industry Canada

multilateral forums: ASEAN, ASEAN Regional Forum, United Nations, World Trade Organization (WTO), and the Francophone (Government of Canada 2012).

Despite the fact that the global economy was hit hard by recession in 2011, bilateral trade between Canada and Vietnam hit an all-time high of almost $1.6 billion. Currently, Canadian companies continue to expand into a variety of sectors in Vietnam, including IT, forestry, oil and gas, and agriculture (Table 7.2). Though the CIDA's focus in Vietnam has been toward improvement in agricultural productivity, it has also supported a policy and institutional reforms aimed towards an overall advancement of the business environment and living standards in Vietnam (Government of Canada 2012).

In Fig. 7.4 are shown the main indicators of Canada's economy.

7.2 Canada–Vietnam Treaty

The Government of the Socialist Republic of Vietnam and the Government of Canada, desiring to conclude an agreement for the avoidance of double taxation and the prevention of fiscal evasion with respect to taxes on income, have agreed as follows:

Article 1 – Personal Scope

This Agreement shall apply to persons who are residents of one or both of the Contracting States.

Article 2 – Taxes Covered

1. This Agreement shall apply to taxes on income imposed on behalf of each Contracting State, irrespective of the manner in which they are levied.
2. There shall be regarded as taxes on income all taxes imposed on total income, or on elements of income, including taxes on gains from the alienation of movable or immovable property, as well as taxes on capital appreciation.
3. The existing taxes to which the Agreement shall apply are:

   a. In the case of Vietnam:

   (i) the personal income tax;
   (ii) the profit tax;
   (iii) the profit remittance tax;
   (hereinafter referred to as "Vietnamese tax");

CANADA	
Area	9,970,610 km²
Population	33.6 m

THE ECONOMY	
GDP	$1.805 tn
Avg. growth 2004-09	1.20%
GDP per capita	$51,689
GDP per capita PPP	$41,335
FDI Inflows (2011)	$40.932 bn
FDI Outflows (2011)	$49.569 bn
Total Exports	$481.7 Bn
Total Imports	$480.9 Bn

INFLATION AND FINANCE	
Consumer price inflation (2012)	2.2%
Avg. ann. Inflation 2005-10	1.7%
Unemployment Rate (2012)	7.4%
Household saving rates (2012)	4.2%
Public Deficit (% of GDP) (2012)	-3.7%

MAIN EXPORT DESTINATIONS	
	% of total
United States	75.1
United Kingdom	3.4
China	3.1
Japan	2.3
EU 27	8.3

Fig. 7.4 Canada economic indicators. *Source*: IMF (2013)

    b. In the case of Canada:
    the income taxes imposed by the Government of Canada under the Income Tax Act; (hereinafter referred to as "Canadian tax")

  4. The Agreement shall apply also to any identical or substantially similar taxes, which are imposed after the date of signature of the Agreement in addition to, or in place of, the existing taxes. The competent authorities of the Contracting States shall notify each other of important changes, which have been made in their respective taxation laws.

Article 3 – General Definitions

  1. For the purposes of this Agreement, unless the context otherwise requires:

    a. The term "Vietnam" means the Socialist Republic of Vietnam and, when used in a geographical sense, it means the territory of Vietnam, including:

      (i) Any area beyond the territorial seas of Vietnam which, in accordance with international law and the laws of Vietnam, is an area within which Vietnam may exercise rights with respect to the seabed and subsoil and their natural resources;

(ii) the seas and airspace above every area referred to in subparagraph (i) in respect of any activity carried on in connection with the exploration for or the exploitation of the natural resources referred to therein;

b. The term "Canada" used in a geographical sense, means the territory of Canada, including:

(i) any area beyond the territorial seas of Canada which, in accordance with international law and the laws of Canada, is an area within which Canada may exercise rights with respect to the seabed and subsoil and their natural resources;
(ii) the seas and airspace above every area referred to in subparagraph (i) in respect of any activity carried on in connection with the exploration for or the exploitation of the natural resources referred to therein;

c. The terms "a Contracting State" and "the other Contracting State" mean, as the context requires, Vietnam or Canada;
d. The term "person" includes an individual, a company, a partnership and any other body of persons;
e. The term "company" means any body corporate or any entity which is treated as a body corporate for tax purposes;
f. The terms "enterprise of a Contracting State" and "enterprise of the other Contracting State" mean respectively an enterprise carried on by a resident of a Contracting State and an enterprise carried on by a resident of the other Contracting State;
g. The term "national" means:

(i) any individual possessing the nationality of a Contracting State;
(ii) any legal person, partnership and association deriving its status as such from the laws in force in a Contracting State;

h. The term "competent authority" means:

(i) In the case of Vietnam, the Minister of Finance or the Minister's authorized representative;
(ii) in the case of Canada, the Minister of National Revenue or the Minister's authorized representative;
(iii) the term "international traffic" means any voyage of a ship or aircraft to transport passengers or property except where the principal purpose of the voyage is to transport passengers or property between places within a Contracting State.

2. As regards the application of the Agreement by a Contracting State at any time, any term not defined therein shall, unless the context otherwise requires, have the meaning which it has at that time under the law of that State concerning the taxes to which the Agreement applies.

Article 4 – Resident

1. For the purposes of this Agreement, the term "resident of a Contracting State" means any person who, under the laws of that State, is liable to tax therein by reason of his domicile, residence, place of management, place of registration, place of incorporation or any other criterion of a similar nature.
2. Where by reason of the provisions of paragraph 1 an individual is a resident of both Contracting States, then his status shall be determined as follows:

a. He shall be deemed to be a resident of the State in which he has a permanent home available to him; if he has a permanent home available to him in both States, he shall

be deemed to be a resident of the State with which his personal and economic relations are closer (centre of vital interests);
   b. If the State in which he has his center of vital interests cannot be determined, or if he has not a permanent home available to him in either State, he shall be deemed to be a resident of the State in which he has an habitual abode;
   c. If he has an habitual abode in both States or in neither of them, he shall be deemed to be a resident of the State of which he is a national;
   d. If he is a national of both States or of neither of them, the competent authorities of the Contracting States shall settle the question by mutual agreement.

3. Where by reason of the provisions of paragraph 1 a company is a resident of both Contracting States, then its status shall be determined as follows:
   a. It shall be deemed to be a resident of the State of which it is a national;
   b. If it is a national of neither of the States, it shall be deemed to be a resident of the State in which its place of effective management is situated.

4. Where by reason of the provisions of paragraph 1 a person other than an individual or a company is a resident of both Contracting States, the competent authorities of the Contracting States shall by mutual agreement endeavor to settle the question and to determine the mode of application of the Agreement to such person.

Article 5 – Permanent Establishment

1. For the purposes of this Agreement, the term "permanent establishment" means a fixed place of business through which the business of an enterprise is wholly or partly carried on.
2. The term "permanent establishment" includes especially:
   a. A place of management;
   b. A branch;
   c. An office;
   d. A factory;
   e. A workshop; and
   f. A mine, an oil or gas well, a quarry or any other place relating to the exploration for or the exploitation of natural resources.
3. The term "permanent establishment" shall likewise encompasses:
   a. A building site, construction, assembly or installation project or supervisory activities in connection therewith, but only where such site, project or activities continue for a period of more than six months;
   b. The furnishing of services, including consultancy services, by an enterprise of a Contracting State through employees or other personnel in the other Contracting State, but only where activities of that nature continue (for the same or a connected project) within the country for a period or periods aggregating more than six months within any twelve month period.
4. Notwithstanding the preceding provisions of this Article, the term "permanent establishment" shall be deemed not to include:
   a. The use of facilities solely for the purpose of storage or display of goods or merchandise belonging to the enterprise;
   b. The maintenance of a stock of goods or merchandise belonging to the enterprise solely for the purpose of storage or display;
   c. The maintenance of a stock of goods or merchandise belonging to the enterprise solely for the purpose of processing by another enterprise;

d. The maintenance of a fixed place of business solely for the purpose of purchasing goods or merchandise or of collecting information, for the enterprise;
e. The maintenance of a fixed place of business solely for the purpose of carrying on, for the enterprise, any other activity of a preparatory or auxiliary character;
f. The maintenance of a fixed place of business solely for any combination of activities mentioned in subparagraphs (a) to (e) provided that the overall activity of the fixed place of business resulting from this combination is of a preparatory or auxiliary character.

5. Notwithstanding the provisions of paragraphs 1 and 2, where a person - other than an agent of an independent status to whom paragraph 7 applies - is acting in a Contracting State on behalf of an enterprise of the other Contracting State, that enterprise shall be deemed to have a permanent establishment in the first-mentioned State in respect of any activities which that person undertakes for the enterprise, if such person:

   a. Has, and habitually exercises, in that State an authority to conclude contracts in the name of the enterprise, unless the activities of such person are limited to those mentioned in paragraph 4 which, if exercised through a fixed place of business, would not make this fixed place of business a permanent establishment under the provisions of that paragraph; or
   b. Has no such authority, but habitually maintains in the first-mentioned State a stock of goods or merchandise from which he regularly delivers goods or merchandise on behalf of the enterprise.

6. Notwithstanding the preceding provisions of this Article, an insurance enterprise of a Contracting State shall, except in regard to re-insurance, be deemed to have a permanent establishment in the other Contracting State if it collects premiums in the territory of that other State or insures risks situated therein through a person other than an agent of an independent status to whom paragraph 7 applies.

7. An enterprise of a Contracting State shall not be deemed to have a permanent establishment in the other Contracting State merely because it carries on business in that other State through a broker, general commission agent or any other agent of an independent status, or merely because it maintains in that other State a stock of goods or merchandise with an agent of an independent status from which deliveries are made by that agent, provided that such persons are acting in the ordinary course of their business. However, when the activities of such an agent are devoted wholly or almost wholly on behalf of that enterprise, he will not be considered an agent of an independent status within the meaning of this paragraph.

8. The fact that a company which is a resident of a Contracting State controls or is controlled by a company which is a resident of the other Contracting State, or which carries on business in that other State (whether through a permanent establishment or otherwise), shall not of itself constitute either company a permanent establishment of the other.

Article 6 – *Income from Immovable Property*

1. Income derived by a resident of a Contracting State from immovable property (including income from agriculture or forestry) situated in the other Contracting State may be taxed in that other State.
2. For the purposes of this Agreement, the term "immovable property" shall have the meaning, which it has under the taxation law of the Contracting State in which the property in question is situated. The term shall in any case include property accessory to immovable property, livestock and equipment used in agriculture and forestry, rights to which the provisions of law respecting landed property apply, usufruct of immovable property and rights to variable or fixed payments as consideration for the working of, or

the right to work, mineral deposits, sources and other natural resources; ships and aircrafts shall not be regarded as immovable property.
3. The provisions of paragraph 1 shall apply to income derived from the direct use, letting, or use in any other form of immovable property and to income from the alienation of such property.
4. The provisions of paragraphs 1 and 3 shall also apply to the income from immovable property of an enterprise and to income from immovable property used for the performance of independent personal services.

Article 7 – Business Profits

1. The profits of an enterprise of a Contracting State shall be taxable only in that State unless the enterprise carries on business in the other Contracting State through a permanent establishment situated therein. If the enterprise carries on or has carried on business as aforesaid, the profits of the enterprise may be taxed in the other State but only so much of them as is attributable to that permanent establishment.
2. Subject to the provisions of paragraph 3, where an enterprise of a Contracting State carries on business in the other Contracting State through a permanent establishment situated therein, there shall in each Contracting State be attributed to that permanent establishment the profits which it might be expected to make if it were a distinct and separate enterprise engaged in the same or similar activities under the same or similar conditions and dealing wholly independently with the enterprise of which it is a permanent establishment.
3. In determining the profits of a permanent establishment, there shall be allowed as deduction expenses which are incurred for the purposes of the business of the permanent establishment including executive and general administrative expenses so incurred, whether in the State in which the permanent establishment is situated or elsewhere. However, no such deduction shall be allowed in respect of amounts, if any, paid (otherwise than as a reimbursement of actual expenses) by the permanent establishment to the head office of the enterprise or any of its other offices, by way of royalties, fees or other similar payments in return for the use of patens or other rights, or by way of commission, for specific services performed or for management, or, except in the case of a banking enterprise, by way of interest on moneys lent to the permanent establishment. Likewise, no account shall be taken in the determination of the profits of a permanent establishment, for amounts charged (otherwise than towards reimbursement of actual expenses), by the permanent establishment to the head office of the enterprise or any of its other offices, by way of royalties, fees or other similar payments in return for the use of patents or other rights, or by way of commission for specific services performed or for management, or, except in the case of a banking enterprise, by way of interest on moneys lent to the head office of the enterprise or any of its other offices.
4. Nothing in this Article shall affect the application of any law of a Contracting State relating to the determination of the tax liability of a person in cases where the information available to the competent authority of that State is inadequate to determine the profits to be attributed to a permanent establishment, provided that that law shall be applied, so far as the information available to the competent authority permits, consistently with the principles contained in this Article.
5. Insofar as it has been customary in a Contracting State to determine the profits to be attributed to a permanent establishment on the basis of an apportionment of the total profits of the enterprise to its various parts, nothing in paragraph 2 shall preclude that Contracting State from determining the profits to be taxed by such apportionment as may be customary; the method of apportionment adopted shall, however, be such that the result shall be in accordance with the principles contained in this Article.
6. No profits shall be attributed to a permanent establishment by reason of the mere purchase by that permanent establishment of goods or merchandise for the enterprise.

7. For the purposes of the preceding paragraphs, the profits to be attributed to the permanent establishment shall be determined by the same method year by year unless there is good and sufficient reason to the contrary.
8. Where profits include items of income, which are dealt with separately in other Articles of this Agreement, then the provisions of those Articles shall not be affected by the provisions of this Article.

Article 8 – Shipping and Air Transport

1. Profits derived by an enterprise of a Contracting State from the operation of ships or aircraft in international traffic shall be taxable only in that State.
2. Notwithstanding the provisions of paragraph 1 and of Article 7, profits derived by an enterprise of a Contracting State from a voyage of a ship or aircraft where the principal purpose of the voyage is to transport passengers or property between places in the other Contracting State may be taxed in that other State.
3. The provisions of paragraphs 1 and 2 shall also apply to profits from the participation in a pool, a joint business or an international operating agency.
4. For the purposes of this Article, profits from the operation of ships or aircraft in international traffic include:
   a. Income from the rental on a bareboat basis of ships or aircraft; and
   b. Profits from the use, maintenance or rental of containers (including trailers and related equipment for the transport of containers) used for the transport of goods or merchandise, where such rental, use or maintenance, as the case may be, is incidental to the operation of ships or aircraft in international traffic.

Article 9 – Associated Enterprises

1. Where:
   a. An enterprise of a Contracting State participates directly or indirectly in the management, control or capital of an enterprise of the other Contracting State, or
   b. The same persons participate directly or indirectly in the management, control or capital of an enterprise of a Contracting State and an enterprise of the other Contracting State, and in either case conditions are made or imposed between the two enterprises in their commercial or financial relations which differ from those which would be made between independent enterprises, then any income which would, but for those conditions, have accrued to one of the enterprises, but, by reason of those conditions, have not so accrued, may be included in the income of that enterprise and taxed accordingly
2. Where a Contracting State includes in the income of an enterprise of that State - and taxes accordingly - income on which an enterprise of the other Contracting State has been charged to tax in that other State and the income so included is income which would have accrued to the enterprise of the first-mentioned State if the conditions made between the two enterprises had been those which would have been made between independent enterprises, then that other State shall make an appropriate adjustment to the amount of tax charged therein on that income. In determining such adjustment, due regard shall be had to the other provisions of this Agreement and the competent authorities of the Contracting States shall if necessary consult each other.
3. A Contracting State shall not change the income of an enterprise in the circumstances referred to in paragraph 1 after the expiry of the time limits provided in its national laws and, in any case, after five years from the end of the year in which the income which would be subject to such change would, but for the conditions referred to in paragraph 1, have accrued to that enterprise.
4. The provisions of paragraphs 2 and 3 shall not apply in the case of fraud, willful default or neglect.

Article 10 – Dividends

1. Dividends paid by a company, which is a resident of a Contracting State to a resident of the other Contracting State, may be taxed in that other State.
2. However, such dividends may also be taxed in the Contracting State of which the company paying the dividends is a resident and according to the laws of that State, but if the recipient is the beneficial owner of the dividends the tax so charged shall not exceed:
    a. 5 per cent of the gross amount of the dividends if the beneficial owner is a company that controls at least 70 per cent of the voting power in the company paying the dividends;
    b. 10 per cent of the gross amount of the dividends if the beneficial owner is a company that controls at least 25 per cent but less than 70 per cent of the voting power in the company paying the dividends; and
    c. 15 per cent of the gross amount of the dividends in all other cases. The provisions of this paragraph shall not affect the taxation of the company on the profits out of which the dividends are paid.
3. The term "dividends" as used in this Article means income from shares, "jouissance" shares or "jouissance" rights, mining shares, founders' shares or other rights, not being debt-claims, participating in profits, as well as income which is subjected to the same taxation treatment as income from shares by the laws of the State of which the company making the distribution is a resident.
4. The provisions of paragraph 2 shall not apply if the beneficial owner of the dividends, being a resident of a Contracting State, carries on business in the other Contracting State of which the company paying the dividends is a resident, through a permanent establishment situated therein, or performs in that other State independent personal services from a fixed base situated therein, and the holding in respect of which the dividends are paid is effectively connected with such permanent establishment or fixed base. In such case the provisions of Article 7 or Article 14, as the case may be, shall apply.
5. Where a company which is a resident of a Contracting State derives profits or income from the other Contracting State, that other State may not impose any tax on the dividends paid by the company, except insofar as such dividends are paid to a resident of that other State or insofar as the holding in respect of which the dividends are paid is effectively connected with a permanent establishment or a fixed base situated in that other State, nor subject the company's undistributed profits to a tax on the company's undistributed profits, even if the dividends paid or the undistributed profits consist wholly or partly of profits or income arising in such other State.

Article 11 – Interest

1. Interest arising in a Contracting State and paid to a resident of the other Contracting State may be taxed in that other State.
2. However, such interest may also be taxed in the Contracting State in which it arises and according to the laws of that State, but if the recipient is the beneficial owner of the interest the tax so charged shall not exceed 10 per cent of the gross amount of the interest.
3. Notwithstanding the provisions of paragraph 2:
    a. Interest arising in a Contracting State and paid in respect of indebtedness of the Government of that State or of a political subdivision or local authority thereof shall, provided that the interest is beneficially owned by a resident of the other Contracting State, be taxable only in that other State;
    b. Interest arising in a Contracting State and paid to a resident of the other Contracting State shall be taxable only in that other State if it is paid in respect of a loan made,

guaranteed or insured, or a credit extended, guaranteed or insured by any institution, the capital of which is wholly owned by the Government of that other Sate, which is specified and agreed in letters exchanged between the competent authorities of the Contracting States.
4. The term "interest" as used in this Article means income from debt-claims of every kind, whether or not secured by mortgage, and in particular, income from government securities and income from bonds or debentures, including premiums and prizes attaching to such securities, bonds or debentures, as well as income which is subjected to the same taxation treatment as income from money lent by the laws of the State in which the income arises. However, the term "interest" does not include income dealt with in Article 10.
5. The provisions of paragraph 2 shall not apply if the beneficial owner of the interest, being a resident of a Contracting State, carries on business in the other Contracting State in which the interest arises through a permanent establishment situated therein, or performs in that other State independent personal services from a fixed base situated therein, and the debt-claim in respect of which the interest is paid is effectively connected with such permanent establishment or fixed base. In such case the provisions of Article 7 or Article 14, as the case may be, shall apply.
6. Interest shall be deemed to arise in a Contracting State when the payer is a resident of that State. Where, however, the person paying the interest, whether he is a resident of a Contracting State or not, has in a Contracting State a permanent establishment or a fixed base in connection with which the indebtedness on which the interest is paid was incurred, and such interest is borne by such permanent establishment or fixed base, then such interest shall be deemed to arise in the State in which the permanent establishment or fixed base is situated.
7. Where, by reason of a special relationship between the payer and the beneficial owner or between both of them and some other person, the amount of the interest, having regard to the debt-claim for which it is paid, exceeds the amount which would have been agreed upon by the payer and the beneficial owner in the absence of such relationship, the provisions of this Article shall apply only to the last-mentioned amount. In such case, the excess part of the payments shall remain taxable according to the laws of each Contracting State, due regard being had to the other provisions of this Agreement.

Article 12 – Royalties and Fees for Technical Services

1. Royalties and fees for technical services arising in a Contracting State and paid to a resident of the other Contracting State may be taxed in that other State.
2. However, such royalties and fees for technical services may also be taxed in the Contracting State in which they arise and according to the laws of that State, but if the recipient is the beneficial owner of the royalties or of the fees for technical services the tax so charged shall not exceed:
   a. In the case of royalties 10 per cent of the gross amount of such royalties;
   b. In the case of fees for technical services 7.5 per cent of the gross amount of such fees.
3. The term "royalties" as used in this Article means payments of any kind received as a consideration for the use of, or the right to use, any copyright of literary, artistic or scientific work (including payments of any kind in respect of motion picture films and works on film, tape or other means of reproduction for radio or television broadcasting), any patent, trade mark, design or model, plan, secret formula or process or for the use of, or the right to use, industrial, commercial or scientific equipment, or for information concerning industrial, commercial or scientific experience.
4. The term "fees for technical services" as used in this Article means payments of any kind to any person, other than payments to an employee of the person making the

payments, in consideration for any services of a managerial, technical or consultancy nature rendered in the Contracting State of which the payer is a resident.
5. The provisions of paragraph 2 shall not apply if the beneficial owner of the royalties or fees for technical services, being a resident of a Contracting State, carries on business in the other Contracting State in which the royalties or fees for technical services arise through a permanent establishment situated therein, or performs in that other State independent personal services from a fixed base situated therein, and the right, property or contract in respect of which the royalties or fees for technical services are paid is effectively connected with such permanent establishment or fixed base. In such case the provisions of Article 7 or Article 14, as the case may be, shall apply.
6. Royalties or fees for technical services shall be deemed to arise in a Contracting State when the payer is a resident of that State. Where, however, the person paying the royalties or fees for technical services, whether he is a resident of a Contracting State or not, has in a Contracting State a permanent establishment or a fixed base in connection with which the obligation to make the payment was incurred, and such royalties or fees for technical services are borne by that permanent establishment or fixed base, then such royalties or fees for technical services shall be deemed to arise in the State in which the permanent establishment or fixed base is situated.
7. Where, by reason of a special relationship between the payer and the beneficial owner or between both of them and some other person, the amount of the royalties or fees for technical services paid exceeds, for whatever reason, the amount which would have been agreed upon by the payer and the beneficial owner in the absence of such relationship, the provisions of this Article shall apply only to the last-mentioned amount. In such case, the excess part of the payments shall remain taxable according to the laws of each Contracting State, due regard being had to the other provisions of this Agreement.

Article 13 – Capital Gains

1. Gains derived by a resident of a Contracting State from the alienation of immovable property situated in the other Contracting State may be taxed in that other State.
2. Gains from the alienation of movable property forming part of the business property of a permanent establishment which an enterprise of a Contracting State has in the other Contracting State or of movable property pertaining to a fixed base available to a resident of a Contracting State in the other Contracting State for the purpose of performing independent personal services, including such gains from the alienation of such a permanent establishment (alone or with the whole enterprise) or of such a fixed base may be taxed in that other State.
3. Gains derived by an enterprise of a Contracting State from the alienation of ships or aircraft operated in international traffic or movable property pertaining to the operation of such ships or aircraft shall be taxable only in that State.
4. Gains from the alienation of shares of a company that is a resident of a Contracting State may be taxed in that State.
5. Gains from the alienation of any property, other than that referred to in paragraphs 1, 2, 3 and 4 may be taxed in both Contracting States in accordance with the respective laws of those States.

Article 14 – Independent Personal Services

1. Income derived by an individual who is a resident of a Contracting State in respect of professional services or other activities of an independent character shall be taxable only in that State unless he has a fixed base regularly available to him in the other Contracting State for the purpose of performing his activities. If he has or had such a fixed base, the income may be taxed in the other State but only so much of it as is attributable to that fixed base.

2. The term "professional services" includes especially independent scientific, literary, artistic, educational or teaching activities as well as the independent activities of physicians, lawyers, engineers, architects, dentists and accountants.

Article 15 – Dependent Personal Services

1. Subject to the provisions of Articles 16, 18 and 19, salaries, wages and other remuneration derived by a resident of a Contracting State in respect of an employment shall be taxable only in that State unless the employment is exercised in the other Contracting State. If the employment is so exercised, such remuneration as is derived therefrom may be taxed in that other State.
2. Notwithstanding the provisions of paragraph 1, remuneration derived by a resident of a Contracting State in respect of an employment exercised in the other Contracting State shall be taxable only in the first-mentioned State if:
    a. The recipient is present in the other State for a period or period not exceeding in the aggregate 183 days in any twelve month period commencing or ending in the fiscal year concerned, and
    b. The remuneration is paid by, or on behalf of, an employer who is not a resident of the other State, and
    c. The remuneration is not borne by a permanent establishment or a fixed base, which the employer has in the other State.
3. Notwithstanding the preceding provisions of this Article, remuneration derived in respect of an employment exercised aboard a ship or aircraft operated in international traffic by an enterprise of a Contracting State, shall be taxable only in that State unless the remuneration is derived by a resident of the other Contracting State.

Article 16 – Directors' Fees

Directors' fees and other similar payments derived by a resident of a Contracting State in his capacity as a member of the board of directors of a company which is a resident of the other Contracting State, may be taxed in that other State.

Article 17 – Artists and Sportsmen

1. Notwithstanding the provisions of Articles 14 and 15, income derived by a resident of a Contracting State as an entertainer, such as a theatre, motion picture, radio or television artiste, or a musician, or as a sportsman, from his personal activities as such exercised in the other Contracting State, may be taxed in that other State.
2. Where income in respect of personal activities exercised by an entertainer or a sportsman in his capacity as such accrues not to the entertainer or sportsman himself but to another person, that income may, notwithstanding the provisions of Articles 7, 14 and 15, be taxed in the Contracting State in which the activities of the entertainer or sportsman are exercised.
3. The provisions of paragraph 2 shall not apply if it is established that neither the entertainer or the sportsman nor persons related thereto, participate directly or indirectly in the profits of the person referred to in that paragraph.
4. The provisions of paragraphs 1 and 2 shall not apply to income derived from activities performed in a Contracting State by a resident of the other Contracting State in the context of a visit in the first-mentioned State of a non-profit organization of the other State, provided the visit is substantially supported by public funds.

Article 18 – Pensions and Annuities

1. Pensions and annuities arising in a Contracting State and paid to a resident of the other Contracting State may be taxed in that other State.
2. Pensions arising in a Contracting State and paid to a resident of the other Contracting State may also be taxed in the State in which they arise and according to the law of that State. However, in the case of periodic pension payments, other than payments under the social security legislation in a Contracting State, the tax so charged shall not exceed 15 per cent of the gross amount of the payment.
3. Annuities arising in a Contracting State and paid to a resident of the other Contracting State may also be taxed in the State in which they arise and according to the law of that State.
4. Notwithstanding anything in this Agreement, alimony and other similar payments arising in a Contracting State and paid to a resident of the other Contracting State who is subject to tax therein in respect thereof, shall be taxable only in that other State.

Article 19 – Government Service

1. a. Salaries, wages and similar remuneration, other than a pension, paid by a Contracting State or a political subdivision or a local authority thereof to an individual in respect of services rendered to that State or subdivision or authority in any other State shall be taxable only in the first-mentioned State.
   b. However, such salaries, wages or similar remuneration shall be taxable only in the other Contracting State if the services are rendered in that State and the individual is a resident of that State who:
      (i) Is a national of that State; or
      (ii) Did not become a resident of that State solely for the purpose of rendering the services.
2. The provisions of paragraph 1 shall not apply to remuneration in respect of services rendered in connection with a business carried on by a Contracting State or a political subdivision or a local authority thereof.

Article 20 – Students

Payments which a student, apprentice or business trainee who is, or was immediately before visiting a Contracting State, a resident of the other Contracting State and who is present in the first-mentioned State solely for the purpose of his education or training receives for the purpose of his maintenance, education or training shall not be taxed in that State, provided that such payments arise from sources outside that State.

Article 21 – Other Income

1. Subject to the provisions of paragraph 2, items of income of a resident of a Contracting State, wherever arising, not dealt with in the foregoing Articles of this Agreement shall be taxable only in that State.
2. However, if such income is derived by a resident of a Contracting State from sources in the other Contracting State, such income may also be taxed in the State in which it arises, and according to the law of that State. Where such income is income from an estate or a trust, other than a trust to which Contributions were deductible, the tax so charged shall, provided that the income is taxable in the Contracting State in which the beneficial owner is a resident, not exceed 15 per cent of the gross amount of the income.

Article 22 – Elimination of Double Taxation

1. In the case of Vietnam, double taxation shall be avoided as follows: where a resident of Vietnam derives income which, in accordance with the provisions of this Agreement, may be taxed in Canada, Vietnam shall allow as a deduction from the tax on the income of that resident an amount equal to the income tax paid in Canada. Such deduction shall not, however, exceed that part of the income tax, as computed before the deduction is given, which is attributable to the income which may be taxed in Canada.
2. In the case of Canada, double taxation shall be avoided as follows:
    a. Subject to the existing provisions of the law of Canada regarding the deduction from tax payable in Canada of tax paid in a territory outside Canada and to any subsequent modification of those provisions - which shall not affect the general principle hereof - and unless a greater deduction or relief is provided under the laws of Canada, tax payable in Vietnam on profits, income or gains arising in Vietnam shall be deducted from any Canadian tax payable in respect of such profits, income or gains;
    b. Subject to the existing provisions of the law of Canada regarding the taxation of income from a foreign affiliate and to any subsequent modification of those provisions - which shall not affect the general principle hereof - for the purpose of computing Canadian tax, a company which is a resident of Canada shall be allowed to deduct in computing its taxable income any dividend received by it out of the exempt surplus of a foreign affiliate which is a resident of Vietnam; and
    c. Where, in accordance with any provision of the Agreement, income derived by a resident of Canada is exempt from tax in Canada, Canada may nevertheless, in calculating the amount of tax on other income, take into account the exempted income. The term "exempt surplus" shall have the meaning that it has under the Income Tax Act of Canada.
3. For the purpose of subparagraph (a) of paragraph 2, tax payable in Vietnam by a company engaged primarily in the manufacturing or natural resources sector which is a resident of Canada in respect of:
    a. Interest, other than interest which is exempted in Vietnam in accordance with paragraph 3 of Article 11, or
    b. Payments of any kind received as a consideration for the use of, or the right to use, any patent, design or model, plan, secret formula or process, or for information concerning industrial or scientific experience,
    c. Paid by a company engaged primarily in the same sector which is a resident of Vietnam shall be deemed to have been paid at the rate of 10 per cent of the gross amount of the payment. The provisions of this paragraph shall apply for the first five years for which the Agreement is effective, but the competent authorities of the Contracting States may consult with each other to determine whether this period shall be extended.
4. For the purposes of subparagraph (a) of paragraph 2, tax payable in Vietnam by a company which is a resident of Canada in respect of profits attributable to manufacturing activities or to the exploration or exploitation of natural resources carried on by it in Vietnam shall be deemed to include any amount which would have been payable thereon as Vietnamese tax for any year but for an exemption from, or reduction of, tax granted for that year or any part thereof under specific provisions of Vietnamese legislation and provided always that the competent authority of Vietnam has certified that any such exemption from or reduction of Vietnamese tax given under these provisions has been granted in other to promote economic development in Vietnam. Relief from Canadian tax by virtue of this paragraph shall be given for a period of ten years only, beginning with the date on which the Agreement entered into force.

5. For the purposes of this Article, profits, income or gains of a resident of a Contracting State that may be taxed in the other Contracting State in accordance with this Agreement shall be deemed to arise from sources in that other State.

Article 23 – Non-discrimination

1. Nationals of a Contracting State shall not be subjected in the other Contracting State to any taxation or any requirement connected therewith which is other or more burdensome than the taxation and connected requirements to which nationals of that other State in the same circumstances are or may be subjected.
2. The taxation on a permanent establishment which an enterprise of a Contracting State has in the other Contracting State shall not be less favorably levied in that other State than the taxation levied on enterprises of that other State carrying on the same activities.
3. Nothing in this Article shall be construed as obliging a Contracting State to grant to residents of the other Contracting State any personal allowances, reliefs and reductions for taxation purposes on account of civil status or family responsibilities which it grants to its own residents.
4. Enterprises of a Contracting State, the capital of which is wholly or partly owned or controlled, directly or indirectly, by one or more residents of the other Contracting State, shall not be subjected in the first-mentioned State to any taxation or any requirement connected therewith which is other or more burdensome than the taxation and connected requirements to which other similar enterprises of the first-mentioned State, the capital of which is wholly or partly owned or controlled, directly or indirectly, by one or more residents of a third State, are or may be subjected.
5. In this Article, the term "taxation" means taxes, which are the subject of this Agreement.

Article 24 – Mutual Agreement Procedure

1. Where a person considers that the actions of one or both of the Contracting States result or will result for him in taxation not in accordance with the provisions of this Agreement, he may, irrespective of the remedies provided by the domestic law of those States, address to the competent authority of the Contracting State of which he is a resident an application in writing stating the grounds for claiming the revision of such taxation. To be admissible, the said application must be submitted within two years from the first notification of the action, which gives rise to taxation not in accordance with the Agreement.
2. The competent authority referred to in paragraph 1 shall endeavor, if the objection appears to it to be justified and if it is not itself able to arrive at a satisfactory solution, to resolve the case by mutual agreement with the competent authority of the other Contracting State, with a view to the avoidance of taxation not in accordance with the Agreement.
3. A Contracting State shall not, after the expiry of the time limits provided in its national laws and, in any case, after five years from the end of the taxable period in which the income concerned has accrued, increase the tax base of a resident of either of the Contracting State by including therein items of income which have also been charged to tax in the other Contracting State. This paragraph shall not apply in the case of fraud, willful default or neglect.
4. The competent authorities of the Contracting States shall endeavor to resolve by mutual agreement any difficulties or doubts arising as to the interpretation or application of the Agreement.
5. The competent authorities of the Contracting States may consult together for the elimination of double taxation in cases not provided for in the Agreement and may communicate with each other directly for the purpose of applying the Agreement.

Article 25 – Exchange of Information

1. The competent authorities of the Contracting States shall exchange such information as is necessary for carrying out the provisions of this Agreement or of the domestic laws of the Contracting States concerning taxes covered by the Agreement insofar as the taxation thereunder is not contrary to the Agreement. The exchange of information is not restricted by Article 1. Any information received by a Contracting State shall be treated as secret in the same manner as information obtained under the domestic laws of that State and shall be disclosed only to persons or authorities (including courts and administrative bodies) involved in the assessment or collection of, the enforcement in respect of, or the determination of appeals in relation to taxes. Such persons or authorities shall use the information only for such purposes. They may disclose the information in public court proceedings or in judicial decisions.
2. Nothing in paragraph 1 shall be construed so as to impose on a Contracting State the obligation:
   a. To carry out administrative measures at variance with the laws or the administrative practice of that or of the other Contracting State;
   b. To supply information which is not obtainable under the laws or in the normal course of the administration of that or of the other Contracting State;
   c. To supply information, which would disclose any trade, business, industrial, commercial or professional secret or trade process, or information, the disclosure of which would be contrary to public policy (ordre public).
3. If information is requested by a Contracting State in accordance with this Article, the other Contracting State shall endeavor to obtain the information to which the request relates in the same way as if its own taxation were involved notwithstanding the fact that the other State does not, at that time, need such information. If specifically requested by the competent authority of a Contracting State, the competent authority of the other Contracting State shall endeavor to provide information under this Article in the form requested, such as depositions of witnesses and copies of unedited original documents (including books, papers, statements, records, accounts or writings), to the same extent such depositions and documents can be obtained under the laws and administrative practices of that other State with respect to its own taxes.

Article 26 – Diplomatic Agents and Consular Officers

1. Nothing in this Agreement shall affect the fiscal privileges of diplomatic agents or consular officers under the general rules of international law or under the provisions of special agreements.
2. Notwithstanding Article 4, an individual who is a member of a diplomatic mission, consular post or permanent mission of a Contracting State which is situated in the other Contracting State or in a third State shall be deemed for the purposes of the Agreement to be a resident of the sending State if he is liable in the sending State to the same obligations in relation to tax on his total income as are residents of that sending State.
3. The Agreement shall not apply to international organizations, to organs or officials thereof and to persons who are members of a diplomatic mission, consular post or permanent mission of a third State or group of States, being present in a Contracting State and who are not liable in either Contracting State to the same obligations in relation to tax on their total income as are residents thereof.

Article 27 – Entry into Force

1. Each of the Contracting States shall notify the other Contracting State of the completion of the procedures required by the laws of the respective Contracting State for bringing

into force this Agreement. This Agreement shall enter into force on the date of the later of these notifications.
2. The provisions of the Agreement shall have effect:

   a. In respect of tax withheld at the source on amounts paid or credited to non-residents on or after the first day of January in the calendar year following that in which the Agreement enters into force; and
   b. In respect of other taxes for taxation years beginning on or after the first day of January in the calendar year following that in which the Agreement enters into force.

Article 28 – Termination

This Agreement shall remain in force until terminated by a Contracting State. Either Contracting State may terminate the Agreement, through the diplomatic channel, by giving to the other Contracting State a written notice of termination on or before June 30 in any calendar year from the fifth year after the year in which the Agreement entered into force. In such event, the Agreement shall cease to have effect:

   a. In respect of tax withheld at the source on amounts paid or credited to non-residents on or after the first day of January of the calendar year following that in which the notice of termination is given; and
   b. In respect of other taxes for taxation years beginning on or after the first day of January of the calendar year following that in which the notice of termination is given.

DONE in duplicate at Hanoi, this 11th day of November of the year one thousand nine hundred and ninety-seven.

In the Vietnamese, French and English languages, each version being equally authentic.
This Agreement entered into force on 16 December 1998.

Chapter 8
Asian Area Treaties

8.1 Vietnam–Asian Area Bilateral Agreements' History

8.1.1 Vietnam–India Bilateral Agreement's History and Evolution

India and Vietnam signed a bilateral trade agreement in 1978. India has supported Vietnam through its independence from the French, has openly opposed the U.S. during the Vietnam War, and was the one of few non-communist nations to assist Vietnam in the Cambodian–Vietnam War. After first establishing diplomatic ties in 1972, India, which has registered an average growth rate of around 8 % over the past decade, granted Vietnam "Most Favored Nation" in 1975, established the India–Vietnam Joint Business Council in 1993, and signed the Bilateral Investment Promotion and Protection Agreement (BIPPA) in March 1997. Moreover, both nations propagated the Joint Declaration on Comprehensive Cooperation in 2003 in which the nations envisioned the creation of the "Arc of Advantage and Prosperity" (Indian Business Chamber in Vietnam 2012).

In addition to signing agreements and MOUs to avoid double taxation, for cultural exchange, education exchange, and cooperation in science, technology, agriculture, and fisheries, Vietnam, whose foreign trade to GDP ratio has exceeded 150 % over the past 5 years, and India have also established the Joint Working Group and the Bilateral Joint Commission (Ministry of External Affairs, India). Yet, potential for trade and investment remains largely untapped.

While India is currently one of the ten largest exporters to Vietnam with bilateral trade exceeding $4 billion, both parties have set a $7 billion target by 2015. Top 5 commodities (of which raw materials constitute the highest proportion) account for over 50 % of India's total exports to Vietnam, whereas Vietnam's top 5 commodity exports, which constitute over 60 % of its total exports, include a diverse range of products such as chemicals, fuel, coffee and high-tech machinery.

In Fig. 8.1 below is shown a breakdown of the main trade between Vietnam and India.

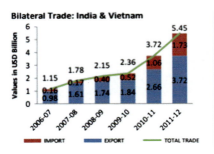 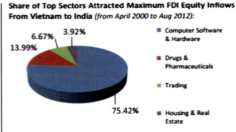

Fig. 8.1 Bilateral trade between India and Vietnam with sector-wise breakdown. *Source*: Department of Commerce, Ministry of Commerce and Industry, Government of India

The Indian Prime Minister, Dr. Manmohan Singh, and the Vietnamese President, Truong Tan Sang, have had high-level discussions to further boost strategic ties. While increased bilateral trade is bound to benefit both economies, India's motivation behind strengthening alliance with Vietnam (whose FDI as a percentage of total investments and GDP is thrice India's percentage, given the relative sizes of the economies) seems to be largely driven by China's belligerence. With numerous potential opportunities for significant mutual investment in energy, financial services, and urban infrastructure, there is a significant number of trade incentives.

8.1.2 Vietnam–Singapore Bilateral Agreement's History and Evolution

Since the establishment of diplomatic relations in 1973, the 40 years of bilateral trade ties between Vietnam and Singapore have been much more robust since Vietnam joined the Bali Treaty in July 1992 and became a full member of the ASEAN 3 years later. To make effective bilateral trade flow possible, the Vietnam–Singapore Cooperation Commission was set up in May 1993, followed by the Vietnam–Singapore Joint Steering Committee in Investment in 2003. In addition to that, the Annual Bilateral Consultation at Deputy Foreign Minister Level between the two Foreign Ministries was set up to discuss bilateral cooperation on international and domestic matters of mutual concern to the two nations. Nevertheless, the Vietnam–Singapore Training Centre (VSTC) was established in 2001 as part of Singapore's commitment to the Initiative for ASEAN Integration (IAI) in order to train Vietnamese officials.

Furthermore, in 2005, the Singaporean Minister of Trade and Industry, in collaboration with the Vietnamese Minister of Planning and Investment (at the time), set up with the Singapore–Vietnam Connectivity Framework (Ministry of Trade and Industry, Singapore 2011). The Connectivity Framework, which came into effect on 6 January 2006, had the primary objective of implementing policies of mutual benefit to both states in regard to investment and commerce.

The agreement covers six sectors of cooperation: Finance, Education and Training, Information and Computer Technology (ICT), Telecommunications, Investment, Transportation, and Trade and Services.

Along with those landmark agreements, many smaller, yet significant agreements have been signed between Vietnam and Singapore over the years: the Shipping Trade Agreement of 1992, the Agreement of Air Transport of 1992, the Trade Agreement of 1992, the Agreement on the Promotion and Protection of Investments of 1992, the Agreement on Cooperation in the field of Management and Environmental Protection of 1993, the Agreement on Avoidance of Double Taxation of 1994, and the Agreement on Tourism Cooperation of 1994.

All those efforts have yielded fruit; with investments worth over US$23 billion (Vietnamese investment FDI in Singapore is much smaller in comparison) in over 900 different projects covering 17/21 sectors of the economy and 39/63 provinces of Vietnam, Singapore is the third largest foreign investor in the country, and Vietnam's political stability, proximity to Singapore, and a dynamic 46 million-people workforce are some of the things that make Vietnam an attractive FDI destination for Singaporean companies; as proof of Vietnam becoming one of the top recipients of aid under the Singapore Cooperation Programme (SCP) by 2012, over 13,000 Vietnamese had received training in Singapore in a variety of sectors under this program. Consequently, limitations on land and labor are driving investors in the industrial sector out of Singapore. The Vietnam Singapore Industrial Parks (VSIPs) are concrete examples of Singaporean investors' obsession with Vietnam.

To elevate the existing trade links (Table 8.1), both countries are currently working toward the signing of a Strategic Partnership Agreement in 2013 to celebrate the 40th anniversary of diplomatic ties between Vietnam and Singapore (Government of Singapore).

8.1.3 Vietnam–Korea Bilateral Agreement's History and Evolution

The two countries, historically friendly and having shared a common cultural heritage of Buddhism, Confucianism, and Taoism, fell prey to international divide-and-rule politics in the period following the Second World War. The fact that over 300,000 Koreans fought on the side of the U.S. against Communist Vietnam became a problem when both sides attempted to normalize relations after the Cold War ended. In order to normalize relations with socialist countries, South Korea launched its Nordpolitik-Northern Policy around the same era when Vietnam adopted the Doi Moi reform policy in 1986 (Park 2012).

The two nations, however, worked to resolve their differences and cooperate to attain future synergies—thus in 1992, both nations established embassies in each other's capitals. Since then, governments of both countries have had no reservations

Table 8.1 Vietnam–Singapore bilateral trade

	2010	2011
Imports	2,193,042	2,084,599
Exports	10,061,102	12,834,900
Total trade	12,254,144	14,919,499

Source: IE Singapore's Statlink

in implementing policies to make those synergies possible—over the past two decades, several top leaders of both nations have visited the other party and signed important agreements such as the Comprehensive Partnership Agreement in 2001 and the Strategic Cooperative Partnership Agreement in 2009.

Given Korea's proactive approach towards Vietnamese commerce among other factors, it comes as no surprise that South Korea, Vietnam's number one investor with an FDI of $23.5 billion spread across more than 3,000 projects, has created over 500,000 jobs in Vietnam with companies like Samsung Electronics and POSCO having made major investments in different Vietnamese provinces. With Korea being Vietnam's fourth largest trading partner and Vietnam being Korea's ninth largest trading partner (second largest among ASEAN countries), bilateral trade reached $13.6 billion in 2011 (though historically, Vietnam's exports to Korea have been less diverse than those of Korea) and both nations' Presidents have established a $20 billion target for 2015 and more or less three times that by 2020. In addition to the number one recipient of Korea's Economic Cooperation and Development Fund (ECDF) (Korea has provided over $1.2 billion for over 37 different projects), Korea has also given Vietnam more than $130 million over the last 20 years spread across 35 projects. Moreover, in addition to helping Vietnam invest in IT and high-tech industry, Korea has also built vocational schools and hospitals in remote Vietnamese locations as part of development aid to Vietnam (Park 2012).

Ironically, while Vietnam has promoted economic cooperation with South Korea, it has maintained its traditional friendly relations with North Korea, being its former Cold War ally, as well as socialist comrade. While 20 years after the establishment of diplomatic relations Vietnam and South Korea have achieved much more than they may have conceived possible back in the day, some obstacle to future progress remain—tension exists regarding the aftereffects of the Vietnam War and Korea's participation in it. Though both the countries' major trading partner now is China, being middle powers of the region and through expanded trade links with each other and other ASEAN nations, Vietnam and Korea have the potential to play a major role in the continent's geopolitics.

8.1.4 Vietnam–Japan Bilateral Agreement's History and Evolution

Vietnam has steadily developed a bilateral trading relationship with Japan, one of the world's largest economies, for a long time. Though their relations were scarred by World War II, Japan agreed to pay a war compensation (disguised as non-refundable aid) of $49 million and set up an embassy in Hanoi in 1975, while Vietnam established an embassy in Tokyo the following year (Vietnam Ministry of Foreign Affairs 2007a). Over the years, the level of mutual trust between the nations improved despite huge economic gaps between them. In order to improve Vietnam's capabilities in the development roadmap, Japan committed US$1.76 billion towards infrastructure upgrades and projects for environmental safety and elimination of poverty.

In 2011, bilateral trade between the countries, valued at over $21 billion, was 26 % higher than that of 2010 (of this, the value of Vietnam's exports was $10.7 billion). In addition to Vietnam being a member of the ASEAN–Japan Center (AJC), under which Vietnam has become better equipped to help its companies export high-quality products to Japan, the signing of the ASEAN–Japan Economic Partnership Agreement (AJCP) and the Vietnam–Japan Economic Partnership Agreement (VJEPA) has been a catalyst to the expansion of bilateral trade between the two countries.

Vietnam has had and continues to have excellent prospects in Japan as far as export of seafood is concerned—the Japanese have the world's highest per capita consumption of seafood products (70–80 kg/person/year). In addition to that, Vietnam has equally good prospects in Japan as far as wooden, leather, and shoe products are concerned. Consequently, Japan exports equipment, machinery, and material for domestic production to Vietnam—these are generally of a value equaling Vietnam's exports to Japan; this is unlike Vietnam's bilateral relationships with many other countries in Southeast Asia and Northeast Asia, in which Vietnam bears trade deficits. Japan, as of 2011, being the fourth largest investor in Vietnam, with investments in over 1,600 projects, has made its brands like Hitachi, Toyota, and Toshiba familiar to ordinary Vietnamese (Fig. 8.2). Despite that, Vietnam's brand positioning in Japan is weak since imports from Vietnam constitute a small percentage of Japan's total imports (1/3 of total) and less than 2 % of Japan's total exports are to Vietnam.

Vietnam has historically lagged behind Thailand, Indonesia, and Malaysia when it comes to bilateral trade with Japan. This is for several reasons: Vietnamese companies, other than failing to understand the Japanese business culture and not making use of all the available benefits, are also often unable to afford participation in trade fairs and fail to meet Japanese safety standards on manufacturing and food processing. Thus, there continues to be plenty of room for expansion in bilateral trade—while Japanese companies are more successfully penetrating the Vietnamese market, Vietnamese companies can do the same by overcoming regulatory and industrial barriers.

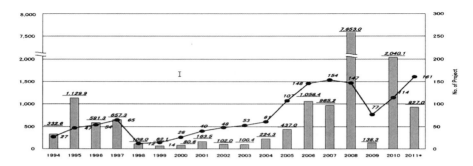

Fig. 8.2 Japanese FDI toward Vietnam (approval basis) in millions of US$. *Source*: Japan External Trade Organization (JETRO)

8.1.5 Vietnam–China Bilateral Agreement's History and Evolution

The Vietnamese embassy in Beijing celebrated the 63rd anniversary of diplomatic ties between Vietnam and China on 18 January 2013. Despite sharing similar socialist backgrounds and having diplomatic ties since 1950, Vietnam and the People's Republic of China (a nation over 15 times the size of Vietnam) have had a turbulent relationship due to history—primarily the Vietnam War and Vietnam's occupation of Cambodia. However, since the normalization of relations in 1991, both countries have engaged in trade cooperation and have signed over 53 agreements to date, especially after the creation of the China–ASEAN free trade—though bilateral trade amounted to only slightly over $30 million, it had exceeded $30 billion by 2011 (Fig. 8.3) and reached nearly $41 billion in 2012. The governments, however, have set a more ambitious target of $60 billion in bilateral trade revenues by 2015. Even in 2009, though both economies were somewhat affected by the international financial crises, bilateral trade volume increased by 8 % to over $21 billion.

By the end of July 2012, with over 850 investment projects and over 893,000 tourists visiting Vietnam, China ranked in the top 15 in terms of investments in Vietnam. Chinese investment volume appears to be heavily concentrated in industrial parks, motor vehicle spare parts, food processing, mineral extraction, and electricity. In fact, Chinese business' invasion of Vietnam has been so aggressive that Vietnam's industrial production would suffer major crises should China discontinue trading with it for some reason.

In addition to that, a majority of engineering, procurement, and construction contracts for industrial projects in Vietnam have been given to Chinese companies due to their ability to offer cheap technology and secure funding from Chinese banks. The problem with such investment, however, is that the cheap technology has worse environmental consequences and often times the technology that Chinese contractors use in Vietnam is banned in China itself due to concerns regarding safety and efficiency. Moreover, massive purchases of agricultural commodities by

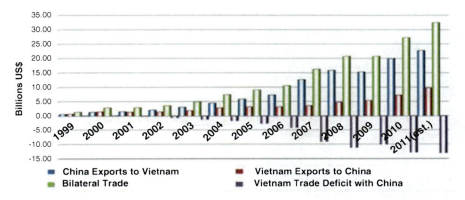

Fig. 8.3 Vietnam–China bilateral trade and trade balance. *Source*: Vietnam Ministry of Industry and Trade

Chinese merchants have driven food prices in Vietnam and thus significantly contributed to national inflation (Zhang 2012).

Going forward, the perception of the rest of the world on the Vietnam–China relationship is more of the kind of relationship where China is the bully in Asia and Vietnam is being forced to trade with China to prevent hostility. While the Vietnamese have not expressed frustration with Chinese takeover of its markets, there exists significant mutual suspicion. While bilateral trade will reach new records if current trends continue, mutual trust will improve only through more people-to-people contact between citizens of the two nations—while the trends in that regard are positive, there is much room for improvement.

8.1.6 Vietnam–Thailand Bilateral Agreement's History and Evolution

After formally establishing diplomatic relations 37 years ago in 1976, bilateral trade between Vietnam and Thailand got a significant boost since 1991—especially after Vietnam's admission to ASEAN in 1995. Today, it is not uncommon to see vast varieties of Thai goods in Vietnamese markets and vice versa.

Following their first joint cabinet session in Danang in 2004, a second one was held on 27 October 2012 at which Prime Minister Yingluck Shinawatra of Thailand and Prime Minister Nguyen Tan Dung signed a joint statement between the Thai and Vietnamese Foreign Ministers, the Thai-Vietnam Security Outlook (2012–2016), and a memorandum of understanding relating to the establishment of the Thai-Vietnamese Business Council. With 295 projects and capital investments in Vietnam worth over US$6 billion, Thailand was the tenth largest investor in Vietnam in 2011.

Table 8.2 Thai imports from Vietnam in 2011 (in US$)

Thai imports from Vietnam 2011	Value (US$1,000s)	% total imports
Coffee, tea, mate and spices	84,158.00	48.46
Meat, fish and seafood food preparations nes	22,709.00	15.37
Silk	2,168.00	11.87
Sugars and sugar confectionery	16,327.00	11.04
Manmade filaments	81,993.00	10.86
Manufactures of plaiting material, basketwork, etc.	475.00	8.54
Edible fruit, nuts, peel of citrus fruit, melons	40,932.00	8.11
Other made textile articles, sets, worn clothing etc.	16,253.00	7.83
Footwear, gaiters and the like, parts thereof	21,271.00	7.37
Miscellaneous manufactured articles	17,990.00	6.00

Source: Government of Thailand

While bilateral trade between the nations was around $9 billion in 2011, both the governments have set a double target by 2015, i.e., a growth rate of 20 % per annum over the next couple of years. Given the fact that both nations are among the world's leading producers of rice, increased trade cooperation between them will stabilize rice prices, output quality, and food security. In addition, both nations also boosted bilateral trade in fresh fruit—especially Vietnam's exports to Thailand (Tables 8.2 and 8.3).

In addition to rice trade, Thailand's welcome to Vietnam's attendance at the tri-party rubber trade meeting in Thailand in December 2012 signaled seriousness by both nations' leaders to achieve the $18 billion bilateral trade target. Vietnam reciprocated the tri-party invitation by supporting Thailand's role in solving the South China Sea dispute in ASEAN. In order to ensure that the 20 % bilateral trade growth target is reached, in 2012, leaders of both nations requested their respective Ministries of Foreign Affairs to coordinate the other ministries to their counterparts in both nations in order to establish and strengthen bilateral ties for peace, prosperity, and stability in the region. This not only will help Vietnam and Thailand boost their bilateral trade but also will increase intra-ASEAN trade as a whole and aid it in expanding its influence globally.

8.1.7 Vietnam–Taiwan Bilateral Agreement's History and Evolution

Vietnam adheres to the one-China policy and formally recognizes the People's Republic of China only, though it engages in a lot of trade with Taiwan, also known as the Republic of China. After Vietnam and Taiwan promulgated their respective foreign investment laws, Taiwanese businessmen were some of Vietnam's earliest foreign investors. In 1993, the two nations signed four important agreements: protection of Taiwanese investors in Vietnam, double taxation avoidance, agricultural and fishing cooperation, and labor agreements. Initially, Taiwan's investment

8.1 Vietnam–Asian Area Bilateral Agreements' History

Table 8.3 Thailand's exports to Vietnam in 2011 (in US$)

Thailand exports to Vietnam 2011	Value (US$1,000s)	% total exports
Knitted or crocheted fabric	55,089	20.19
Raw hides and skins (other than furskins) and leather	89,562	17.75
Products of animal origin, nes	7,030	15.91
Zinc and articles thereof	16,295	15.86
Oil seed, oleagic fruits, grain, seed, fruit, etc., nes	19,790	15.71
Pharmaceutical products	53,746	15.49
Beverages, spirits and vinegar	119,777	13.65
Impregnated, coated or laminated textile fabric	21,351	12.43
Miscellaneous chemical products	96,914	12.11
Ships, boats and other floating structures	174,361	11.03
Manmade filaments	91,086	10.27

Source: Government of Thailand

in Vietnam was mainly concentrated in the South due to better infrastructure and abundance of land and labor; however, over time the FDI has spread nationwide due to the government's incentive policies to adjust capital distribution. Thus, Taiwanese projects are now scattered across over 40 provinces throughout Vietnam, though a majority of them are still located in Hanoi, Ho Chi Minh City, Dong Nai, and Binh Duong.

Taiwan's FDI contributions in Vietnam are proportionate with overall FDI contributions in Vietnam. Most of Taiwanese projects are small scale and labor intensive since they rely on low- or medium-level technology. While this has generated jobs in Vietnam and produced value for Taiwan, Vietnam's increasing labor costs and inevitably increasing demand of high-end technology may lead to Taiwan's FDI contributions to become discordant with Vietnam's development and Taiwanese investors may thus lag behind the Chinese and Koreans, among others. Below is an analysis from a historical perspective, which is useful in understanding how Taiwan got to where it is today in regard to FDI contributions in Vietnam.

Taiwan utilized its research organizations such as the Chung Hua Institution for Economic Research (CIER) and the Taiwan Institute for Economic Research (TIER) to evaluate the risk and probability of Taiwan's isolation in the East Asian economic integration process shortly after the establishment of the ASEAN Free Trade Area (AFTA) in 1992. This came as no surprise, given the fact that Taiwan's economic structure is shifting toward a more service-oriented economy—thus driving up its cost of labor. Additionally, the appreciation of the New Taiwan dollar against the U.S. dollar since the late 1980s has steadily hurt its export industry.

Such factors led the Taiwanese government to implement a "Go South" policy that resulted in a number of trade, investment, and double taxation avoidance agreements while facilitating Taiwan's development with investment FDI in labor-intensive industries such as leather and textiles. While the paranoia of isolation drove Taiwan to act fast, ASEAN integration did not happen that fast anyway—even after AFTA's creation, several non-trade barriers were not removed and the ASEAN financial crises of 1997 weakened several of ASEAN's key players such as Indonesia and Malaysia. Thus, despite findings of the CIER and the TIER, AFTA's establishment did not have a significant impact on Taiwan's trade relations with other ASEAN nations, including Vietnam.

Just like the AFTA, the establishment of the China–ASEAN Free Trade Area (CAFTA) that took effect in 2010 but was agreed upon in 2002 put pressure on the Taiwanese government to be proactive in seeking good bilateral trade relations with ASEAN economies, including China. This led to Taipei launching its second "Go South" policy, which focused on international business development and marketing of Taiwan's business environment abroad and is heavily based on the provisions of the WTO. As predicted by the studies done by Taiwanese scholars, the ASEAN's macro trends have not had any significant impact on Taiwan's trade relations with Vietnam (though Taiwan may face a serious risk once FTAs between ASEAN and Japan, Korea, India, New Zealand, and Australia come into effect). While Taipei is still considering options for the long haul, it has placed focus on "track two" or non-direct activities such as cultural and academic exchanges, non-governmental organizations' cooperation, and so forth. Despite that, the growth rate of trade and investment between Taiwan and Vietnam remains lower than that of China and ASEAN and China and Taiwan.

Furthermore, the Economic Cooperation Framework Agreement (ECFA), which opens new investment corridors for Taiwan, is expected to cause a slowdown in investment flow between Taiwan and Vietnam—particularly since unstable macroeconomic factors have tensed the Vietnam–Taiwan economic relationship. Hence, the trade deficit of Vietnam with Taiwan may fall. Thus, it can be said that regional and global integration is bound to pose new challenges for both Taiwan's and Vietnam's economies. Having said that, their efforts thus far and the results of those efforts cannot be discredited—Taiwan has consistently been Vietnam's leading investor, though the future tasks of restructuring economies to create new comparative advantages while changing current growth patterns, and empowering domestic enterprises to add significant value to transnational supply chains, are indeed arduous.

8.1.8 Vietnam–Hong Kong Bilateral Agreement's History

A double taxation agreement between Hong Kong and Vietnam was signed on 16 December 2008.

Given that Hong Kong has a simple territorial-based tax system with relatively low tax rates compared to other developed economies, and with capital gains, interests and dividends being exempt from profits tax, double taxation of income does not generally arise out of operations. Nevertheless, the treaty has been welcomed as it does create some incentives and legal avenues for Hong Kong companies and individuals doing business in Vietnam, as well as for foreign

Table 8.4 Withholding tax rate benefits provided by Hong Kong–Vietnam DTA

	Dividends	Royalties	Interest
Vietnam non-treaty rate	Nil	10 %	10 %
HK non-treaty rate	Nil	4.95 %/4.5 %	Nil
HK/Vietnam DTA rate	10 %	7 %/10 %	0/10 %

companies that may invest in Vietnam through a Hong Kong intermediary company.

The HK/Vietnam DTA provides limited benefits in withholding tax rates. The following Table 8.4 sets out the withholding tax rates for dividends, royalties, and interest with or without the treaty.

Without the treaty, foreign companies carrying out business in Vietnam or having contracts with Vietnamese customers without establishing a legal entity in Vietnam are subject to "Foreign Contractor Withholding Tax" ("FCWT"), which taxes the foreign company at various rates, depending on the business activities performed.

Under Article 5 of the treaty, a permanent establishment is defined as including the provision of services by an enterprise if the services continue (for the same or a connected project) for a period or periods aggregating more than 180 days within any 12-month period.

There is a capital gains exemption for gains derived by a Hong Kong resident, except for gains on:

- The sale of immovable property situated in Vietnam,
- The sale of movable property forming part of the business property of a permanent establishment in Vietnam,
- The sale of the shares of, or equivalent economic stake in, a company that mainly derives its assets value directly or indirectly from immovable property in Vietnam.

Hong Kong employees working in Vietnam will be exempt from Vietnamese personal income tax provided that (1) they do not spend more than 183 days in Vietnam in any 12-month period commencing or ending in the fiscal year concerned; (2) their remuneration is not paid by, or on behalf of, an employer who is a resident of Vietnam; and (3) the remuneration is not borne by a permanent establishment in Vietnam.

8.2 Thailand–Vietnam Treaty

The Government of the Socialist Republic of Vietnam and the Government of the Kingdom of Thailand, desiring to conclude an Agreement for the avoidance of double taxation and the prevention of fiscal evasion with respect to taxes on income, have agreed as follows:

Article 1 – Personal Scope

This Agreement shall apply to persons who are residents of one or both of the Contracting States.

Article 2 – Taxes Covered

1. This Agreement shall apply to taxes on income imposed on behalf of a Contracting State or of its political subdivisions or local authorities, irrespective of the manner in which they are levied.
2. There shall be regarded as taxes on income all taxes imposed on total income, or on elements of income, including taxes on gains from the alienation of movable or immovable property, taxes on the total amounts of wages or salaries paid by enterprises as well as taxes on capital appreciation.
3. The existing taxes to which the Agreement shall apply are:

    a. In Vietnam:

    (i) the personal income tax;
    (ii) the profit tax;
    (iii) the profit remittance tax;
    (iv) the foreign contractor tax;
    And
    (v) the petroleum foreign sub - contractor tax;
    (hereinafter referred to as "Vietnamese tax");

    b. In Thailand:

    (i) the income tax;
    (ii) the petroleum income tax;
    (hereinafter referred to as "Thai tax").

4. The Agreement shall also apply to any identical or substantially similar taxes, which are imposed after the date of signature of this Agreement in addition to, or in place of the existing taxes. The competent authorities of the Contracting States shall notify each other of important changes, which have been made in their respective taxation laws.

Article 3 – General Definitions

1. For the purposes of this Agreement, unless the context otherwise requires:

    a. The term "Vietnam" means the Socialist Republic of Vietnam, when used in a geographical sense, it means all its national territory, including its territorial sea and any area beyond its territorial sea, within which Vietnam, by Vietnamese legislation and in accordance with international law, has sovereign rights of exploration for and exploitation of natural resources of the seabed and its subsoil and superjacent water mass;
    b. The term "Thailand" means the Kingdom of Thailand and includes any area adjacent to the territorial waters of the Kingdom of Thailand which by Thai legislation, and in accordance with the international law, falls under the jurisdiction of the Kingdom of Thailand;
    c. The terms "a Contracting State" and "the other Contracting State" mean Vietnam or Thailand as the context requires;

d. The term "person" includes an individual, a company and any body of persons as well as any entity treated as a taxable unit under the taxation laws in force in either Contracting State;
   e. The term "company" means any body corporate or any entity which is treated as a body corporate for tax purposes;
   f. The terms "enterprise of a Contracting State" and "enterprise of the other Contracting State" mean respectively an enterprise carried on by a resident of a Contracting State and an enterprise carried on by a resident of the other Contracting State;
   g. The term "national" means:
      (i) any individual possessing the nationality of a Contracting State;
      (ii) any legal person, partnership, association and any other entity deriving its status as such from the laws in force in a Contracting State;
   h. The term "international traffic" means any transport by a ship or aircraft operated by an enterprise of a Contracting State, except when the ship or aircraft is operated solely between places in the other Contracting State; and
   i. The term "competent authority" means, in the case of Vietnam, the Minister of Finance or his authorized representative, and, in the case of Thailand, the Minister of Finance or his authorized representative.
2. As regards the application of the Agreement by a Contracting State, any term not defined therein shall, unless the context otherwise requires, have the meaning which it has under the law of that State concerning the taxes to which the Agreement applies.

Article 4 – Resident

1. For the purposes of this Agreement, the term "resident of a Contracting State" means any person who, under the laws of that State, is liable to tax therein by reason of his domicile, residence, place of incorporation, place of management or any other criterion of a similar nature. But this term does not include any person who is liable to tax in that State in respect only of income from sources in that State.
2. Where by reason of the provisions of paragraph 1 an individual is a resident of both Contracting States, then his status shall be determined as follows:
   a. He shall be deemed to be a resident of the State in which he has a permanent home available to him; if he has a permanent home available to him in both States, he shall be deemed to be a resident of the State with which his personal and economic relations are closer (centre of vital interests);
   b. If the Contracting State in which he has his centre of vital interests cannot be determined, or if he has not a permanent home available to him in either State, he shall be deemed to be a resident of the State in which he has an habitual abode;
   c. If he has an habitual abode in both States or in neither of them, he shall be deemed to be a resident of the State of which he is a national;
   d. If he is a national of both States or of neither of them, the competent authorities of the Contracting States shall settle the question by mutual agreement.
3. Where by reason of the provisions of paragraph 1, a person other than an individual is a resident of both Contracting States, then it shall be deemed to be a resident of the State where it was incorporated.

Article 5 – Permanent Establishment

1. For the purposes of this Agreement, the term "permanent establishment" means a fixed place of business through which the business of the enterprise is wholly or partly carried on.
2. The term "permanent establishment" includes especially:
   a. A place of management;
   b. A branch;
   c. An office;
   d. A factory;
   e. A workshop;
   f. A mine, an oil or gas well, a quarry or any other place of extraction of natural resources;
   g. A building site, a construction installation or assembly project or supervisory activities in connection therewith, where such site, project or activities continue for a period of more than six months.
3. Notwithstanding the preceding provisions of this Article, the term "permanent establishment" shall be deemed not to include:
   h. The use of facilities solely for the purpose of storage, display or delivery of goods or merchandise belonging to the enterprise;
   i. The maintenance of a stock of goods or merchandise belonging to the enterprise solely for the purpose of storage, display or delivery;
   j. The maintenance of a stock of goods or merchandise belonging to the enterprise solely for the purpose of processing by another enterprise;
   k. The maintenance of a fixed place of business solely for the purpose of purchasing goods or merchandise, or of collecting information, for the enterprise;
   l. The maintenance of a fixed place of business solely for the purpose of advertising, for the supply of information, for scientific research or for similar activities which have a preparatory or auxiliary character, for the enterprise;
   m. The maintenance of a fixed place of business solely for any combination of activities, mentioned in subparagraphs a. to e., provided that the overall activity of the fixed place of business resulting from this combination is of a preparatory or auxiliary character.
4. Notwithstanding the provisions of paragraphs 1 and 2, where a person - other than an agent of an independent status to whom paragraph 5 applies - is acting on behalf of an enterprise and has, and habitually exercises, in a Contracting State an authority to conclude contracts in the name of the enterprise, that enterprise shall be deemed to have a permanent establishment in that State in respect of any activities which that person undertakes for the enterprise, unless the activities of such person are limited to those mentioned in paragraph 3 which, if exercised through a fixed place of business, would not make this fixed place of business a permanent establishment under the provisions of that paragraph.
5. An enterprise of a Contracting State shall not be deemed to have a permanent establishment in the other Contracting State merely because it carries on business in that other State through a broker, general commission agent or any other agent of independent status, provided that such persons are acting in the ordinary course of their business.
6. The fact that a company which is a resident of a Contracting State controls or is controlled by a company which is a resident of the other Contracting State, or which carries on business in that other State (whether through a permanent establishment or otherwise), shall not of itself constitute either company a permanent establishment of the other.

Article 6 – Income from Immovable Property

1. Income derived by a resident of a Contracting State from immovable property (including income from agriculture or forestry) situated in the other Contracting State may be taxed in that other State.
2. The term "immovable property" shall have the meaning, which it has under the law of the Contracting State in which the property in question is situated. The term shall in any case include property accessory to immovable property, livestock and equipment used in agriculture and forestry, rights to which the provisions of general law respecting landed property apply, usufruct of immovable property and rights to variable or fixed payments as consideration for the working of, or the right to work, mineral deposits, sources and other natural resources; ships, boats and aircraft shall not be regarded as immovable property.
3. The provisions of paragraph 1 shall apply to income derived from the direct use, letting, or use in any other form of immovable property.
4. The provisions of paragraphs 1 and 3 shall also apply to the income from immovable property of an enterprise and to income from immovable property used for the performance of independent personal services.

Article 7 – Business Profits

1. The income or profits of an enterprise of a Contracting State shall be taxable only in that State unless the enterprise carries on business in the other Contracting State through a permanent establishment situated therein. If the enterprise carries on business as aforesaid, the income or profits of the enterprise may be taxed in the other State but only so much of them as is attributable to that permanent establishment.
2. Subject to the provisions of paragraph 3, where an enterprise of a Contracting State carries on business in the other Contracting State through a permanent establishment situated therein, there shall in each Contracting State be attributed to that permanent establishment the income or profits which it might be expected to make if it were a distinct and separate enterprise engaged in the same or similar activities under the same or similar conditions and dealing wholly independently with the enterprise of which it is a permanent establishment.
3. In determining the profits of a permanent establishment, there shall be allowed as deductions expenses which are incurred for the purposes of the business of the permanent establishment, including executive and general administrative expenses so incurred, whether in the State in which the permanent establishment is situated or elsewhere.
4. Insofar as it has been customary in a Contracting State to determine the profits to be attributed to a permanent establishment on the basis of a certain percentage of the gross receipt of the enterprise or of the permanent establishment or on the basis of an apportionment of the total profits of the enterprise to its various parts, nothing in paragraph 2 shall preclude that Contracting State from determining the profits to be taxed by such a method as may be customary; the method adopted shall, however, be such that the result shall be in accordance with the principles contained in this Article.
5. No income or profits shall be attributed to a permanent establishment by reason of the mere purchase by that permanent establishment of goods or merchandise for the enterprise.
6. For the purposes of the preceding paragraphs, the income or profits to be attributed to the permanent establishment shall be determined by the same method year by year unless there is good and sufficient reason to the contrary.
7. Where income or profits include items of income, which are dealt with separately in other Articles of this Agreement, then the provisions of those Articles shall not be affected by the provisions of this Article.

Article 8 – Shipping and Air Transport

1. Income or profits derived by an enterprise of a Contracting State from the operation of aircraft in international traffic shall be taxable only in that Contracting State.
2. Income or profits derived by an enterprise of a Contracting State from the operation of ships in international traffic may be taxed in the other Contracting State, but the tax imposed in that other State shall be reduced by an amount equal to 50 percent thereof.
3. The provisions of paragraphs 1 and 2 shall also apply to income or profits from the participation in a pool, a joint business or an international operating agency.

Article 9 – Associated Enterprises

Where

a. An enterprise of a Contracting State participates directly or indirectly in the management, control or capital of an enterprise of the other Contracting State, or
b. The same persons participate directly or indirectly in the management, control or capital of an enterprise of a Contracting State and an enterprise of the other Contracting State, and in either case conditions are made or imposed between the two enterprises in their commercial or financial relations which differ from those which would be made between independent enterprises, then any income or profits which would, but for those conditions, have accrued to one of the enterprises, but, by reason of those conditions, have not so accrued, may be included in the income or profits of that enterprise and taxed accordingly.

Article 10 – Dividends

1. Dividends paid by a company, which is a resident of a Contracting State to a resident of the other Contracting State, may be taxed in that other State.
2. However, such dividends may also be taxed in the Contracting State of which the company paying the dividends is a resident and according to the laws of that State, but if the recipient is the beneficial owner of the dividends the tax so charged shall not exceed 15 percent of the gross amount of the dividends. This paragraph shall not affect the taxation of the company in respect of the profits out of which the dividends are paid.
3. The term "dividends" as used in this Article means income from shares, mining shares, founders' shares or other rights, not being debt-claims, participating in profits, as well as income from other corporate rights which is subjected to the same taxation treatment as income from shares by the laws of the State of which the company making the distribution is a resident.
4. The provisions of paragraphs 1 and 2 shall not apply if the beneficial owner of the dividends, being a resident of a Contracting State, carries on business in the other Contracting State of which the company paying the dividends is a resident, through a permanent establishment situated therein, or performs in that other State independent personal services from a fixed base situated therein, and the holding in respect of which the dividends are paid is effectively connected with such permanent establishment or fixed base. In such case the provisions of Article 7 or Article 14, as the case may be, shall apply.
5. Where a company which is a resident of a Contracting State derives income or profits from the other Contracting State, that other State may not impose any tax on the dividends paid by the company, except insofar as such dividends are paid to a resident of that other State or insofar as the holding in respect of which the dividends are paid is effectively connected with a permanent establishment or a fixed base situated in that other State, nor subject the company's undistributed profits to a tax on the company's undistributed profits, even if the dividends paid or the undistributed profits consist

wholly or partly of income or profits arising in such other State. Nothing in this paragraph shall be construed as preventing a Contracting State from imposing income tax, according to the laws of that State, on the disposal of profits made by a permanent establishment situated therein.

Article 11 – Interest

1. Interest arising in a Contracting State and paid to a resident of the other Contracting State may be taxed in that other State.
2. However, such interest may also be taxed in the Contracting State in which it arises and according to the laws of that State, but if the recipient is the beneficial owner of the interest the tax so charged shall not exceed:
   a. 10 percent of the gross amount of the interest if it is received by any financial institution (including an insurance company);
   b. 15 percent of the gross amount of the interest in other cases.
3. Notwithstanding the provisions of paragraph 2, interest arising in a Contracting State and paid to the Government of the other Contracting State shall be exempt from tax in the first-mentioned Contracting State. For the purposes of this paragraph, the term "Government"
   a. In the case of Vietnam, means the Government of the Socialist Republic of Vietnam and shall include:
      (i) the State Bank of Vietnam;
      (ii) the local authorities; and
      (iii) such institutions, the capital of which is wholly owned by the Government of the Socialist Republic of Vietnam or any local authorities as may be agreed from time to time between the competent authorities of the two Contracting States;
   b. In the case of Thailand, means the Government of the Kingdom of Thailand and shall include:
      (i) the Bank of Thailand;
      (ii) the local authorities; and
      (iii) such institutions, the capital of which is wholly owned by the Government of the Kingdom of Thailand or any local authorities as may be agreed from time to time between the competent authorities of the two Contracting States.
4. The term "interest" as used in this Article means income, from debt-claims of every kind, whether or not secured by mortgage, and whether or not carrying a right to participate in the debtor's profits, and in particular, income from government securities and income from bonds or debentures, including premiums and prizes attaching to such securities, bonds or debentures, as well as income assimilated to income from money lent by the taxation law of the Contracting State in which the income arises. Penalty charges for late payment shall not be regarded as interest for the purpose of this Article.
5. The provisions of paragraphs 1 and 2 shall not apply if the beneficial owner of the interest, being a resident of a Contracting State, carries on business in the other Contracting State in which the interest arises, through a permanent establishment situated therein, or performs in that other State independent personal services from a fixed base situated therein, and the debt - claim in respect of which the interest is paid is effectively connected with such permanent establishment or fixed base. In such case the provisions of Article 7 or Article 14, as the case may be, shall apply.
6. Interest shall be deemed to arise in a Contracting State when the payer is that State itself, a political subdivision, a local authority or a resident of that State. Where, however, the

person paying the interest, whether he is a resident of a Contracting State or not, has in a Contracting State a permanent establishment or a fixed base in connection with the indebtedness on which the interest is paid was incurred, and such interest is borne by such permanent establishment or fixed base, then such interest shall be deemed to arise in the State in which the permanent establishment or fixed base is situated.
7. Where, by reason of a special relationship between the payer and the beneficial owner or between both of them and some other person, the amount of the interest, having regard to the debt - claim for which it is paid, exceeds the amount which would have been agreed upon by the payer and the beneficial owner in the absence of such relationship, the provisions of this Article shall apply only to the last - mentioned amount. In such case, the excess part of the payments shall remain taxable according to the laws of each Contracting State, due regard being had to the other provisions of this Agreement.

Article 12 – Royalties

1. Royalties arising in a Contracting State and paid to a resident of the other Contracting State may be taxed in that other State.
2. However, such royalties may also be taxed in the Contracting State in which they arise and according to the laws of that State, but if the recipient is the beneficial owner of the royalties, the tax so charged shall not exceed 15 percent of the gross amount of the royalties.
3. The term "royalties" as used in this Article means payments of any kind received as a consideration for the use of, or the right to use, any copyright of literary, artistic or scientific work including cinematograph films, or films or tapes used for radio or television broadcasting, any patent, trade mark, design or model, plan, secret formula or process, or for the use of, or the right to use, industrial, commercial, or scientific equipment, or for information concerning industrial, commercial or scientific experience.
4. The provisions of paragraphs 1 and 2 shall not apply if the beneficial owner of the royalties, being a resident of a Contracting State, carries on business in the other Contracting State in which the royalties arise, through a permanent establishment situated therein, or performs in that other State independent personal services from a fixed base situated therein, and the right or property in respect of which the royalties are paid is effectively connected with such permanent establishment or fixed base. In such cases the provisions of Article 7 or Article 14, as the case may be, shall apply.
5. Royalties shall be deemed to arise in a Contracting State when the payer is that State itself, a political subdivision, a local authority or a resident of that State. Where, however, the person paying the royalties, whether he is a resident of a Contracting State or not, has in a Contracting State a permanent establishment or a fixed base in connection with which the liability to pay the royalties was incurred, and such royalties are borne by such permanent establishment or fixed base, then such royalties shall be deemed to arise in the State in which the permanent establishment or fixed base is situated.
6. Where, by reason of a special relationship between the payer and the beneficial owner or between both of them and some other person, the amount of the royalties, having regard to the use, right or information for which they are paid, exceeds the amount which would have been agreed upon by the payer and the beneficial owner in the absence of such relationship, the provisions of this Article shall apply only to the last-mentioned amount. In such case, the excess part of the payments shall remain taxable according to the laws of each Contracting State, due regard being had to the other provisions of this Agreement.

Article 13 – Capital Gains

1. Gains derived by a resident of a Contracting State from the alienation of immovable property referred to in Article 6 and situated in the other Contracting State may be taxed in that other State.
2. Gains from the alienation of movable property forming part of the business property of a permanent establishment which an enterprise of a Contracting State has in the other Contracting State or of movable property pertaining to fixed base available to a resident of a Contracting State in the other Contracting State for the purpose of performing independent personal services, including such gains from the alienation of such a permanent establishment (alone or with the whole enterprise) or of such a fixed base, may be taxed in that other State.
3. Gains derived by an enterprise of a Contracting State from the alienation of ships or aircraft operated in international traffic or movable property pertaining to the operation of such ships or aircraft, shall be taxable only in that State.
4. Gains from the alienation of any property, other than those referred to in paragraphs 1, 2 and 3 shall be taxable only in the Contracting State of which the alienator is a resident. Nothing in this paragraph shall prevent either Contracting State from taxing the gains or income from the sale or transfer of shares or other securities.

Article 14 – Independent Personal Services

1. Income derived by a resident of a Contracting State in respect of professional services or other activities of an independent character shall be taxable only in that State unless he has a fixed base regularly available to him in the other Contracting State for the purpose of performing his activities, for a period or periods amounting to or exceeding in the aggregate 183 days in the fiscal year concerned; in that case, only so much of the income as is attributable to that fixed base may be taxed in that other State.
2. The term "professional services" includes especially independent scientific, literary, artistic, educational or teaching activities as well as the independent activities of physicians, lawyers, engineers, architects, dentists and accountants.

Article 15 – Dependent Personal Services

1. Subject to the provisions of Articles 16, 18 and 19, salaries, wages and other similar remuneration derived by a resident of a Contracting State in respect of an employment shall be taxable only in that State unless the employment is exercised in the other Contracting State. If the employment is so exercised, such remuneration as is derived therefrom may be taxed in that other State.
2. Notwithstanding the provisions of paragraph 1, remuneration derived by a resident of a Contracting State in respect of an employment exercised in the other Contracting State shall be taxable only in the first-mentioned State if:
    a. The recipient is present in the other State for a period or periods not exceeding in the aggregate 183 days in the fiscal year concerned, and
    b. The remuneration is paid by, or on behalf of, an employer who is not a resident of the other State, and
    c. The remuneration is not borne by a permanent establishment or a fixed base, which the employer has in the other State.
3. Notwithstanding the preceding provisions of this Article, remuneration derived in respect of an employment exercised aboard a ship or aircraft operated in international traffic, by an enterprise of a Contracting State shall be taxable only in that State.

Article 16 – Directors' Fees

Directors' fees and other similar payments derived by a resident of a Contracting State in his capacity as a member of the board of directors of a company which is a resident of the other Contracting State may be taxed in that other State.

Article 17 – Artists and Athletes

1. Notwithstanding the provisions of Articles 14 and 15, income derived by a resident of a Contracting State as an entertainer, such as a theatre, motion picture, radio or television artiste, or a musician, or as an athlete, from his personal activities as such exercised in the other Contracting State, may be taxed in that other State.
2. Where income in respect of personal activities exercised by an entertainer or an athlete in his capacity as such accrues not to the entertainer or athlete himself but to another person, that income may, notwithstanding the provisions of Articles 7, 14 and 15, be taxed in the Contracting State in which the activities of the entertainer or athlete are exercised.
3. The provisions of paragraphs 1 and 2 shall not apply to remuneration or profits, salaries, wages and other similar income derived from activities performed in a Contracting State by an entertainer or an athlete if the visit to that Contracting State is substantially supported by public funds of the other Contracting State.

Article 18 – Pensions

Subject to the provisions of paragraph 2 of Article 19, pensions and other similar remuneration paid to a resident of a Contracting State in consideration of past employment shall be taxable only in that State.

Article 19 – Governmental Function

1. a. Remuneration, other than a pension, paid by a Contracting State or a political subdivision or a local authority thereof to an individual in respect of services rendered to that State or subdivision or authority shall be taxable only in that State.
   b. However, such remuneration shall be taxable only in the other Contracting State if the services are rendered in that State and the individual is a resident of that State who:
      (i) Is a national of that State; or
      (ii) Did not become a resident of that State solely for the purpose of rendering the services.

2. a. Any pension paid by, or out of funds created by, a Contracting State or a political subdivision or a local authority thereof to an individual in respect of services rendered to that State or subdivision or authority shall be taxable only in that State.
   b. However, such pension shall be taxable only in the other Contracting State if the individual is a resident of, and a national of, that State.

3. The provisions of Articles 15, 16 and 18 shall apply to remuneration and pensions in respect of services rendered in connection with a business carried on by a Contracting State or a political subdivision or a local authority thereof.

Article 20 – Students

Payments which a student or business apprentice who is or was immediately before visiting a Contracting State a resident of the other Contracting State and who is present in the first-mentioned State solely for the purpose of his education or training receives for the purpose of his maintenance, education or training shall not be taxed in that State, provided that such payments arise from sources outside that State.

Article 21 – Professors, Teachers and Researchers

1. An individual who is a resident of a Contracting State immediately before making a visit to the other Contracting State, and who, at the invitation of any university, college, school or other similar educational institution which is recognized by the competent authority in that other Contracting State, visits that other Contracting State for a period not exceeding two years solely for the purpose of teaching or research or both at such educational institution shall be exempt from tax in that other Contracting State on any remuneration for such teaching or research.
2. This Article shall only apply to income from research if such research is undertaken by the individual for the public interest and not primarily for the benefit of some other private person or persons.

Article 22 – Other Income

Items of income of a resident of a Contracting State not dealt with in the foregoing Articles of this Agreement may be taxed in the State where the income arises.

Article 23 – Methods for Elimination of Double Taxation

1. The laws in force in either of the Contracting States shall continue to govern the taxation of income in the respective Contracting States except when an express provision to the contrary is made in this Agreement. When income is subject to tax in both Contracting States, relief from double taxation shall be given in accordance with the following paragraphs of this Article.
2. a. Where a resident of Thailand derives income, which, in accordance with the provisions of this Agreement, may be taxed in Vietnam, Thailand shall allow as a deduction from the tax on the income of that resident an amount equal to the tax paid in Vietnam. Such deduction shall not, however, exceed that part of the Thai tax, as computed before the deduction is given, which is attributable to that income.
   b. For the purposes of subparagraph a. above, the term "tax paid in Vietnam" shall be deemed to include the amount of Vietnamese tax which, under the laws of Vietnam and in accordance with this Agreement, would have been paid had the Vietnamese tax not been exempted or reduced in accordance with:
      (i) The provisions of the parts 27, 28, 32 or 33 of the Law on Foreign Investment in Vietnam (1987) and connected regulations, as effective on the date of signature of this Agreement or as modified only in minor respects after the date of signature of this Agreement; or
      (ii) Any other special incentive measures designed to promote economic development in Vietnam, which may be introduced hereafter in modification of, or in addition to, the existing laws, provided that an agreement is made between the two competent authorities.
3. a. Where a resident of Vietnam derives income, which, in accordance with the provisions of this Agreement, may be taxed in Thailand, Vietnam shall allow as a

deduction from the tax on the income of that resident an amount equal to the tax paid in Thailand. Such deduction shall not, however, exceed that part of the Vietnamese tax, as computed before the deduction is given, which is attributable to that income.
b. For the purposes of subparagraph a. above, the term "tax paid in Thailand" shall be deemed to include the amount of Thai tax which, under the laws of Thailand and in accordance with this Agreement, would have been paid had the Thai tax not been exempted or reduced in accordance with:

(i) The provisions of the parts 31, 33, 34, 35 (2), 35 (3), 35 (4) or 36 (4) of the Investment promotion Act, B. E. 2520 (1977), and connected regulations, as effective on the date of signature of this Agreement or as modified only in minor respects after the date of signature of this Agreement; or
(ii) Any other special incentive measures designed to promote economic development in Thailand, which may be introduced hereafter in modification of, or in addition to, the existing laws, provided that an agreement is made between the two competent authorities.

Article 24 – Mutual Agreement Procedure

1. Where a person who is a resident of a Contracting State considers that the actions of the competent authority of one or both of the Contracting States result or will result for him in taxation not in accordance with the provisions of this Agreement, he may, irrespective of the remedies provided by the domestic laws of those States, present his case to the competent authority of the Contracting State of which the person is a resident. The case must be presented within three years from the first notification of the action resulting in taxation not in accordance with the provisions of the Agreement.
2. The competent authority shall endeavor, if the objection appears to it be justified and if it is not itself able to arrive at a satisfactory solution, to resolve the case by mutual agreement with the competent authority of the other Contracting State, with a view to the avoidance of taxation which is not in accordance with the Agreement.
3. The competent authorities of the Contracting States shall endeavor to resolve by mutual agreement any difficulties or doubts arising as to the interpretation or application of the Agreement. They may also consult together for the elimination of double taxation in cases not provided for in the Agreement.
4. The competent authorities of the Contracting States may communicate with each other directly for the purposes of reaching an agreement in the sense of the preceding paragraphs.

Article 25 – Exchange of Information

1. The competent authorities of the Contracting States shall exchange such information as is necessary for carrying out the provisions of this Agreement or of the domestic laws of the Contracting States concerning taxes covered by the Agreement insofar as the taxation thereunder is not contrary to the Agreement. Any information received by a Contracting State shall be treated as secret in the same manner as information obtained under the domestic laws of that State and shall be disclosed only to persons or authorities (including courts and administrative bodies) involved in the assessment or collection of, the enforcement or prosecution in respect of, or the determination of appeals in relation to, the taxes covered by the Agreement. Such persons or authorities shall use the information only for such purposes. They may disclose the information in public court proceedings or in judicial decisions.
2. In no case shall the provisions of paragraph 1 be construed so as to impose on a Contracting State the obligation:

a. To carry out administrative measures at variance with the laws and administrative practice of that or of the other Contracting State;
b. To supply information which is not obtainable under the laws or in the normal course of the administration of that or of the other Contracting State;
c. To supply information, which would disclose any trade, business, industrial, commercial or professional secret or trade process, or information, the disclosure of which would be contrary to public policy (ordre public).

Article 26 – Diplomatic Agents and Consular Officers

Nothing in this Agreement shall affect the fiscal privileges of diplomatic agents or consular officers under the general rules of international law or under the provisions of special agreements.

Article 27 – Entry into Force

1. This Agreement shall be ratified and the instruments of ratification shall be exchanged at Hanoi as soon as possible.
2. The Agreement shall enter into force upon the exchange of instruments of ratification and its provisions shall have effect:
   a. In respect of taxes withheld at source, on amounts paid or remitted on or after the first day of January next following that in which the exchange of instruments of ratification takes place;
   b. In respect of other taxes on income, for taxable years or accounting periods beginning on or after the first day of January next following that in which the exchange of instruments of ratification takes place.

Article 28 – Termination

This Agreement shall remain in force indefinitely, but either of the Contracting States may, on or before 30th of June in any calendar year beginning after the expiration of a period of five years from the date of its entry into force, give to the other Contracting State, through diplomatic channels, written notice of termination.

In such event the Agreement shall cease to have effect:

a. In respect of taxes withheld at source, on amounts paid or remitted on or after the first day of January next following that in which the notice is given;
b. In respect of other taxes on income, for taxable years or accounting periods beginning on or after the first day of January next following that in which the notice is given.

Done in duplicate at Hanoi on this 23rd day of December, one thousand nine hundred and ninety two year of the Christian Era, each in the Vietnamese, Thai and English languages, all texts being equally authoritative, except in the case of doubt when the English text shall prevail.

8.3 Korea–Vietnam Treaty

The Government of the Socialist Republic of Vietnam and the Government of the Republic of Korea, desiring to conclude an Agreement for the avoidance of double taxation and the prevention of fiscal evasion with respect to taxes on income, have agreed as follows:

Article 1 – Personal Scope

This Agreement shall apply to persons who are residents of one or both of the Contracting States.

Article 2 – Taxes Covered

1. This Agreement shall apply to taxes on income imposed on behalf of a Contracting State or of its political subdivisions or local authorities, irrespective of the manner in which they are levied.
2. There shall be regarded as taxes on income all taxes imposed on total income, or on elements of income including taxes on gains from the alienation of movable or immovable property, taxes on the total amounts of wages or salaries paid by enterprises as well as taxes on capital appreciation.
3. The existing taxes to which the Agreement shall apply are in particular:

    a. In the case of Vietnam:

    (i) the personal income tax;
    (ii) the profit tax; and
    (iii) the profit remittance tax,
    (hereinafter referred to as "Vietnamese tax");

    b. In the case of Korea:

    (i) the income tax;
    (ii) the corporation tax; and
    (iii) the inhabitant tax,
    (hereinafter referred to as "Korean tax").

4. The Agreement shall also apply to any identical or substantially similar taxes, which are imposed after the date of signature of this Agreement in addition to, or in place of the existing taxes. The competent authorities of the Contracting States shall notify each other of any substantial changes, which have been made in their respective taxation laws.

Article 3 – General Definitions

1. For the purposes of this Agreement, unless the context otherwise requires:

    a. The term "Vietnam" means the Socialist Republic of Vietnam; when used in a geographical sense, it means all its national territory, including its territorial sea and any area beyond its territorial sea, within which Vietnam, by Vietnamese legislation and in accordance with international law, has sovereign rights of exploration for and exploitation of natural resources of the sea-bed and its sub-soil and superjacent water mass;

b. The term "Korea" means the territory of the Republic of Korea including any area adjacent to the territorial sea of the Republic of Korea which, in accordance with international law, has been or may hereafter be designated under the laws of the Republic of Korea as an area within which the sovereign rights of the Republic of Korea with respect to the sea-bed and sub-soil and their natural resources may be exercised;
c. The terms "a Contracting State" and "the other Contracting State" mean Vietnam or Korea, as the context requires;
d. The term "tax" means Vietnamese tax or Korean tax, as the context requires;
e. The term "person" includes an individual, a company and any other body of persons;
f. The term "company" means any body corporate or any entity which is treated as a body corporate for tax purposes;
g. The terms "enterprise of a Contracting State" and "enterprise of the other Contracting State" mean respectively an enterprise carried on by a resident of a Contracting State and an enterprise carried on by a resident of the other Contracting State;
h. The term "nationals" means:

   (i) all individuals possessing the nationality of a Contracting State;
   (ii) all legal person, partnership and association deriving its status as such from the laws in force in a Contracting State;

i. The term "international traffic" means any transport by a ship or aircraft operated by an enterprise of a Contracting State, except when the ship or aircraft is operated solely between places in the other Contracting State;
j. The term "competent authority" means:

   (i) in the case of Vietnam, the Minister of Finance or his authorized representative; and
   (ii) in the case of Korea, the Minister of Finance or his authorized representative.

2. As regards the application of the Agreement by a Contracting State, any term not defined therein shall, unless the context otherwise requires, have the meaning which it has under the laws of that State concerning the taxes to which the Agreement applies.

Article 4 – Resident

1. For the purposes of this Agreement, the term "resident of a Contracting State" means any person who, under the laws of that State, is liable to tax therein by reason of his domicile, residence, place of head or main office, place of management or any other criterion of a similar nature.
2. Where by reason of the provisions of paragraph 1 an individual is a resident of both Contracting States, then his status shall be determined as follows:

   a. He shall be deemed to be a resident of the State in which he has a permanent home available to him. If he has a permanent home available to him in both States, he shall be deemed to be a resident of the State with which his personal and economic relations are closer (centre of vital interests);
   b. If the Contracting State in which he has his centre of vital interests can not be determined, or if he has no permanent home available to him in either State, he shall be deemed to be a resident of the State in which he has an habitual abode;
   c. If he has an habitual abode in both States or in neither of them, he shall be deemed to be a resident of the State of which he is a national;
   d. If he is a national of both States or of neither of them, the competent authorities of the Contracting States shall settle the question by mutual agreement.

3. Where by reason of the provisions of paragraph 1, a person other than an individual is a resident of both Contracting States, then it shall be deemed to be a resident of the State in which its place of effective management is situated. In case of doubts, the competent authorities of the Contracting States shall settle the question by mutual agreement.

Article 5 – Permanent Establishment

1. For the purposes of this Agreement, the term "permanent establishment" means a fixed place of business through which the business of an enterprise is wholly or partly carried on.
2. The term "permanent establishment" includes especially:
   a. A place of management;
   b. A branch;
   c. An office;
   d. A factory;
   e. A workshop; and
   f. A mine, an oil or gas well, a quarry or any other place of extraction of natural resources.
3. A building site or construction or installation project constitutes a permanent establishment only if it lasts more than six months.
4. Notwithstanding the preceding provisions of this Article, the term "permanent establishment" shall be deemed not to include:
   a. The use of facilities solely for the purpose of storage or display of goods or merchandise belonging to the enterprise;
   b. The maintenance of a stock of goods or merchandise belonging to the enterprise solely for the purpose of storage or display;
   c. The maintenance of a stock of goods or merchandise belonging to the enterprise solely for the purpose of processing by another enterprise;
   d. The maintenance of a fixed place of business solely for the purpose of purchasing goods or merchandise or of collecting information, for the enterprise;
   e. The maintenance of a fixed place of business solely for the purpose of carrying on, for the enterprise, any other activity of a preparatory or auxiliary character;
   f. The maintenance of a fixed place of business solely for any combination of activities mentioned in sub-paragraphs a) to e), provided that the overall activity of the fixed place of business resulting from this combination is of a preparatory or auxiliary character.
5. Notwithstanding the provisions of paragraphs 1 and 2, where a person - other than an agent of an independent status to whom paragraph 6 applies - is acting on behalf of an enterprise and has, and habitually exercises, in a Contracting State an authority to conclude contracts in the name of the enterprise, that enterprise shall be deemed to have a permanent establishment in that State in respect of any activities which that person undertakes for the enterprise, unless the activities of such person are limited to those mentioned in paragraph 4 which, if exercised through a fixed place of business, would not make this fixed place of business a permanent establishment under the provisions of that paragraph.
6. An enterprise shall not be deemed to have a permanent establishment in a Contracting State merely because it carries on business in that State through a broker, general commission agent or any other agent of an independent status, - provided that such persons are acting in the ordinary course of their business.
7. The fact that a company which is a resident of a Contracting State controls or is controlled by a company which is a resident of the other Contracting State, or which

carries on business in that other State (whether through a permanent establishment or otherwise), shall not of itself constitute either company a permanent establishment of the other.

Article 6 – Income from Immovable Property

1. Income derived by a resident of a Contracting State from immovable property (including income from agriculture or forestry) situated in the other Contracting State may be taxed in that other State.
2. The term "immovable property" shall have the meaning, which it has under the law of the Contracting State in which the property in question is situated. The term shall in any case include property accessory to immovable property, livestock and equipment used in agriculture and forestry, rights to which the provisions of general law respecting landed property apply, usufruct of immovable property and rights to variable or fixed payments as consideration for the working of, or the right to work, mineral deposits, sources and other natural resources; ships, boats and aircraft shall not be regarded as immovable property.
3. The provisions of paragraph 1 shall apply to income derived from the direct use, letting, or use in any other form of immovable property.
4. The provisions of paragraphs 1 and 3 shall also apply to the income from immovable property of an enterprise and to income from immovable property used for the performance of independent personal services.

Article 7 – Business Profits

1. The profits of an enterprise of a Contracting State shall be taxable only in that State unless the enterprise carries on business in the other Contracting State through a permanent establishment situated therein. If the enterprise carries on business as aforesaid, the profits of the enterprise may be taxed in the other State but only so much of them as is attributable to that permanent establishment.
2. Subject to the provisions of paragraph 3, where an enterprise of a Contracting State carries on business in the other Contracting State through a permanent establishment situated therein, there shall in each Contracting State be attributed to that permanent establishment the profits which it might be expected to make if it was a distinct and separate enterprise engaged in the same or similar activities under the same or similar conditions and dealing wholly independently with the enterprise of which it is a permanent establishment.
3. In determining the profits of a permanent establishment, there shall be allowed as deductions expenses which are incurred for the purposes of the business of the permanent establishment, including executive and general administrative expenses so incurred, whether in the State in which the permanent establishment is situated or elsewhere.
4. No profits shall be attributed to a permanent establishment by reason of the mere purchase by that permanent establishment of goods or merchandise for the enterprise.
5. For the purposes of the preceding paragraphs, the profits to be attributed to the permanent establishment shall be determined by the same method year by year unless there is good and sufficient reason to the contrary.
6. Where profits include items of income, which are dealt with separately in other Articles of this Agreement, then the provisions of those Articles shall not be affected by the provisions of this Article.

Article 8 – Shipping and Air Transport

1. Profits derived by an enterprise of a Contracting State from the operation of ships or aircraft in international traffic shall be taxable only in that Contracting State.
2. The provisions of paragraph 1 shall also apply to profits from the participation in a pool, a joint business or an international operating agency.

Article 9 – Associated Enterprises

Where

a. An enterprise of a Contracting State participates directly or indirectly in the management, control or capital of an enterprise of the other Contracting State, or
b. The same persons participate directly or indirectly in the management, control or capital of an enterprise of a Contracting State and an enterprise of the other Contracting State, and in either case conditions are made or imposed between the two enterprises in their commercial or financial relations which differ from those which would be made between independent enterprises, then any profits which would, but for those conditions, have accrued to one of the enterprises, but, by reason of those conditions, have not so accrued, may be included in the profits of that enterprise and taxed accordingly.

Article 10 – Dividends

1. Dividends paid by a company, which is a resident of a Contracting State to a resident of the other Contracting State, may be taxed in that other State.
2. However, such dividends may also be taxed in the Contracting State of which the company paying the dividends is a resident and according to the laws of that State, but if the recipient is the beneficial owner of the dividends the tax so charged shall not exceed 10 per cent of the gross amount of the dividends.
This paragraph shall not affect the taxation of the company in respect of the profits out of which the dividends are paid.
3. The term "dividends" as used in this Article means income from shares or other rights, not being debt-claims, participating in profits, as well as income from other corporate right is subjected to the same taxation treatment as income from shares by the laws of the State of which the company making the distribution is a resident.
4. The provisions of paragraphs 1 and 2 shall not apply if the beneficial owner of the dividends, being a resident of a Contracting State, carries on business in the other Contracting State of which the company paying the dividends is a resident through a permanent establishment situated therein, or performs in that other State independent personal services from a fixed base situated therein, and the holding in respect of which the dividends are paid is effectively connected with such permanent establishment or fixed base. In such case, the provisions of Article 7 or Article 14, as the case may be, shall apply.
5. Where a company which is a resident of a Contracting State derives profits or income from the other Contracting State, that other State may not impose any tax on the dividends paid by the company, except insofar as such dividends are paid to a resident of that other Contracting State or insofar as the holding in respect of which the dividends are paid is effectively connected with a permanent establishment or a fixed base situated in that other State, nor subject the company's undistributed profits to a tax on the company's undistributed profits, even if the dividends paid or the undistributed profits consist wholly or partly of profits or income arising in such other State.

Article 11 – Interest

1. Interest arising in a Contracting State and paid to a resident of the other Contracting State may be taxed in that other State.
2. However, such interest may also be taxed in the Contracting State in which it arises and according to the laws of that State, but if the recipient is the beneficial owner of the interest the tax so charged shall not exceed 10 per cent of the gross amount of the interest.
3. Notwithstanding the provisions of paragraph 2, interest arising in a Contracting State and derived by the Government of the other Contracting State including political subdivisions and local authorities thereof, the central bank of that other Contracting State or any financial institution performing functions of a governmental nature of by any resident of the other Contracting State with respect to debt-claims guaranteed or indirectly financed by the Government of that other Contracting State including political subdivisions and local authorities thereof, the central bank of that other Contracting State or any financial institution performing functions of a governmental nature shall be exempt from tax in the first-mentioned Contracting State.
4. For the purpose of paragraph 3, the terms "the central bank and any financial institution performing functions of a governmental nature" mean:

    a. In the case of Vietnam:

    (i) the State Bank of Vietnam;
    (ii) the bank for Foreign Trade of Vietnam (Vietcombank) and such other financial institution performing functions of a governmental nature as may be specified and agreed upon in letters exchanged between the competent authorities of the Contracting States;

    b. In the case of Korea:

    (i) the Bank of Korea;
    (ii) the Export–import Bank of Korea, the Korea Development Bank and such other financial institution performing functions of a governmental nature as may be specified and agreed upon in letters exchanged between the competent authorities of the Contracting States.

5. The term "interest" as used in this Article means income from debt-claims of every kind, whether or not secured by mortgage, and whether or not carrying a right to participate in the debtor's profits, and, in particular, income from Government securities and income from bonds or debentures, including premiums and prizes attaching to such securities, bonds or debentures.
6. The provisions of paragraphs 1 and 2 shall not apply if the beneficial owner of the interest, being a resident of a Contracting State, carries on business in the other Contracting State in which the interest arises, through a permanent establishment situated therein, or performs in that other State independent personal services from a fixed base situated therein and the debt-claim in respect of which the interest is paid is effectively connected with such permanent establishment or fixed base. In such case the provisions of Article 7 or Article 14, as the case may be, shall apply.
7. Interest shall be deemed to arise in a Contracting State when the payer is that State itself, a political sub-division, a local authority or a resident of that State. Where, however, the person paying the interest, whether he is a resident of a Contracting State or not, has in a Contracting State a permanent establishment or a fixed base in connection with which the indebtedness on which the interest is paid was incurred, and such interest is borne by such permanent establishment or fixed base, then such interest shall be deemed to arise in the State in which the permanent establishment or fixed base is situated.

8. Where, by reason of a special relationship between the payer and the beneficial owner or between both of them and some other persons, the amount of the interest, having regard to the debt-claim for which it is paid, exceeds the amount which would have been agreed upon by the payer and the beneficial owner in the absence of such relationship, the provisions of this Article shall apply only to the last-mentioned amount. In such case, the excess part of the payments shall remain taxable according to the laws of each Contracting State, due regard being had to the other provisions of this Agreement.

Article 12 – Royalties

1. Royalties arising in a Contracting State and paid to a resident of the other Contracting State may be taxed in that other State.
2. However, such royalties may also be taxed in the Contracting State in which they arise, and according to the laws of that Contracting State, but if the beneficial owner of the royalties is a resident of the other Contracting State, the tax so charged shall not exceed:
   a. 5 per cent of the gross amount of the royalties in respect of payments of any kind received as a consideration for the use of, or the right to use, any patent, design or model, plan, secret formula or process, or for the use of, or the right to use, industrial, commercial or scientific equipment, or for information concerning industrial, commercial or scientific experience;
   b. 15 per cent of the gross amount of the royalties in all other cases.
3. The term "royalties" as used in this Article means payments of any kind received as a consideration for the use of, or the right to use, any copyright of literary, artistic or scientific work including cinematograph films, or films or tapes used for radio or television broadcasting, any patent, trade mark, design or model, plan, secret formula or process, or for the use of, or the right to use, industrial, commercial or scientific equipment, or for information concerning industrial, commercial or scientific experience.
4. The provisions of paragraphs 1 and 2 shall not apply if the beneficial owner of the royalties, being a resident of a Contracting State, carries on business in the other Contracting State in which the royalties arise, through a permanent establishment situated therein, or performs in that other State independent personal services from a fixed base situated therein, and the right or property in respect of which the royalties are paid is effectively connected with such permanent establishment or fixed base. In such case, the provisions of Article 7 or Article 14, as the case may be, shall apply.
5. Royalties shall be deemed to arise in a Contracting State when the payer is that State itself, a political subdivision, a local authority or a resident of that State. Where, however, the person paying the royalties, whether he is a resident of a Contracting State or not, has in a Contracting State a permanent establishment or fixed base in connection with which the liability to pay the royalties was incurred, and such royalties are borne by such permanent establishment or fixed base, then such royalties shall be deemed to arise in the State in which the permanent establishment or fixed base is situated.
6. Where, by reason of a special relationship between the payer and the beneficial owner or between both of them and some other person, the amount of the royalties, having regard to the use, right or information for which they are paid, exceeds the amount which would have been agreed upon by the payer and the beneficial owner in the absence of such relationship, the provisions of this Article shall apply only to the last-mentioned amount. In such case, the excess part of the payments shall remain taxable according to the laws of each Contracting State, due regard being had to the other provisions of this Agreement.

Article 13 – Capital Gains

1. Gains derived by a resident of a Contracting State from the alienation of immovable property referred to in Article 6 and situated in the other Contracting State may be taxed in that other State.
2. Gains from the alienation of movable property forming part of the business property of a permanent establishment which an enterprise of a Contracting State has in the other Contracting State or of movable property pertaining to a fixed base available to a resident of a Contracting State in the other Contracting State for the purpose of performing independent personal services, including gains from the alienation of such a permanent establishment (alone or with the whole enterprise) or of such fixed base, may be taxed in that other State.
3. Gains from the alienation of ships or aircraft operated in international traffic, or movable property pertaining to the operation of such ships or aircraft, shall be taxable only in the Contracting State of which the enterprise is a resident.
4. Gains from the alienation of shares of the capital stock of a company the property of which consists directly or indirectly principally of immovable property situated in a Contracting State may be taxed in that State.
5. Gains from the alienation of any property other than that referred to in paragraphs 1, 2 and 3 shall be taxable only in the State of which the alienator is a resident.

Article 14 – Independent Personal Services

1. Income derived by a resident of a Contracting State in respect of professional services or other activities of an independent character shall be taxable only in that State unless he has a fixed base regularly available to him in the other Contracting State for the purpose of performing his activities. If he has such a fixed base, the income may be taxed in the other Contracting State but only so much of it as is attributable to that fixed base.
2. The term "professional services" includes especially independent scientific, literary, artistic, educational or teaching activities as well as the independent activities of physicians, lawyers, engineers, architects, dentists and accountants.

Article 15 – Dependent Personal Services

1. Subject to the provisions of Articles 16, 18, 19, 20 and 21, salaries, wages and other similar remuneration derived by a resident of a Contracting State in respect of an employment shall be taxable only in that State unless the employment is exercised in the other Contracting State. If the employment is so exercised, such remuneration as is derived therefrom may be taxed in that other State.
2. Notwithstanding the provisions of paragraph 1, remuneration derived by a resident of a Contracting State in respect of an employment exercised in the other Contracting State shall be taxable only in the first-mentioned State if:
    a. The recipient is present in the other State for a period or periods not exceeding in the aggregate 183 days in any twelve month period, and
    b. The remuneration is paid by, or on behalf of, an employer who is not a resident of the other State, and
    c. The remuneration is not borne by a permanent establishment or a fixed base, which the employer has on the other State.
3. Notwithstanding the preceding provisions of this Article, remuneration derived in respect of an employment exercised aboard a ship or aircraft operated in international traffic by an enterprise of a Contracting State shall be taxable only in that State.

Article 16 – Directors' Fees

Directors' fees and other similar payments derived by a resident of a Contracting State in his capacity as a member of the board of directors of a company which is a resident of the other Contracting State may be taxed in that other Contracting State.

Article 17 – Artists and Sportsmen

1. Notwithstanding the provisions of Articles 14 and 15, income derived by a resident of a Contracting State as an entertainer, such as a theatre, motion picture, radio or television artiste, or a musician, or as a sportsman, from his personal activities as such exercised in the other Contracting State, may be taxed in that other State.
2. Where income in respect of personal activities exercised by an entertainer or a sportsman in his capacity as such accrues not to the entertainer or sportsman himself but to another person, that income may, notwithstanding the provisions of Articles 7, 14 and 15, be taxed in the Contracting State in which the activities of the entertainer or sportsman are exercised.
3. Notwithstanding the provisions of paragraphs 1 and 2 of this Article, income derived by entertainers or sportsmen who are residents of a Contracting State from the activities exercised in the other Contracting State under a special programme of cultural exchange agreed upon between the Governments of both Contracting States, shall be exempt from tax in that other State.

Article 18 – Pensions

Subject to the provisions of paragraph 2 of Article 19, pensions and other similar remuneration paid to a resident of a Contracting State in consideration of past employment shall be taxable only on that State.

Article 19 – Government Service

1. a. Remuneration, other than a pension, paid by a Contracting State or a political subdivision or a local authority thereof to an individual in respect of services rendered to that State or subdivision or authority shall be taxable only in that State.
   b. However, such remuneration shall be taxable only in the other Contracting State if the services are rendered in that State and the individual is a resident of that State who:
      (i) is a national of that State; or
      (ii) did not become a resident of that State solely for the purpose of rendering the services.
2. a. Any pension paid by, or out of funds created by, a Contracting State or a political subdivision or a local authority thereof to an individual in respect of services rendered to that State or subdivision or authority shall be taxable only in that State.
   b. However, such pension shall be taxable only in the other Contracting State if the individual is a resident of, and a national of, that State.
3. The provisions of Articles 15, 16 and 18 shall apply to remuneration and pensions in respect of services rendered in connection with a business carried on by a Contracting State or a political subdivision or a local authority thereof.
4. The provisions of paragraphs 1 and 2 of this Article shall likewise apply in respect of remuneration or pensions paid by:

a. In the case of Vietnam:
   The State Bank of Vietnam, the Bank for Foreign Trade of Vietnam (Vietcombank), the Vietnamese Chamber of Commerce and Industry and other institutions performing functions of a governmental nature as may be specified and agreed upon in letters exchanged between the competent authorities of the Contracting States;
b. In the case of Korea:
   The Bank of Korea, the Export–import Bank of Korea, the Korea Development Bank, the Korea Trade Promotion Corporation and other institutions performing functions of a governmental nature as may be specified and agreed upon in letters exchanged between the competent authorities of the Contracting States.

Article 20 – Students

1. Payments which a student or business apprentice who is or was immediately before visiting a Contracting State a resident of the other Contracting State and who is present in the first-mentioned Contracting State solely for the purpose of his education or training receives for the purpose of his maintenance, education or training shall not be taxed in that State, provided that such payments arise from sources outside that State.
2. Notwithstanding the provisions of Article 15, remuneration for services rendered by a student or a business apprentice in a Contracting State shall not be taxed in that State, provided that such services are in connection with his studies or training.

Article 21 – Professors and Teachers

An individual who is or was a resident of a Contracting State immediately before making a visit to the other Contracting State, who, at the invitation of any university, school or other similar educational institution, which is recognized as non-profitable by the Government of that other State, visits that other Contracting State for a period not exceeding two years from the date of his first arrival in that other State, solely for the purposes of teaching or research or both as such educational institution shall be exempt from tax in that other State on his remuneration for such teaching or research.

Article 22 – Other Income

1. Items of income of a resident of a Contracting State, wherever arising, not dealt with in the foregoing Articles of this Agreement shall be taxable only in that State.
2. The provisions of paragraph 1 shall not apply to income, other than income from immovable property as defined in paragraph 2 of Article 6, if the recipient of such income, being a resident of a Contracting State, carries on business in the other Contracting State through a permanent establishment situated therein, or performs in that other State independent personal services from a fixed base situated therein, and the right or property in respect of which the income is paid is effectively connected with such permanent establishment or fixed base. In such case the provisions of Article 7 or Article 14, as the case may be, shall apply.

Article 23 – Methods for Elimination of Double Taxation

1. In the case of a resident of Vietnam, double taxation shall be eliminated as follows:
   Subject to the provisions of the law of Vietnam which relate to the allowance of a credit against Vietnamese tax of tax paid in a country outside Vietnam (which shall not affect the general principle of this Article), Korean tax payable under the law of Korea and in accordance with this Agreement, whether directly or by deduction, in respect of income derived by a resident of Vietnam from sources within Korea shall be allowed as a credit against Vietnamese tax payable in respect of that income. The credit shall not, however, exceed the Vietnamese tax as computed by reference to the same income before the credit is given.
2. In the case of a resident of Korea, double taxation shall be eliminated as follows:
   Subject to the provisions of the Korean tax law regarding the allowance as a credit against Korean tax of tax payable in any country other than Korea (which shall not affect the general principle hereof), the Vietnamese tax payable (excluding, in the case of dividends, tax payable in respect of the profits out of which the dividends are paid) under the laws of Vietnam and in accordance with this Agreement, whether directly or by deduction, in respect of income from sources within Vietnam shall be allowed as a credit against Korean tax payable in respect of that income. The credit shall not, however, exceed that proportion of Korean tax, which the income from source within Vietnam bears to the entire income subject to the Korean tax.
3. For the purposes of credit referred to in paragraph 2, the term "Vietnamese tax payable" shall be deemed to include the amount of Vietnamese tax which, under the laws of Vietnam and in accordance with this Agreement, would have been payable had the Vietnamese tax not been exempted or reduced in accordance with:
   a. The provisions of Articles 26, 27, 28, 32 or 33 of the Law on Foreign investment in Vietnam 1987 as amended from time to time and connected regulations, as are effective on the date of signature of this Agreement as have been modified only in minor aspects after the date of signature of this Agreement; or
   b. Any other special incentive measures designed to promote economic development in Vietnam, which may be introduced hereafter in modification of or in addition to, the existing laws, as, may be agreed between the competent authorities of the Contracting States.
4. For the purpose of Korean tax credit referred to in paragraph 2, the Vietnamese tax payable shall, irrespective of the amount of tax actually paid, be deemed to be, in the case of:
   a. Dividends or interest, 10 per cent of the gross amount of the dividends or interest derived from sources within Vietnam; and
   b. Royalties, 15 per cent of the gross amount of the royalties derived from sources within Vietnam.
5. The provisions of paragraphs 3 and 4 of this Article shall apply only during a period of ten years starting from the first day of the calendar year next following that in which this Agreement enters into force in accordance with the provisions of Article 28. The period of application may be extended by mutual agreement between the competent authorities of the Contracting States.

Article 24 – Non-discrimination

1. The nationals of a Contracting State shall not be subject in the other Contracting State to any taxation or any requirement connected therewith, which is other or more

burdensome than the taxation and connected requirements to which nationals of that other State in the same circumstances are or may be subjected.
2. The taxation on a permanent establishment, which an enterprise of a Contracting State has in the other Contracting State, shall not be less favorably levied in that other State than the taxation levied on enterprises of that other State carrying on the same activities. This provision shall not be construed as obliging a Contracting State to grant to residents of the other Contracting State any personal allowances, reliefs and reductions for taxation purposes on account of civil status or family responsibilities which it grants to its own residents.
3. Except where the provisions of Article 9, paragraph 8 of Article 11, or paragraph 6 of Article 12 apply, interest, royalties and other disbursements paid by an enterprise of a Contracting State to a resident of the other Contracting State shall, for the purpose of determining the taxable profits of such enterprise, be deductible under the same conditions as if they had been paid to a resident of the first-mentioned State.
4. Enterprises of a Contracting State, the capital of which is wholly or partly owned or controlled, directly or indirectly, by one or more residents of the other Contracting State, shall not be subjected in the first-mentioned State to any taxation or any requirement connected therewith which is other or more burdensome than the taxation and connected requirements to which other similar enterprises of the first-mentioned State are or may be subjected.
5. The provisions of paragraphs 2 and 4 of this Article shall not apply to the Vietnamese profit remittance tax, which in any case shall not exceed 10 per cent of the gross amount of profits remitted, and the Vietnamese taxation in respect of oil exploration or production activities or in respect of agricultural production activities.
6. Nothing contained in this Article shall be construed as obliging either Contracting State to grant to individuals not resident in that State any of the personal allowances, reliefs and reductions for tax purposes, which are granted to resident individuals.
7. The provisions of this Article shall apply only to taxes covered by this Agreement.

Article 25 – Mutual Agreement Procedure

1. Where a person who is resident of a Contracting State considers that the actions of the competent authority of one or both of the Contracting States result or will result for him in taxation not in accordance with the provisions of this Agreement, he may, irrespective of the remedies provided by the domestic law of those States, present his case to the competent authority of the Contracting State of which he is a resident or, of this case comes under paragraph 1 of Article 24, to that of the Contracting State of which he is a national. The case must be presented within three years from the first notification of the action resulting in taxation not in accordance with the provisions of the Agreement.
2. The competent authority shall endeavor, if the objection appears to it to be justified and if it is not itself able to arrive at a satisfactory solution, to resolve the case by mutual agreement with the competent authority of the other Contracting State, with a view to the avoidance of taxation, which is not in accordance with the Agreement.
3. The competent authorities of the Contracting States shall jointly endeavor to resolve any difficulties or doubts arising as to the interpretation or application of the Agreement. They may also consult together for the elimination of double taxation in cases not provided for in the Agreement.
4. The competent authorities of the Contracting States may communicate with each other directly for the purpose of reaching an agreement in the sense of the preceding

paragraphs. When it seems advisable in order to reach agreement to have an oral exchange of opinions, such exchange may take place through a Commission consisting of representatives of the competent authorities of the Contracting States.

Article 26 – Exchange of Information

1. The competent authorities of the Contracting States shall exchange such information as is necessary for carrying out the provisions of this Agreement or of the domestic laws of the Contracting States concerning taxes covered by the Agreement insofar as the taxation thereunder is not contrary to the Agreement. The exchange of information is not restricted by Article 1. Any information received by a Contracting State shall be treated as secret in the same manner as information obtained under the domestic laws of that State and shall be disclosed only to persons or authorities (including courts and administrative bodies) involved in the assessment or collection of, the enforcement or prosecution is respect of, or the determination of appeals in relation to, the taxes covered by the Agreement. Such persons or authorities shall use the information only for such purposes. They may disclose the information in public court proceedings or in judicial decisions.
2. In no case shall the provisions of paragraph 1 of this Article be construed so as to impose on a Contracting State the obligation:

   a. To carry out administrative measures at variance with the laws and administrative practice of that or of the other Contracting State;
   b. To supply information which is not obtainable under the laws or in the normal course of the administration of that or of the other Contracting State;
   c. To supply information, which would disclose any trade, business, industrial, commercial or professional secret or trade process, or information, the disclosure of which would be contrary to public policy.

Article 27 – Diplomatic Agents and Consular Officers

Nothing in this Agreement shall affect the fiscal privileges of diplomatic agents or consular officers under the general rules of international law or under the provisions of special agreements.

Article 28 – Entry into Force

1. Each of the Contracting States shall notify to the other Contracting State the completion of the domestic procedures required by its law for entering into force of this Agreement. This Agreement shall enter into force 30 days after the later of these notifications.
2. This Agreement shall have effect:

   a. In respect of taxes withheld at source, on amount paid or credited to non-residents on or after the first day of January of the calendar year next following that in which this Agreement enters into force; and
   b. In respect of other taxes, for taxation years beginning on or after the first day of January of the calendar year next following that in which this Agreement enters into force.

Article 29 – Termination

This Agreement shall remain in force indefinitely but either of the Contracting State may, on or before the thirtieth day of June in any calendar year from the fifth year, following that in which this Agreement enters into force, give to the other Contracting State, through diplomatic channels, written notice of termination and, in such event, this Agreement shall cease to have effect:

a. In respect of taxes withheld at source on amounts paid or credited to non-residents on or after the first day of January in the calendar year next following that in which the notice of termination is given; and
b. In respect of other taxes for taxation years beginning on or after the first day of January of the calendar year next following that in which the notice of termination is given.

DONE in duplicate at Hanoi this 20th day of May of the year one thousand nine hundred and ninety-four in the Vietnamese, Korean and English languages, all texts being equally authentic. In case of divergence of interpretation, the English text shall prevail.

Protocol

At the moment of signing the Agreement between the Government of the Socialist Republic of Vietnam and the Government of the Republic of Korea for the Avoidance of Double Taxation and the Prevention of Fiscal Evasion with respect to Taxes on Income, the undersigned have agreed that the following provisions shall form an integral part of the Agreement.

1. In respect of the profit remittance tax in paragraph 3 (a) (iii) of Article 2 "Taxes Covered" it is understood that the remitted profit which is liable to above mentioned tax in Vietnam will be taxed only in accordance with paragraph 2 of Article 10.
2. In respect of paragraph 4 (b) (ii) of Article 11 "Interest" and paragraph 4 (b) of Article 19 "Government Service" it is understood that the Export–import Bank of Korea is a government-invested bank which is established by the "Export–import Bank of Korea Act" to promote, in close conformity with government policies, the sound development of the national economy and economic cooperation with foreign countries by extending the financial aid required for export and import transactions, overseas investment and the development of natural resources abroad, and is operated under the control and supervision of the Korean Government. It is also understood that the Korea Development Bank is a government-owned bank which is established by the "Korea Development Bank Act" to furnish and administer funds, in close conformity with government policies, for the financing of major industrial projects in order to expedite industrial development and expansion of the national economy, and is operated under the control and supervision of the Korean Government. Furthermore, the above two banks do not receive deposits from the public. It is therefore understood that, all these being taken into account, these two banks perform functions of a governmental nature and distinctively differ from commercial banks in these respects.
3. In respect of Article 24 "Non - discrimination", it is understood that, if a Contracting State hereinafter concludes or has already concluded with any other country a tax treaty of which the non-discrimination provisions are less discriminatory to a resident of the other Contracting State than the current provisions of non-discrimination of this Agreement, the first-mentioned provisions shall be applied promptly in place of the last-mentioned provisions.

DONE in duplicate at Hanoi this 20th day of May of the year one thousand nine hundred and ninety-four in the Vietnamese, Korean and English languages, all texts being equally authentic. In case of divergence of interpretation, the English text shall prevail.

8.4 China–Vietnam Treaty

The Government of the Socialist Republic of Vietnam and the Government of the People's Republic of China, desiring to conclude an Agreement for the avoidance of double taxation and the prevention of fiscal evasion with respect to taxes on income, have agreed as follows:

Article 1 – Personal Scope

This Agreement shall apply to persons who are residents of one or both of the Contracting States.

Article 2 – Taxes Covered

1. This Agreement shall apply to taxes on income imposed on behalf of a Contracting State or of its political subdivisions or local authorities, irrespective of the manner in which they are levied.
2. There shall be regarded as taxes on income all taxes imposed on total income, or on elements of income, including taxes on gains from the alienation of movable or immovable property, as well as taxes on capital appreciation.
3. The existing taxes to which the Agreement shall apply are:

   (a) In the Socialist Republic of Vietnam:

   (i) the personal income tax;
   (ii) the profit tax;
   (iii) the profit remittance tax;
   (hereinafter referred to as "Vietnamese tax");

   (b) In the People's Republic of China:

   (i) the individual income tax;
   (ii) the income tax for enterprises with foreign investment and foreign enterprises;
   (iii) the local income tax;
   (hereinafter referred to as "Chinese tax").

4. The Agreement shall also apply to any identical or substantially similar taxes, which are imposed after the date of signature of this Agreement in addition to, or in place of, the existing taxes. The competent authorities of the Contracting States shall notify each other of important changes, which have been made in their respective taxation laws.

Article 3 – General Definitions

1. For the purposes of this Agreement, unless the context otherwise requires:

   (a) The term "Vietnam" means the Socialist Republic of Vietnam; When used in a geographical sense, means all the territory of the Socialist Republic of Vietnam, including its territorial sea, in which the Vietnamese laws relating to taxation apply, and any area beyond its territorial sea, within which the Socialist Republic of Vietnam has sovereign rights of exploration for and exploitation of resources of the seabed and its sub-soil and superjacent water resources in accordance with international law;

(b) The term "China" means the People's Republic of China; when used in a geographical sense, means all the territory of the People's Republic of China, including its territorial sea. In which the Chinese laws relating to taxation apply, and any area beyond its territorial sea, within which the People's Republic of China has sovereign rights of exploration for and exploitation of resources of the seabed and its sub-soil and superjacent water resources in accordance with international law;
(c) The terms "a Contracting State" and "the other Contracting State" mean Vietnam or China as the context requires;
(d) The term "tax" means Vietnamese tax or Chinese tax, as the context requires;
(e) The term "person" includes an individual, a company and any other body of persons;
(f) The term "company" means any body corporate or any entity which is treated as a body corporate for tax purposes;
(g) The terms "enterprise of a Contracting State" and "enterprise of the other Contracting State" mean respectively an enterprise carried on by a resident of a Contracting State and an enterprise carried on by a resident of the other Contracting State;
(h) The term "nationals" means:

  (i) all individuals possessing the nationality of a Contracting State;
  (ii) all legal persons, partnerships and associations deriving their status as such from the laws in force in a Contracting State;

(i) The term "international traffic" means any transport by a ship or aircraft operated by a resident of a Contracting State, except when the ship or aircraft is operated solely between places in the other Contracting State;
(j) The term "competent authority" means:

  (i) In the case of Vietnam, the Minister of Finance or his authorized representative; and
  (ii) In the case of China, the State Administration of Taxation or its authorized representative.

2. As regards the application of the Agreement by a Contracting State, any term not defined therein shall, unless the context otherwise requires, have the meaning which it has under the law of that Contracting State concerning the taxes to which the Agreement applies.

Article 4 – Resident

1. For the purposes of this Agreement, the term "resident of a Contracting State" means any person who, under the laws of that Contracting State, is liable to tax therein by reason of his domicile, residence, place of registration, place of head office or any other criterion of a similar nature.
2. Where by reason of the provisions of paragraph 1 an individual is a resident of both Contracting States, then his status shall be determined as follows:

   (a) He shall be deemed to be a resident of the Contracting State in which he has a permanent home available to him; if he has a permanent home available to him in both Contracting States, he shall be deemed to be a resident of the Contracting State with which his personal and economic relations are closer (centre of vital interests);
   (b) If the Contracting State in which he has his centre of vital interests cannot be determined, or if he has no permanent home available to him in either Contracting State, he shall be deemed to be a resident of the Contracting State in which he has an habitual abode;

(c) If he has an habitual abode in both Contracting States or in neither of them, he shall be deemed to be a resident of the Contracting State of which he is a national;
(d) If he is a national of both Contracting States or of neither of them, the competent authorities of the Contracting States shall settle the question by mutual agreement.

3. Where by reason of the provisions of paragraph 1 a person other than an individual is a resident of both Contracting States, then the competent authorities of the Contracting States shall determine that the person is a resident of a Contracting State for the purposes of this Agreement by mutual agreement.

Article 5 – Permanent Establishment

1. For the purposes of this Agreement, the term "permanent establishment" means a fixed place of business through which the business of an enterprise is wholly or partly carried on.
2. The term "permanent establishment" includes especially:
    (a) A place of management;
    (b) A branch;
    (c) An office;
    (d) A factory;
    (e) A workshop;
    (f) A mine, an oil or gas well, a quarry or any other place of extraction of natural resource.
3. The term "permanent establishment" likewise encompasses:
    (a) A building site, a construction, assembly or installation project or supervisory activities in connection therewith, but only where such site, project or activities continue for a period of more than six months;
    (b) The furnishing of services, including consultancy services, by an enterprise of a Contracting State through employees or other engaged personnel in the other Contracting State, provided that such activities continue (for the same project or a connected project) for a period or periods aggregating more than six months within any 12-month period.
4. Notwithstanding the preceding provisions of this Article, the term "permanent establishment" shall be deemed not to include:
    (a) The use of facilities solely for the purpose of storage, display or delivery of goods or merchandise belonging to the enterprise;
    (b) The maintenance of a stock of goods or merchandise belonging to the enterprise solely for the purpose of storage, display or delivery;
    (c) The maintenance of a stock of goods or merchandise belonging to the enterprise solely for the purpose of processing by another enterprise;
    (d) The maintenance of a fixed place of business solely for the purpose of purchasing goods or merchandise or of collecting information, for the enterprise;
    (e) The maintenance of a fixed place of business solely for the purpose of carrying on, for the enterprise, any other activity of a preparatory or auxiliary character.
5. Notwithstanding the provisions of paragraphs 1 and 2, where a person—other than an agent of an independent status to whom paragraph 7 applies—is acting in a Contracting State on behalf of an enterprise of the other Contracting State, has and habitually exercises an authority to conclude contracts in the name of the enterprise, that enterprise shall be deemed to have a permanent establishment in the first-mentioned Contracting State in respect of any activities which that person undertakes for the enterprise, unless

the activities of such person are limited to those mentioned in paragraph 4 which, if exercised through a fixed place of business, would not make this fixed place of business a permanent establishment under the provisions of that paragraph.
6. Notwithstanding the preceding provisions of this Article, an insurance enterprise of a Contracting State shall, except in regard to re-insurance, be deemed to have a permanent establishment in the other Contracting State if it collects premiums in the territory of that other Contracting State or insures risks situated therein through a person other than an agent of an independent status to whom paragraph 7 applies.
7. An enterprise of a Contracting State shall not be deemed to have a permanent establishment in the other Contracting State merely because it carries on business in that other Contracting State through a broker, general commission agent or any other agent of an independent status, provided that such persons are acting in the ordinary course of their business. However, when the activities of such an agent are devoted wholly or almost wholly on behalf of that enterprise, he will not be considered an agent of an independent status within the meaning of this paragraph.
8. The fact that a company which is a resident of a Contracting State controls or is controlled by a company which is a resident of the other Contracting State, or which carries on business in that other Contracting State (whether through a permanent establishment or otherwise), shall not of itself constitute either company a permanent establishment of the other.

Article 6 – Income from Immovable Property

1. Income derived by a resident of a Contracting State from immovable property (including income from agriculture or forestry) situated in the other Contracting State may be taxed in that other Contracting State.
2. The term "immovable property" shall have the meaning, which it has under the law of the Contracting State in which the property in question is situated. The term shall in any case include property accessory to immovable property, livestock and equipment used in agriculture and forestry, rights to which the provisions of general law respecting landed property apply, usufruct of immovable property and rights to variable or fixed payments as consideration for the working of, or the right to work, mineral deposits, sources and other natural resources; ships, boats and aircraft shall not be regarded as immovable property.
3. The provisions of paragraph 1 shall apply to income derived from the direct use, letting, or use in any other form of immovable property.
4. The provisions of paragraphs 1 and 3 shall also apply to the income from immovable property of an enterprise and to income from immovable property used for the performance of independent personal services.

Article 7 – Business Profits

1. The profits of an enterprise of a Contracting State shall be taxable only in that Contracting State unless the enterprise carries on business in the other Contracting State through a permanent establishment situated therein. If the enterprise carries on business as aforesaid, the profits of the enterprise may be taxed in the other Contracting State, but only so much of them as is attributable to that permanent establishment.
2. Subject to the provisions of paragraph 3, where an enterprise of a Contracting State carries on business in the other Contracting State through a permanent establishment situated therein, there shall in each Contracting State be attributed to that permanent establishment the profits which it might be expected to make if it were a distinct and separate enterprise engaged in the same or similar activities under the same or similar

conditions and dealing wholly independently with the enterprise of which it is a permanent establishment.
3. In determining the profits of a permanent establishment, there shall be allowed as deductions expenses which are incurred for the purposes of the business of the permanent establishment, including executive and general administrative expenses so incurred, whether in the Contracting State in which the permanent establishment is situated or elsewhere. However, no such deduction shall be allowed in respect of amounts, if any, paid (otherwise than towards reimbursement of actual expenses) by the permanent establishment to the head office of the enterprise or any of its other offices, by way of royalties, fees or other similar payments in return for the use of patents or other rights, or by way of commission, for specific services performed or for management, or, except in the case of a banking enterprise, by way of interest on money lent to the permanent establishment. Likewise, no account shall be taken, in the determination of the profits of a permanent establishment, for amounts charged (otherwise than towards reimbursement of actual expenses) by the permanent establishment to the head office of the enterprise or any of its other offices, by way of royalties, fees or other similar payments in return for the use of patents or other rights, or by way of commission for specific services performed or for management, or, except in the case of banking enterprise by way of interest on money lent to the head office of the enterprise or any of its other offices.
4. In so far as it has been customary in a Contracting State to determine the profits to be attributed to a permanent establishment on the basis of an apportionment of the total profits of the enterprise to its various parts, nothing in paragraph 2 shall preclude that Contracting State from determining the profits to be taxed by such an apportionment as may be customary. The method of apportionment adopted shall, however, be such that the result shall be in accordance with the principles contained in this Article.
5. No profits shall be attributed to a permanent establishment by reason of the mere purchase by that permanent establishment of goods or merchandise for the enterprise.
6. For the purposes of the preceding paragraphs, the profits to be attributed to the permanent establishment shall be determined by the same method year by year unless there is good and sufficient reason to the contrary.
7. Where profits include items of income, which are dealt with separately in other Articles of this Agreement, then the provisions of those Articles shall not be affected by the provisions of this Article.

Article 8 – Shipping and Air Transport

1. Profits derived by a resident of a Contracting State from the operation of ships or aircraft in international traffic shall be taxable only in that Contracting State.
2. The provisions of paragraph 1 shall also apply to profits from the participation in a pool, a joint business or an international operating agency.

Article 9 – Associated Enterprises

1. Where
   (a) An enterprise of a Contracting State participates directly or indirectly in the management, control or capital of an enterprise of the other Contracting State, or
   (b) The same persons participate directly or indirectly in the management, control or capital of an enterprise of a Contracting State and an enterprise of the other Contracting State, And in either case conditions are made or imposed between the two enterprises in their commercial or financial relations which differ from those which would be made between independent enterprises, then any profits which would, but for those conditions, have accrued to one of the enterprises, but, by

reason of those conditions, have not so accrued, may be included in the profits of that enterprise and taxed accordingly.

2. Where a Contracting State includes in the profits of an enterprise of that Contracting State—and taxes accordingly—profits on which an enterprise of the other Contracting State has been charged to tax in that other Contracting State and the profits so included are profits which would have accrued to the enterprise of the first-mentioned Contracting State if the conditions made between the two enterprises had been those which would have been made between independent enterprises, then that other Contracting State shall make an appropriate adjustment to the amount of the tax charged therein on those profits. In determining such adjustment, due regard shall be had to the other provisions of the Agreement and the competent authorities of the Contracting States shall, if necessary, consult each other.

Article 10 – Dividends

1. Dividends paid by a company, which is a resident of a Contracting State to a resident of the other Contracting State, may be taxed in that other Contracting State.
2. However, such dividends may also be taxed in the Contracting State of which the company paying the dividends is a resident and according to the laws of that Contracting State, but if the recipient is the beneficial owner of the dividends the tax so charged shall not exceed 10 per cent of the gross amount of the dividends. This paragraph shall not affect the taxation of the company in respect of the profits out of which the dividends are paid.
3. The term "dividends" as used in this Article means income from shares, or other rights, not being debt-claims, participating in profits, as well as income from other corporate rights which is subjected to the same taxation treatment as income from shares by the laws of the Contracting State of which the company making the distribution is a resident.
4. The provisions of paragraphs 1 and 2 shall not apply if the beneficial owner of the dividends, being a resident of a Contracting State, carries on business in the other Contracting State of which the company paying the dividends is a resident, through a permanent establishment situated therein, or performs in that other Contracting State independent personal services from a fixed base situated therein, and the holding in respect of which the dividends are paid is effectively connected with such permanent establishment or fixed base. In such case the provisions of Article 7 or Article 14, as the case may be, shall apply.
5. Where a company, which is a resident of a Contracting State, derives profits or income from the other Contracting State. That other Contracting State may not impose any tax on the dividends paid by the company, except insofar as such dividends are paid to a resident of that other Contracting State or insofar as the holding in respect of which the dividends are paid is effectively connected with a permanent establishment or a fixed base situated in that other Contracting State, nor subject the company's undistributed profits to a tax on the company's undistributed profits, even if the dividends paid or the undistributed profits consist wholly or partly of profits or income arising in such other Contracting State.

Article 11 – Interest

1. Interest arising in a Contracting State and paid to a resident of the other Contracting State may be taxed in that other Contracting State.
2. However, such interest may also be taxed in the Contracting State in which it arises and according to the laws of that Contracting State, but if the recipient is the beneficial owner of the interest the tax so charged shall not exceed 10 per cent of the gross amount of the interest.

3. Notwithstanding the provisions of paragraph 2, interest arising in a Contracting State and paid to the Government of the other Contracting State shall be exempt from tax in the first-mentioned Contracting State. For the purposes of this paragraph, the term "Government":

   (a) In the case of Vietnam, means the Government of the Socialist Republic of Vietnam and shall include:
      (i) the state-owned banks of Vietnam;
      (ii) the political subdivisions or the local authority; and
      (iii) such financial institutions, the capital of which is wholly owned by the Government of the Socialist Republic of Vietnam or any political subdivisions or local authorities thereof, as may be agreed upon from time to time between the competent authorities of the Contracting States;

   (b) In the case of China, means the Government of the People's Republic of China and shall include:
      (i) the Chinese state banks;
      (ii) the political subdivisions or the local authority; and
      (iii) such financial institutions, the capital of which is wholly owned by the Government of the People's Republic of China or any political subdivisions or local authorities thereof, as may be agreed upon from time to time between the competent authorities of the Contracting States.

4. The term "interest" as used in this Article means income from debt-claims of every kind, whether or not secured by mortgage and whether or not carrying a right to participate in the debtor's profits, and in particular, income from government securities and income from bonds or debentures, including premiums and prizes attaching to such securities, bonds or debentures. Penalty charges for late payment shall not be regarded as interest for the purpose of this Article.

5. The provisions of paragraphs 1, 2 and 3 shall not apply if the beneficial owner of the interest, being a resident of a Contracting State, carries on business in the other Contracting State in which the interest arises, through a permanent establishment situated therein, or performs in that other Contracting State independent personal services from a fixed base situated therein, and the debt-claim in respect of which the interest is paid is effectively connected with such permanent establishment or fixed base. In such case the provisions of Article 7 or Article 14, as the case may be, shall apply.

6. Interest shall be deemed to arise in a Contracting State when the payer is the Government of that Contracting State, a political subdivision, a local authority thereof or a resident of that Contracting State. Where, however, the person paying the interest, whether he is a resident of a Contracting State or not, has in a Contracting State a permanent establishment or a fixed base in connection with which the indebtedness on which the interest is paid was incurred, and such interest is borne by such permanent establishment or fixed base, then such interest shall be deemed to arise in the Contracting State in which the permanent establishment or fixed base is situated.

7. Where, by reason of a special relationship between the payer and the beneficial owner or between both of them and some other person, the amount of the interest, having regard to the debt-claim for which it is paid, exceeds the amount which would have been agreed upon by the payer and the beneficial owner in the absence of such relationship, the provisions of this Article shall apply only to the last-mentioned amount. In such case, the excess part of the payments shall remain taxable according to the laws of each Contracting State, due regard being had to the other provisions of this Agreement.

Article 12 – Royalties

1. Royalties arising in a Contracting State and paid to a resident of the other Contracting State may be taxed in that other Contracting State.
2. However, such royalties may also be taxed in the Contracting State in which they arise and according to the laws of that Contracting State, but if the recipient is the beneficial owner of the royalties the tax so charged shall not exceed 10 per cent of the gross amount of the royalties.
3. The term "royalties" as used in this Article means payments of any kind received as a consideration for the use of, or the right to use, any copyright of literary, artistic or scientific work including cinematograph films or films or tapes used for radio or television broadcasting, any patent, trade mark, design or model, plan, secret formula or process, or for the use of, or the right to use, industrial, commercial or scientific equipment, or for information concerning industrial, commercial or scientific experience.
4. The provisions of paragraphs 1 and 2 shall not apply if the beneficial owner of the royalties, being a resident of a Contracting State, carries on business in the other Contracting State in which the royalties arise, through a permanent establishment situated therein, or performs in that other Contracting State independent personal services from a fixed base situated therein, and the right or property in respect of which the royalties are paid is effectively connected with such permanent establishment or fixed base. In such case the provisions of Article 7 or Article 14, as the case may be, shall apply.
5. Royalties shall be deemed to arise in a Contracting State when the payer is the Government of that Contracting State, a political subdivision, or a local authority thereof or a resident of that Contracting State. Where, however, the person paying the royalties, whether he is a resident of a Contracting State or not, has in a Contracting State a permanent establishment or a fixed base in connection with which the liability to pay the royalties was incurred, and such royalties are borne by such permanent establishment or fixed base, then such royalties shall be deemed to arise in the Contracting State in which the permanent establishment or fixed base is situated.
6. Where, by reason of a special relationship between the payer and the beneficial owner or between both of them and some other person, the amount of the royalties, having regard to the use, right or information for which they are paid, exceeds the amount which would have been agreed upon by the payer and the beneficial owner in the absence of such relationship, the provisions of this Article shall apply only to the last-mentioned amount. In such case, the excess part of the payments shall remain taxable according to the laws of each Contracting State, due regard being had to the other provisions of this Agreement.

Article 13 – Capital Gains

1. Gains derived by a resident of a Contracting State from the alienation of immovable property referred to in Article 6 and situated in the other Contracting Stare may be taxed in that other Contracting State.
2. Gains from the alienation of movable property forming part of the business property of a permanent establishment which an enterprise of a Contracting State has in the other Contracting State or of movable property pertaining to a fixed base available to a resident of a Contracting State in the other Contracting State for the purpose of performing independent personal services, including such gains from the alienation of such a permanent establishment (alone or together with the whole enterprise) or of such fixed base, may be taxed in that other Contracting State.

3. Gains derived by a resident of a Contracting State from the alienation of ships or aircraft operated in international traffic or movable property pertaining to the operation of such ships or aircraft shall be taxable only in that Contracting State.
4. Gains from the alienation of shares of the capital stock of a company the property of which consists directly or indirectly principally of immovable property situated in a Contracting State may be taxed in that Contracting State.
5. Gains from the alienation of shares other than those mentioned in paragraph 4 representing a participation of at least 25 per cent in a company, which is a resident of a Contracting State, may be taxed in that Contracting State.
6. Gains from the alienation of any property other than that referred to in paragraphs 1 to 5, shall be taxable only in the Contracting State of which the alienator is a resident.

Article 14 – Independent Personal Services

1. Income derived by a resident of a Contracting State in respect of professional services or other activities of an independent character shall be taxable only in that Contracting State except in the following circumstances, when such income may also be taxed in the other Contracting State:

    (a) If he has a fixed base regularly available to him in the other Contracting State for the purpose of performing his activities; in that case, only so much of the income as is attributable to that fixed base may be taxed in that other Contracting State; or
    (b) If his stay in the other Contracting State is for a period or periods amounting to or exceeding in the aggregate 183 days in the calendar year concerned; in that case, only so much of the income as is derived from his activities performed in that other Contracting State may be taxed in that other Contracting State.

2. The term "professional services" includes especially independent scientific, literary, artistic, educational or teaching activities as well as the independent activities of physicians, lawyers, engineers, architects, dentists and accountants.

Article 15 – Dependent Personal Services

1. Subject to the provisions of Articles 16, 18, 19, 20 and 21, salaries, wages and other similar remuneration derived by a resident of a Contracting State in respect of an employment shall be taxable only in that Contracting State unless the employment is exercised in the other Contracting State. If the employment is so exercised, such remuneration as is derived therefrom may be taxed in that other Contracting State.
2. Notwithstanding the provisions of paragraph 1, remuneration derived by a resident of a Contracting State in respect of an employment exercised in the other Contracting State shall be taxable only in the first-mentioned Contracting State if:

    (a) The recipient is present in the other Contracting State for a period or periods not exceeding in the aggregate 183 days in the calendar year concerned; and
    (b) The remuneration is paid by, or on behalf of. An employer who is not a resident of the other Contracting State; and
    (c) The remuneration is not borne by a permanent establishment or a fixed base, which the employer has in the other Contracting State.

3. Notwithstanding the preceding provisions of this Article, remuneration derived in respect of an employment exercised aboard a ship or aircraft operated in international traffic by a resident of a Contracting State shall be taxable only in that Contracting State.

Article 16 – Directors' Fees

Directors' fees and other similar payments derived by a resident of a Contracting State in his capacity as a member of the board of directors of a company which is a resident of the other Contracting State may be taxed in that other Contracting State.

Article 17 – Artistes and Athletes

1. Notwithstanding the provisions of Articles 14 and 15, income derived by a resident of a Contracting State as an entertainer, such as a theatre, motion picture, radio or television artiste, or a musician, or as an athlete, from his personal activities as such exercised in the other Contracting State, may be taxed in that other Contracting State.
2. Where income in respect of personal activities exercised by an entertainer or an athlete in his capacity as such accrues not to the entertainer or athlete himself but to another person, that income may, notwithstanding the provisions of Articles 7, 14 and 15, be taxed in the Contracting State in which the activities of the entertainer or athlete are exercised.
3. Notwithstanding the provisions of paragraphs 1 and 2, income derived by entertainers or athletes who are residents of a Contracting State from the activities exercised in the other Contracting State under a plan of cultural exchange between the Governments of both Contracting States shall be exempt from tax in that other Contracting State.

Article 18 – Pensions

1. Subject to the provisions of paragraph 2 of Article 19, pensions and other similar remuneration paid to a resident of a Contracting State in consideration of past employment shall be taxable only in that Contracting State.
2. Notwithstanding the provisions of paragraph 1, pensions paid and other similar payments made by the Government of a Contracting State, a political subdivision or a local authority thereof under a public welfare scheme of the social security system of that Contracting State shall be taxable only in that Contracting State.

Article 19 – Government Service

1. (a) Remuneration, other than a pension, paid by the Government of a Contracting State or a political subdivision or a local authority thereof to an individual in respect of services rendered to the Government of that Contracting State or a political subdivision or a local authority thereof, in the discharge of functions of a governmental nature, shall be taxable only in that Contracting State.
   (b) However, such remuneration shall be taxable only in the other Contracting State if the services are rendered in that other Contracting State and the individual is a resident of that other Contracting State who:

   (i) is a national of that other Contracting State; or
   (ii) did not become a resident of that other Contracting State solely for the purpose of rendering the services.

2. (a) Any pension paid by, or out of funds to which contributions are made by the Government of a Contracting State or a political subdivision or a local authority thereof to an individual in respect of services rendered to the Government of that Contracting State or a political subdivision or a local authority thereof shall be taxable only in that Contracting State.
   (b) However, such pension shall be taxable only in the other Contracting State if the individual is a resident of, and a national of, that other Contracting State.

3. The provisions of Articles 15, 16, 17 and 18 shall apply to remuneration and pensions in respect of services rendered in connection with a business carried on by the Government of a Contracting State or a political subdivision or a local authority thereof.

Article 20 – Students, Apprentices and Trainees

A student, business apprentice or trainee who is or was immediately before visiting a Contracting State a resident of the other Contracting State and who is present in the first-mentioned Contracting State solely for the purpose of his education, training shall be exempt from tax in that first-mentioned Contracting State on the following payments or income received or derived by him for the purpose of his maintenance, education or training:

(a) Payments derived from sources outside that Contracting State for the purpose of his maintenance, education, study, research or training;
(b) Grants, scholarships or awards supplied by the Government, or a scientific, educational, cultural or other tax-exempt organization; and
(c) Any remuneration not exceeding 2,000 US dollars or the equivalent in Vietnamese Dong or the equivalent in Chinese RMB per calendar year in respect of personal services in connection with his studies or training.

Article 21 – Teachers, Professors and Researchers

An individual who is, or immediately before visiting a Contracting State was, a resident of the other Contracting State and is present in the first-mentioned Contracting State for the primary purpose of teaching, giving lectures or conducting research at a university, college, school or educational institution or scientific research institution accredited by the Government of the first-mentioned Contracting State shall be exempt from tax in the first-mentioned Contracting State, for a period of two years from the date of his first arrival in the first-mentioned Contracting State, in respect of remuneration for such teaching, lectures or research.

Article 22 – Other Income

1. Items of income of a resident of a Contracting State, wherever arising, not dealt with in the foregoing Articles of this Agreement shall be taxable only in that Contracting State.
2. However, any such income derived by a resident of a Contracting State from sources in the other Contracting State may also be taxed in that other Contracting State.
3. The provisions of paragraph 1 shall not apply to income, other than income from immovable property as defined in paragraph 2 of Article 6, if the recipient of such income, being a resident of a Contracting State, carries on business in the other Contracting State through a permanent establishment situated therein, or performs in that other Contracting State independent personal services from a fixed base situated therein, and the right or property in respect of which the income is paid is effectively connected with such permanent establishment or fixed base. In such case the provisions of Article 7 or Article 14, as the case may be, shall apply.

Article 23 – Methods for Elimination of Double Taxation

1. In Vietnam, double taxation shall be eliminated as follows:
Where a resident of Vietnam derives income, profits or gains which under the law of China and in accordance with this Agreement may be taxed in China, Vietnam shall allow as a credit against its tax on the income, profits or gains an amount equal to the tax paid in China. The amount of credit, however, shall not exceed the amount of the

Vietnamese tax on that income, profits or gains computed in accordance with the taxation laws and regulations of Vietnam.
2. In China, double taxation shall be eliminated as follows:

   (a) Where a resident of China derives income from Vietnam the amount of tax on that income payable in Vietnam in accordance with the provisions of this Agreement, may be credited against the Chinese tax imposed on that resident. The amount of the credit, however, shall not exceed the amount of the Chinese tax on that income computed in accordance with the taxation laws and regulations of China;

   (b) Where the income derived from Vietnam is a dividend paid by a company which is a resident of Vietnam to a company which is a resident of China and which owns not less than 10 per cent of the shares of the company paying the dividend, the credit shall take into account the tax paid in Vietnam by the company paying the dividend in respect of its income.

3. For the purposes of paragraphs 1 and 2, the tax payable in Vietnam or in China, as the context requires, shall be deemed to include the tax which is otherwise payable in a Contracting State but has been reduced or waived by that Contracting State under its legal provisions for economic development. In the case of the provisions of paragraph 2 of Article 10, paragraph 2 of Article 11 and paragraph 2 of Article 12, such tax shall be deemed to be 10 per cent of the gross amount of dividends, interest and royalties.

Article 24 – Non-discrimination

1. Nationals of a Contracting State shall not be subjected in the other Contracting State to any taxation or any requirement connected therewith, which is other or more burdensome than the taxation and connected requirements to which nationals of that other Contracting State in the same circumstances are or may be subjected.
2. The taxation on a permanent establishment, which an enterprise of a Contracting State has in the other Contracting State, shall not be less favorably levied in that other Contracting State than the taxation levied on enterprises of that other Contracting State carrying on the same activities. The provisions of this paragraph shall not be construed as obliging a Contracting State to grant to residents of the other Contracting State any personal allowances, reliefs and reductions for taxation purposes on account of civil status or family responsibilities which it grants to its own residents.
3. Except where the provisions of paragraph 1 of Article 9, paragraph 7 of Article 11, or paragraph 6 of Article 12, apply, interest, royalties and other disbursements paid by an enterprise of a Contracting State to a resident of the other Contracting State shall, for the purpose of determining the taxable profits of such enterprise, be deductible under the same conditions as if they had been paid to a resident of the first-mentioned Contracting State.
4. Enterprises of a Contracting State, the capital of which is wholly or partly owned or controlled, directly or indirectly, by one or more residents of the other Contracting State, shall not be subjected in the first-mentioned Contracting State to any taxation or any requirement connected therewith which is other or more burdensome than the taxation and connected requirements to which other similar enterprises of the first-mentioned Contracting State are or may be subjected.
5. Notwithstanding the provisions from paragraphs 1 to 4 of this Article, where a Contracting State imposes any taxation on its nationals which is other than the taxation it imposes on nationals of the other Contracting State for the purposes to promote economic development in accordance with its taxation laws, the imposition as such shall not be construed as discrimination under the meaning of this Article.
6. The provisions of this Article shall apply only to the taxes, which are the subject of this Agreement.

Article 25 – Mutual Agreement Procedure

1. Where a person considers that the actions of one or both of the Contracting States result or will result for him in taxation not in accordance with the provisions of this Agreement, he may, irrespective of the remedies provided by the domestic law of those Contracting States, present his case to the competent authority of the Contracting State of which he is a resident or, if his case comes under paragraph 1 of Article 24, to that of the Contracting State of which he is a national. The case must be presented within three years from the first notification of the action resulting in taxation not in accordance with the provisions of the Agreement.
2. The competent authority shall endeavor, if the objection appears to it to be justified and if it is not itself able to arrive at a satisfactory solution, to resolve the case by mutual agreement with the competent authority of the other Contracting State, with a view to the avoidance of taxation which is not in accordance with the provisions of this Agreement. Any agreement reached shall be implemented notwithstanding any time limits in the domestic law of the Contracting States.
3. The competent authorities of the Contracting States shall endeavor to resolve by mutual agreement any difficulties or doubts arising as to the interpretation or application of the Agreement. They may also consult together for the elimination of double taxation in cases not provided for in this Agreement.
4. The competent authorities of the Contracting States may communicate with each other directly for the purpose of reaching an agreement in the sense of paragraphs 2 and 3. When it seems advisable for reaching agreement, representatives of the competent authorities of the Contracting States may meet together for an oral exchange of opinions.

Article 26 – Exchange of Information

1. The competent authorities of the Contracting States shall exchange such information as is necessary for carrying out the provisions of this Agreement or of the domestic laws of the Contracting States concerning taxes covered by the Agreement insofar as the taxation thereunder is not contrary to the Agreement, in particular for the prevention of fraud or evasion of such taxes. The exchange of information is not restricted by Article 1. Any information received by a Contracting State shall be treated as secret in the same manner as information obtained under the domestic laws of that Contracting State. However, if the information is originally regarded as secret in transmitting Contracting State it shall be disclosed only to persons or authorities (including courts and administrative bodies) involved in the assessment or collection of, the enforcement or prosecution in respect of, or the determination of appeals in relation to, the taxes which are the subject of the Agreement. Such persons or authorities shall use the information only for such purposes. They may disclose the information in public court proceedings or in judicial decisions.
2. In no case shall the provisions of paragraph 1 be construed so as to impose on a Contracting State the obligation:

    (a) To carry out administrative measures at variance with the laws and administrative practice of that or of the other Contracting State;
    (b) To supply information which is not obtainable under the laws or in the normal course of the administration of that or of the other Contracting State;
    (c) To supply information, which would disclose any trade, business, industrial, commercial or professional secret or trade process, or information, the disclosure of which would be contrary to public policy (ordre public).

Article 27 – Diplomatic Agents and Consular Officers

Nothing in this Agreement shall affect the fiscal privileges of diplomatic agents or consular officers under the general rules of international law or under the provisions of special agreements.

Article 28 – Entry into Force

Each of the Contracting States shall notify to the other in writing through the diplomatic channel the completion of the internal procedures required by the law applied in that Contracting State for the bringing into force of this Agreement. This Agreement shall enter into force on the date of the later of these notifications. This Agreement shall have effect as respects income derived during the taxable years beginning on or after the first day of January in the calendar year next following that in which this Agreement enters into force.

Article 29 – Termination

This Agreement shall remain in force until terminated by a Contracting State. Either Contracting State may, on or before the thirtieth day of June in any calendar year beginning after the expiration of a period of five years from the date of its entry into force, give written notice of termination to the other Contracting State through the diplomatic channels. In such event, this Agreement shall cease to have effect as respects income derived during the taxable years beginning on or after the first day of January in the calendar year next following that in which the notice of termination is given.

DONE in duplicate at Beijing this 17th day of May of the year one thousand nine hundred and ninety-five in the Chinese, Vietnamese and English languages, three texts being equally authentic. In case of divergence of interpretations, the English text shall prevail.

Protocol

At the signing of this Agreement between the Government of the People's Republic of China and the Government of the Socialist Republic of Vietnam for the Avoidance of Double Taxation and the Prevention of Fiscal Evasion with respect to Taxes on Income (hereinafter referred to as "the Agreement"), both sides have agreed upon the following provisions which form an integral part of the Agreement:

1. In connection with Article 8 of the Agreement, nothing in this Agreement shall affect the application of the provisions of the Agreement on Civil Air Transport and the Agreement on Maritime Transport signed between the two Governments on March 8, 1992 in Beijing.
2. It is understood that, as long as, according to the Vietnamese tax law, Vietnam does not levy a tax on dividend, the existing profits remittance tax applicable in Vietnam shall be deemed to be the tax on "dividends" referred to in paragraph 3 of Article 10 of the Agreement.

DONE in duplicate at Beijing this 17th day of May of the year one thousand nine hundred and ninety-five in the Chinese, Vietnamese and English languages, three texts being equally authentic. In case of divergence of interpretations, the English text shall prevail.

8.5 Hong Kong–Vietnam Treaty

The Government of the Socialist Republic of Vietnam and the Government of the Hong Kong Special Administrative Region, desiring to conclude an Agreement for the avoidance of double taxation and the prevention of fiscal evasion with respect to taxes on income, have agreed as follows:

Article 1 – Persons Covered

This Agreement shall apply to persons who are residents of one or both of the Contracting Parties.

Article 2 – Taxes Covered

1. This Agreement shall apply to taxes on income imposed on behalf of a Contracting Party, irrespective of the manner in which they are levied.
2. There shall be regarded as taxes on income all taxes imposed on total income, or on elements of income, including taxes on gains from the alienation of movable or immovable property, taxes on the total amounts of wages or salaries paid by enterprises, as well as taxes on capital appreciation.
3. The existing taxes to which this Agreement shall apply are:

    (a) In the case of the Hong Kong Special Administrative Region:

    (i) profits tax;
    (ii) salaries tax; and
    (iii) property tax,
       whether or not charged under personal assessment;

    (b) In the case of the Socialist Republic of Vietnam:

    (i) business income tax; and
    (ii) personal income tax.

4. This Agreement shall apply also to any identical or substantially similar taxes that are imposed after the date of signature of this Agreement in addition to, or in place of, the existing taxes, as well as any other taxes falling within paragraphs 1 and 2 of this Article, which a Contracting Party may impose in future. The competent authorities of the Contracting Parties shall notify each other of any significant changes that have been made in their taxation laws.
5. The existing taxes, together with the taxes imposed after the signature of this Agreement, are hereinafter referred to as "Hong Kong Special Administrative Region tax" and "Vietnamese tax" respectively.

Article 3 – General Definitions

1. For the purposes of this Agreement, unless the context otherwise requires:

    (a) (i) the term " Hong Kong Special Administrative Region " means the Hong Kong Special Administrative Region of the People's Republic of China;
      (ii) the term "Vietnam" means the Socialist Republic of Vietnam; when used in a geographical sense, it means its land territory, islands, internal waters, territorial sea and airspace above them, the maritime areas beyond territorial sea including seabed and subsoil thereof over which the Socialist Republic of

Vietnam exercises sovereignty, sovereign rights and jurisdiction in accordance with national legislation and international law;

(b) The term "company" means any body corporate or any entity that is treated as a body corporate for tax purposes;
(c) The term "competent authority" means:

   (i) in the case of the Hong Kong Special Administrative Region, the Commissioner of Inland Revenue or his authorized representative or any person or body authorized to perform any functions at present exercisable by the Commissioner or similar functions;
   (ii) in the case of Vietnam, the Minister of Finance or his authorized representative;

(d) The term "Contracting Party" means the Hong Kong Special Administrative Region or Vietnam, as the context requires;
(e) The terms "enterprise of a Contracting Party" and "enterprise of the other Contracting Party" mean, respectively, an enterprise carried on by a resident of a Contracting Party and an enterprise carried on by a resident of the other Contracting Party;
(f) The term "international traffic" means any transport by a ship or aircraft operated by an enterprise of a Contracting Party, except when the ship or aircraft is operated solely between places in the other Contracting Party;
(g) The term "national", in relation to Vietnam, means:

   (i) any individual possessing the nationality of Vietnam; and
   (ii) any legal person, partnership or association deriving its status as such from the laws in force in Vietnam;

(h) The term "person" includes an individual, a company, a trust, a partnership and any other body of persons;
(i) the term "tax" means the Hong Kong Special Administrative Region tax or Vietnamese tax, as the context requires.

2. In this Agreement, the terms "Hong Kong Special Administrative Region tax" and "Vietnamese tax" do not include any penalty or interest imposed under the laws in force in either Contracting Party relating to the taxes to which this Agreement applies by virtue of Article 2.
3. As regards the application of this Agreement at any time by a Contracting Party, any term not defined therein shall, unless the context otherwise requires, have the meaning that it has at that time under the laws of that Party for the purposes of the taxes to which this Agreement applies, any meaning under the applicable tax laws of that Party prevailing over a meaning given to the term under other laws of that Party.

Article 4 – Resident

1. For the purposes of this Agreement, the term "resident of a Contracting Party" means:

   (a) In the case of the Hong Kong Special Administrative Region,

      (i) any individual who ordinarily resides in the Hong Kong Special Administrative Region;
      (ii) any individual who stays in the Hong Kong Special Administrative Region for more than 180 days during a year of assessment or for more than 300 days in two consecutive years of assessment one of which is the relevant year of assessment;

(iii) a company incorporated in the Hong Kong Special Administrative Region or, if incorporated outside the Hong Kong Special Administrative Region, being normally managed or controlled in the Hong Kong Special Administrative Region;

(iv) any other person constituted under the laws of the Hong Kong Special Administrative Region or, if constituted outside the Hong Kong Special Administrative Region, being normally managed or controlled in the Hong Kong Special Administrative Region;

(b) In the case of Vietnam, any person who, under the laws of Vietnam, is liable to tax therein by reason of his domicile, residence, place of incorporation, place of registration, place of management or any other criterion of a similar nature. This term, however, does not include any person who is liable to tax in Vietnam in respect only of income from sources in Vietnam.

2. Where by reason of the provisions of paragraph 1, an individual is a resident of both Contracting Parties, then his status shall be determined as follows:

(a) He shall be deemed to be a resident only of the Party in which he has a permanent home available to him; if he has a permanent home available to him in both Parties, he shall be deemed to be a resident only of the Party with which his personal and economic relations are closer ("centre of vital interests");

(b) If the Party in which he has his centre of vital interests cannot be determined, or if he has not a permanent home available to him in either Party, he shall be deemed to be a resident only of the Party in which he has an habitual abode;

(c) If he has an habitual abode in both Parties or in neither of them, he shall be deemed to be a resident only of the Party in which he has the right of abode (in the case of the Hong Kong Special Administrative Region) or of which he is a national (in the case of Vietnam);

(d) If he has the right of abode in the Hong Kong Special Administrative Region and is also a national of Vietnam, or if he does not have the right of abode in the Hong Kong Special Administrative Region nor is he a national of Vietnam, the competent authorities of the Contracting Parties shall settle the question by mutual agreement.

3. Where by reason of the provisions of paragraph 1 a person other than an individual is a resident of both Contracting Parties, then the competent authorities of the Contracting Parties shall determine that the person is a resident of a Contracting Party for the purposes of this Agreement by mutual agreement.

Article 5 – Permanent Establishment

1. For the purposes of this Agreement, the term "permanent establishment" means a fixed place of business through which the business of an enterprise is wholly or partly carried on.
2. The term "permanent establishment" includes especially:

(a) A place of management;
(b) A branch;
(c) An office;
(d) A factory;
(e) A workshop;
(f) A mine, an oil or gas well, a quarry or any other place of extraction of natural resources;
(g) A warehouse, in relation to a person supplying storage facilities for others; and
(h) An installation structure, or equipment used for the exploration of natural resources.

3. The term "permanent establishment" also encompasses:
   (a) A building site, a construction, assembly or installation project or supervisory activities in connection therewith, but only if such site, project or activities last more than six months;
   (b) The furnishing of services, including consultancy services, by an enterprise through employees or other personnel engaged by the enterprise for such purpose, but only if activities of that nature continue (for the same or a connected project) within a Contracting Party for a period or periods aggregating more than 180 days within any twelve-month period.
4. Notwithstanding the preceding provisions of this Article, the term "permanent establishment" shall be deemed not to include:
   (a) The use of facilities solely for the purpose of storage or display of goods or merchandise belonging to the enterprise;
   (b) The maintenance of a stock of goods or merchandise belonging to the enterprise solely for the purpose of storage or display;
   (c) The maintenance of a stock of goods or merchandise belonging to the enterprise solely for the purpose of processing by another enterprise;
   (d) The maintenance of a fixed place of business solely for the purpose of purchasing goods or merchandise or of collecting information, for the enterprise;
   (e) The maintenance of a fixed place of business solely for the purpose of carrying on, for the enterprise, any other activity of a preparatory or auxiliary character.
5. Notwithstanding the provisions of paragraphs 1 and 2, where a person - other than an agent of an independent status to whom paragraph 6 applies - is acting in a Contracting Party on behalf of an enterprise of the other Contracting Party, that enterprise shall be deemed to have a permanent establishment in the first-mentioned Contracting Party in respect of any activities which that person undertakes for the enterprise, if such a person:
   (a) Has, and habitually exercises, in the first-mentioned Contracting Party an authority to conclude contracts in the name of the enterprise, unless the activities of such person are limited to those mentioned in paragraph 4 which, if exercised through a fixed place of business, would not make this fixed place of business a permanent establishment under the provisions of that paragraph; or
   (b) Has no such authority, but habitually maintains in the first-mentioned Party a stock of goods or merchandise from which he regularly delivers goods or merchandise on behalf of the enterprise.
6. An enterprise shall not be deemed to have a permanent establishment in a Contracting Party merely because it carries on business in that Party through a broker, general commission agent or any other agent of an independent status, provided that such persons are acting in the ordinary course of their business. However, when the activities of such an agent are devoted wholly or almost wholly on behalf of that enterprise, and conditions are made or imposed between that enterprise and the agent in their commercial and financial relations which differ from those which would have been made between independent enterprises, he will not be considered an agent of an independent status within the meaning of this paragraph.
7. The fact that a company which is a resident of a Contracting Party controls or is controlled by a company which is a resident of the other Contracting Party, or which carries on business in that other Party (whether through a permanent establishment or otherwise), shall not of itself constitute either company a permanent establishment of the other.

Article 6 – Income from Immovable Property

1. Income derived by a resident of a Contracting Party from immovable property (including income from agriculture or forestry) situated in the other Contracting Party may be taxed in that other Party.
2. The term "immovable property" shall have the meaning, which it has under the laws of the Contracting Party in which the property in question is situated. The term shall in any case include property accessory to immovable property, livestock and equipment used in agriculture and forestry, rights to which the provisions of general law respecting landed property apply, usufruct of immovable property and rights to variable or fixed payments as consideration for the working of, or the right to explore for or work, mineral deposits, quarries, sources and other natural resources; ships, boats and aircraft shall not be regarded as immovable property.
3. The provisions of paragraph 1 shall apply to income derived from the direct use, letting, or use in any other form of immovable property.
4. The provisions of paragraphs 1 and 3 shall also apply to the income from immovable property of an enterprise and to income from immovable property used for the performance of independent personal services.

Article 7 – Business Profits

1. The profits of an enterprise of a Contracting Party shall be taxable only in that Party unless the enterprise carries on business in the other Contracting Party through a permanent establishment situated therein. If the enterprise carries on business as aforesaid, the profits of the enterprise may be taxed in the other Party, but only so much of them as is attributable to:

    (a) That permanent establishment;
    (b) Sales in that other Party of goods or merchandise of the same or similar kind as those sold through that permanent establishment; or
    (c) Other business activities carried on in that other Party of the same or similar kind as those effected through that permanent establishment; provided that (b) or (c) shall not apply where an enterprise is able to demonstrate that the sales or business activities were carried out for reasons other than obtaining treaty benefits.

2. Subject to the provisions of paragraph 3, where an enterprise of a Contracting Party carries on business in the other Contracting Party through a permanent establishment situated therein, there shall in each Contracting Party be attributed to that permanent establishment the profits which it might be expected to make if it were a distinct and separate enterprise engaged in the same or similar activities under the same or similar conditions and dealing wholly independently with the enterprise of which it is a permanent establishment or with other enterprises with which it deals.
3. In determining the profits of a permanent establishment, there shall be allowed as deductions expenses which are incurred for the purposes of the business of the permanent establishment, including executive and general administrative expenses so incurred, whether in the Party in which the permanent establishment is situated or elsewhere. However, no such deduction shall be allowed in respect of amounts, if any, paid (otherwise than towards reimbursement of actual expenses) by the permanent establishment to the head office of the enterprise or any of its other offices, by way of royalties, fees or other similar payments in return for the use of patents or other rights, or by way of commission, for specific services performed or for management, or, except in the case of a banking enterprise, by way of interest on moneys lent to the permanent establishment. Likewise, no account shall be taken, in the determination of the profits of a permanent establishment, of amounts charged (otherwise than towards reimbursement of actual expenses) by the permanent establishment to the head office of the enterprise or

any of its other offices, by way of royalties, fees or other similar payments in return for the use of patents or other rights, or by way of commission for specific services performed or for management, or, except in the case of a banking enterprise, by way of interest on moneys lent to the head office of the enterprise or any of its other offices.
4. Insofar as it has been customary in a Contracting Party to determine the profits to be attributed to a permanent establishment on the basis of an apportionment of the total profits of the enterprise to its various parts, nothing in paragraph 2 shall preclude that Contracting Party from determining the profits to be taxed by such an apportionment as may be customary; the method of apportionment adopted shall, however, be such that the result shall be in accordance with the principles contained in this Article.
5. If the information available to the taxation authority of a Contracting Party is inadequate to determine the profits to be attributed to the permanent establishment of an enterprise, nothing in this Article shall affect the application of any law of that Contracting Party relating to the determination of the tax liability of a person provided that that law shall be applied in accordance with the principles of this Article, so far as the information available to the taxation authority permits.
6. For the purposes of the preceding paragraphs, the profits to be attributed to the permanent establishment shall be determined by the same method year by year unless there is good and sufficient reason to the contrary.
7. Where profits include items of income, which are dealt with separately in other Articles of this Agreement, then the provisions of those Articles shall not be affected by the provisions of this Article.

Article 8 – Shipping and Air Transport

1. Profits of an enterprise of a Contracting Party from the operation of ships or aircraft in international traffic shall be taxable only in that Party.
2. The provisions of paragraph 1 shall also apply to profits from the participation in a pool, a joint business or an international operating agency.

Article 9 – Associated Enterprises

1. Where
   (a) An enterprise of a Contracting Party participates directly or indirectly in the management, control or capital of an enterprise of the other Contracting Party; or
   (b) The same persons participate directly or indirectly in the management, control or capital of an enterprise of a Contracting Party and an enterprise of the other Contracting Party, and in either case conditions are made or imposed between the two enterprises in their commercial or financial relations which differ from those which would be made between independent enterprises, then any profits which would, but for those conditions, have accrued to one of the enterprises, but, by reason of those conditions, have not so accrued, may be included in the profits of that enterprise and taxed accordingly.
2. Where a Contracting Party includes in the profits of an enterprise of that Party - and taxes accordingly - profits on which an enterprise of the other Contracting Party has been charged to tax in that other Party and the profits so included are profits which would have accrued to the enterprise of the first-mentioned Party if the conditions made between the two enterprises had been those which would have been made between independent enterprises, then that other Party shall make an appropriate adjustment to the amount of the tax charged therein on those profits. In determining such adjustment, due regard shall be had to the other provisions of this Agreement and for this purpose the competent authorities of the Contracting Parties shall if necessary consult each other.

Article 10 – Dividends

1. Dividends paid by a company, which is a resident of a Contracting Party to a resident of the other Contracting Party, may be taxed in that other Party.
2. However, such dividends may also be taxed in the Contracting Party of which the company paying the dividends is a resident and according to the laws of that Party, but if the beneficial owner of the dividends is a resident of the other Contracting Party, the tax so charged shall not exceed 10 per cent of the gross amount of the dividends. This paragraph shall not affect the taxation of the company in respect of the profits out of which the dividends are paid.
3. The term "dividends" as used in this Article means income from shares or other rights, not being debt-claims, participating in profits, as well as income from other corporate rights which is subjected to the same taxation treatment as income from shares by the laws of the Party of which the company making the distribution is a resident.
4. The provisions of paragraphs 1 and 2 shall not apply if the beneficial owner of the dividends, being a resident of a Contracting Party, carries on business in the other Contracting Party of which the company paying the dividends is a resident, through a permanent establishment situated therein, or performs in that other Party independent personal services from a fixed base situated therein, and the holding in respect of which the dividends are paid is effectively connected with such permanent establishment or fixed base. In such case, the provisions of Article 7 or Article 14, as the case may be, shall apply.
5. Where a company which is a resident of a Contracting Party derives profits or income from the other Contracting Party, that other Party may not impose any tax on the dividends paid by the company, except insofar as such dividends are paid to a resident of that other Party or insofar as the holding in respect of which the dividends are paid is effectively connected with a permanent establishment or a fixed base situated in that other Party, nor subject the company's undistributed profits to a tax on the company's undistributed profits, even if the dividends paid or the undistributed profits consist wholly or partly of profits or income arising in such other Party.

Article 11 – Interest

1. Interest arising in a Contracting Party and paid to a resident of the other Contracting Party may be taxed in that other Party.
2. However, such interest may also be taxed in the Contracting Party in which it arises and according to the laws of that Party, but if the beneficial owner of the interest is a resident of the other Contracting Party, the tax so charged shall not exceed 10 per cent of the gross amount of the interest.
3. Notwithstanding the provisions of paragraph 2 of this Article,

    (a) Interest arising in the Hong Kong Special Administrative Region shall be exempt from Hong Kong Special Administrative Region tax if the interest is paid to:

    (i) the Government of Vietnam;
    (ii) the State Bank of Vietnam;
    (iii) the Bank for Foreign Trade of Vietnam;
    (iv) other financial institution the capital of which is wholly owned by the Government of Vietnam;
    (v) a financial establishment appointed by the Government of Vietnam and mutually agreed upon by the competent authorities of the two Contracting Parties;

    (b) Interest arising in Vietnam shall be exempt from Vietnamese tax if the interest is paid to:

(i) the Government of the Hong Kong Special Administrative Region;
(ii) the Hong Kong Monetary Authority;
(iii) a financial establishment appointed by the Government of the Hong Kong Special Administrative Region and mutually agreed upon by the competent authorities of the two Contracting Parties.

4. The term "interest" as used in this Article means income from debt-claims of every kind, whether or not secured by mortgage, and whether or not carrying a right to participate in the debtor's profits, and in particular, income from government securities and income from bonds or debentures, including premiums and prizes attaching to such securities, bonds or debentures. Penalty charges for late payment shall not be regarded as interest for the purpose of this Article.
5. The provisions of paragraphs 1, 2 and 3 shall not apply if the beneficial owner of the interest, being the Government of a Contracting Party or a resident of that Party, carries on business in the other Contracting Party in which the interest arises, through a permanent establishment situated therein, or performs in that other Party independent personal services from a fixed base situated therein and the debt-claim in respect of which the interest is paid is effectively connected with (a) such permanent establishment or fixed base, or with (b) business activities referred to in (c) of paragraph 1 of Article 7. In such cases the provisions of Article 7 or Article 14, as the case may be, shall apply.
6. Interest shall be deemed to arise in a Contracting Party when the payer is the Government of that Party or a resident of that Party. Where, however, the person paying the interest, whether he is the Government of a Contracting Party or a resident of that Party or not, has in a Contracting Party a permanent establishment or a fixed base in connection with which the indebtedness on which the interest is paid was incurred, and such interest is borne by such permanent establishment or fixed base, then such interest shall be deemed to arise in the Party in which the permanent establishment or fixed base is situated.
7. Where, by reason of a special relationship between the payer and the beneficial owner or between both of them and some other person, the amount of the interest, having regard to the debt-claim for which it is paid, exceeds the amount which would have been agreed upon by the payer and the beneficial owner in the absence of such relationship, the provisions of this Article shall apply only to the last-mentioned amount. In such case, the excess part of the payments shall remain taxable according to the laws of each Contracting Party, due regard being had to the other provisions of this Agreement.

Article 12 – Royalties

1. Royalties arising in a Contracting Party and paid to a resident of the other Contracting Party may be taxed in that other Party.
2. However, such royalties may also be taxed in the Contracting Party in which they arise and according to the laws of that Party, but if the beneficial owner of the royalties is a resident of the other Contracting Party, the tax so charged shall not exceed:

    (a) 7 per cent of the gross amount of the royalties if they are made as a consideration for the use of, or the right to use, any patent, design or model, plan, secret formula or process;
    (b) 10 per cent of the gross amount of the royalties in all other cases.

3. The term "royalties" as used in this Article means payments of any kind received as a consideration for the use of, or the right to use, any copyright of literary, artistic or scientific work including cinematograph films, or films or tapes or discs used for radio or television broadcasting, any patent, trade mark, design or model, computer software program, plan, secret formula or process, or for the use of, or the right to use, industrial,

commercial or scientific equipment, or for information concerning industrial, commercial or scientific experience.
4. The provisions of paragraphs 1 and 2 shall not apply if the beneficial owner of the royalties, being the Government of a Contracting Party or a resident of that Party, carries on business in the other Contracting Party in which the royalties arise, through a permanent establishment situated therein, or performs in that other Party independent personal services from a fixed base situated therein, and the right or property in respect of which the royalties are paid is effectively connected with (a) such permanent establishment or fixed base, or with (b) business activities referred to in (c) of paragraph 1 of Article 7. In such cases the provisions of Article 7 or Article 14, as the case may be, shall apply.
5. Royalties shall be deemed to arise in a Contracting Party when the payer is the Government of that Party or a resident of that Party. Where, however, the person paying the royalties, whether he is the Government of a Contracting Party or a resident of that Party or not, has in a Contracting Party a permanent establishment or a fixed base in connection with which the liability to pay the royalties was incurred, and such royalties are borne by such permanent establishment or fixed base, then such royalties shall be deemed to arise in the Party in which the permanent establishment or fixed base is situated.
6. Where, by reason of a special relationship between the payer and the beneficial owner or between both of them and some other person, the amount of the royalties, having regard to the use, right or information for which they are paid, exceeds the amount which would have been agreed upon by the payer and the beneficial owner in the absence of such relationship, the provisions of this Article shall apply only to the last-mentioned amount. In such case, the excess part of the payments shall remain taxable according to the laws of each Contracting Party, due regard being had to the other provisions of this Agreement.

Article 13 – Gains from the Alienation of Property

1. Gains derived by a resident of a Contracting Party from the alienation of immovable property referred to in Article 6 and situated in the other Contracting Party may be taxed in that other Party.
2. Gains from the alienation of movable property forming part of the business property of a permanent establishment which an enterprise of a Contracting Party has in the other Contracting Party or of movable property pertaining to a fixed base available to a resident of a Contracting Party in the other Contracting Party for the purpose of performing independent personal services, including such gains from the alienation of such a permanent establishment (alone or with the whole enterprise) or of such fixed base, may be taxed in that other Party.
3. Gains derived by an enterprise of a Contracting Party from the alienation of ships or aircraft operated in international traffic or movable property pertaining to the operation of such ships or aircraft shall be taxable only in that Party.
4. Gains derived by a resident of a Contracting Party from the alienation of shares of or comparable participation in a company, the assets of which consist, directly or indirectly, mainly of immovable property situated in the other Contracting Party may be taxed in that other Party.
5. Gains derived from the alienation of shares, other than the shares referred to in paragraph 4, of not less than 15 per cent of the entire shareholding of a company, which is a resident of a Contracting Party, may be taxed in that Contracting Party.
6. Gains from the alienation of any property, other than that referred to in paragraphs 1, 2, 3, 4 and 5, shall be taxable only in the Contracting Party of which the alienator is a resident.

Article 14 – Independent Personal Services

1. Income derived by a resident of a Contracting Party in respect of professional services or other activities of an independent character shall be taxable only in that Party except in the following circumstances, when such income may also be taxed in the other Contracting Party:

    (a) If he has a fixed base regularly available to him in the other Contracting Party for the purpose of performing his activities; in that case, only so much of the income as is attributable to that fixed base may be taxed in that other Contracting Party; or
    (b) If his stay in the other Contracting Party is for a period or periods amounting to or exceeding in the aggregate 183 days in any twelve-month period commencing or ending in the fiscal year concerned; in that case, only so much of the income as is derived from his activities performed in that other Party may be taxed in that other Party.

2. The term "professional services" includes especially independent scientific, literary, artistic, educational or teaching activities as well as the independent activities of physicians, lawyers, engineers, architects, dentists and accountants.

Article 15 – Dependent Personal Services

1. Subject to the provisions of Articles 16, 18, 19 and 20, salaries, wages and other similar remuneration derived by a resident of a Contracting Party in respect of an employment shall be taxable only in that Party unless the employment is exercised in the other Contracting Party. If the employment is so exercised, such remuneration as is derived therefrom may be taxed in that other Party.
2. Notwithstanding the provisions of paragraph 1, remuneration derived by a resident of a Contracting Party in respect of an employment exercised in the other Contracting Party shall be taxable only in the first-mentioned Party if:

    (a) The recipient is present in the other Party for a period or periods not exceeding in the aggregate 183 days in any twelve-month period commencing or ending in the fiscal year concerned; and
    (b) The remuneration is paid by, or on behalf of, an employer who is not a resident of the other Party; and
    (c) The remuneration is not borne by a permanent establishment or a fixed base, which the employer has in the other Party.

3. Notwithstanding the preceding provisions of this Article, remuneration derived in respect of an employment exercised aboard a ship or aircraft operated in international traffic by an enterprise of a Contracting Party shall be taxable only in that Party.

Article 16 – Directors' Fees

Directors' fees and other similar payments derived by a resident of a Contracting Party in his capacity as a member of the board of directors of a company which is a resident of the other Contracting Party may be taxed in that other Party.

Article 17 – Artistes and Sportsmen

1. Notwithstanding the provisions of Articles 14 and 15, income derived by a resident of a Contracting Party as an entertainer, such as a theatre, motion picture, radio or television artiste, or a musician, or as a sportsman, from his personal activities as such exercised in the other Contracting Party, may be taxed in that other Party.

2. Where income in respect of personal activities exercised by an entertainer or a sportsman in his capacity as such accrues not to the entertainer or sportsman himself but to another person, that income may, notwithstanding the provisions of Articles 7, 14 and 15, be taxed in the Contracting Party in which the activities of the entertainer or sportsman are exercised.
3. Notwithstanding the provisions of paragraphs 1 and 2, income derived by entertainers or sportsmen who are residents of a Contracting Party from activities in the other Contracting Party under a plan of cultural exchange between the Governments of both Contracting Parties shall be exempt from tax in that other Contracting Party.

Article 18 – Pensions

1. Subject to the provisions of paragraph 2 of Article 19, pensions and other similar remuneration (including a lump sum payment) paid to a resident of a Contracting Party in consideration of past employment or self-employment shall be taxable only in that Contracting Party.
2. Notwithstanding the provisions of paragraph 1, pensions and other payments (including a lump sum payment) made under a pension or retirement scheme which is:

    (a) A public scheme which is part of the social security system of a Contracting Party; or

    (b) An arrangement in which individuals may participate to secure retirement benefits and which is recognized for tax purposes in a Contracting Party, shall be taxable only in that Contracting Party.

Article 19 – Government Service

1. (a) Salaries, wages and other similar remuneration, other than a pension, paid by the Government of a Contracting Party to an individual in respect of services rendered to that Party shall be taxable only in that Party.

    (b) However, such salaries, wages and other similar remuneration shall be taxable only in the other Contracting Party if the services are rendered in that other Party and the individual is a resident of that Party who:

    (i) in the case of the Hong Kong Special Administrative Region, has the right of abode therein and in the case of Vietnam, is a national thereof; or

    (ii) did not become a resident of that Party solely for the purpose of rendering the services.

2. (a) Any pension (including a lump sum payment) paid by, or out of funds created or contributed by, the Government of a Contracting Party to an individual in respect of services rendered to that Party shall be taxable only in that Party.

    (b) However, such pension (including a lump sum payment) shall be taxable only in the other Contracting Party if the individual is a resident of that other Party and, in the case of the Hong Kong Special Administrative Region, has the right of abode therein and in the case of Vietnam, is a national thereof, and the pension (including a lump sum payment) is paid in respect of services referred to in sub-paragraph (b) of paragraph 1 of this Article.

3. The provisions of Articles 15, 16, 17 and 18 shall apply to salaries, wages and other similar remuneration, and to pensions (including a lump sum payment), in respect of services rendered in connection with a business carried on by the Government of a Contracting Party.

Article 20 – Students

1. Payments which a student or business trainee or apprentice who is or was immediately before visiting a Contracting Party a resident of the other Contracting Party and who is present in the first-mentioned Party solely for the purpose of his education or training receives for the purpose of his maintenance, education or training shall not be taxed in that Party, provided that such payments arise from sources outside that Party.
2. Notwithstanding the provisions of Article 15, remuneration for services rendered by a student mentioned in the preceding paragraph in a Contracting Party shall not be taxed in that Party, provided that such services are in connection with his studies.

Article 21 – Other Income

1. Items of income of a resident of a Contracting Party, wherever arising, not dealt with in the foregoing Articles of this Agreement shall be taxable only in that Party.
2. The provisions of paragraph 1 shall not apply to income, other than income from immovable property as defined in paragraph 2 of Article 6, if the recipient of such income, being a resident of a Contracting Party, carries on business in the other Contracting Party through a permanent establishment situated therein, or performs in that other Party independent personal services from a fixed base situated therein, and the right or property in respect of which the income is paid is effectively connected with such permanent establishment or fixed base. In such case the provisions of Article 7 or Article 14, as the case may be, shall apply.
3. Notwithstanding the provisions of paragraphs 1 and 2, items of income of a resident of a Contracting Party not dealt with in the foregoing Articles of this Agreement and arising in the other Contracting Party may also be taxed in that other Party.

Article 22 – Methods for Elimination of Double Taxation

1. (a) In the case of the Hong Kong Special Administrative Region, subject to the provisions of the laws of the Hong Kong Special Administrative Region relating to the allowance of a credit against Hong Kong Special Administrative Region tax of tax paid in a jurisdiction outside the Hong Kong Special Administrative Region (which shall not affect the general principle of this Article), Vietnamese tax paid under the laws of Vietnam and in accordance with this Agreement, whether directly or by deduction, in respect of income derived by a person who is a resident of the Hong Kong Special Administrative Region from sources in Vietnam, shall be allowed as a credit against Hong Kong Special Administrative Region tax payable in respect of that income, provided that the credit so allowed does not exceed the amount of Hong Kong Special Administrative Region tax computed in respect of that income in accordance with the tax laws of the Hong Kong Special Administrative Region.
    (b) For the purpose of paragraph 1 (a) of this Article, the income tax paid in Vietnam shall be deemed to include any amount of tax which would have been payable as Vietnamese tax for any year but for an exemption from or a reduction of tax granted for that year or any part thereof as a result of the application of the provisions of Vietnamese law designed to extend time limited tax incentives to promote foreign investment for development purpose. The provision of this sub-paragraph shall only apply for a period of 10 years from the day on which this Agreement comes into effect according to paragraph 2 of Article 28.
2. (a) In the case of Vietnam, where a resident of Vietnam derives income, profits or gains which under the laws of the Hong Kong Special Administrative Region and in accordance with this Agreement may be taxed in the Hong Kong Special Administrative Region, Vietnam shall allow as a credit against its tax on the income, profits

or gains an amount equal to the tax paid in the Hong Kong Special Administrative Region. Such deduction shall not, however, exceed that part of the tax on income, profits or gains, as computed before the deduction is given, which is attributable to the income, profits or gains which may be taxed in the Hong Kong Special Administrative Region.
   (b) Where, in accordance with any provision of this Agreement, income derived by a resident of Vietnam is exempt from tax in Vietnam, Vietnam may nevertheless, in calculating the amount of tax on the remaining income take into account the exempted income.
3. Where a company which is a resident of a Contracting Party pays dividends to a company which is a resident of the other Contracting Party and the latter company, directly or indirectly, controls not less than 10 per cent of the shares of the company which pays the dividends, the credit that the company which is a resident of that other Party is entitled to shall include the tax paid by the company which pays the dividends in respect of the profits from which such dividends are derived (but not exceeding the appropriate portion of profits incidental to the derivation of such dividends).

Article 23 – Non-Discrimination

1. Persons who, in the case of the Hong Kong Special Administrative Region, have the right of abode or are incorporated or otherwise constituted therein, and, in the case of Vietnam, are Vietnam nationals, shall not be subjected in the other Contracting Party to any taxation or any requirement connected therewith, which is other or more burdensome than the taxation and connected requirements to which persons who have the right of abode or are incorporated or otherwise constituted in that other Party (where that other Party is the Hong Kong Special Administrative Region) or nationals of that other Party (where that other Party is Vietnam) in the same circumstances, in particular with respect to residence, are or may be subjected.
2. The taxation on a permanent establishment, which an enterprise of a Contracting Party has in the other Contracting Party, shall not be less favorably levied in that other Party than the taxation levied on enterprises of that other Party carrying on the same activities.
3. Except where the provisions of paragraph 1 of Article 9, paragraph 7 of Article 11, or paragraph 6 of Article 12, apply, interest, royalties and other disbursements paid by an enterprise of a Contracting Party to a resident of the other Contracting Party shall, for the purpose of determining the taxable profits of such enterprise, be deductible under the same conditions as if they had been paid to a resident of the first-mentioned Party.
4. Enterprises of a Contracting Party, the capital of which is wholly or partly owned or controlled, directly or indirectly, by one or more residents of the other Contracting Party, shall not be subjected in the first-mentioned Party to any taxation or any requirement connected therewith which is other or more burdensome than the taxation and connected requirements to which other similar enterprises of the first-mentioned Party are or may be subjected.
5. Nothing contained in this Article shall be construed as obliging a Contracting Party to grant to residents of the other Contracting Party any personal allowances, reliefs and reductions for taxation purposes on account of civil status or family responsibilities which it grants to its own residents.
6. Notwithstanding the provisions of this Article, for so long as Vietnam continues to grant to investors licenses under the Law on Foreign Investment in Vietnam, which specify the taxation to which the investor shall be subjected, the imposition of such taxation shall not be regarded as breaching the terms of paragraphs 2 and 4 of this Article.

Article 24 – Mutual Agreement Procedure

1. Where a person considers that the actions of one or both of the Contracting Parties result or will result for him in taxation not in accordance with the provisions of this Agreement, he may, irrespective of the remedies provided by the domestic laws of those Parties, present his case to the competent authority of the Contracting Party of which he is a resident or, if his case comes under paragraph 1 of Article 23, to that of the Contracting Party in which he has the right of abode or is incorporated or otherwise constituted (in the case of the Hong Kong Special Administrative Region) or of which he is a national (in the case of Vietnam). The case must be presented within three years from the first notification of the action resulting in taxation not in accordance with the provisions of this Agreement.
2. The competent authority shall endeavor, if the objection appears to it to be justified and if it is not itself able to arrive at a satisfactory solution, to resolve the case by mutual agreement with the competent authority of the other Contracting Party, with a view to the avoidance of taxation, which is not in accordance with this Agreement. Any agreement reached shall be implemented notwithstanding any time limits in the domestic laws of the Contracting Parties.
3. The competent authorities of the Contracting Parties shall endeavor to resolve by mutual agreement any difficulties or doubts arising as to the interpretation or application of this Agreement. They may also consult together for the elimination of double taxation in cases not provided for in this Agreement.
4. The competent authorities of the Contracting Parties may communicate with each other directly, including through a joint commission consisting of themselves or their representatives, for the purpose of reaching an agreement in the sense of the preceding paragraphs.

Article 25 – Exchange of Information

1. The competent authorities of the Contracting Parties shall exchange such information as is necessary for carrying out the provisions of this Agreement or of the domestic laws of the Contracting Parties concerning taxes covered by this Agreement, insofar as the taxation thereunder is not contrary to this Agreement, as well as to prevent fiscal evasion in relation to such taxes. Any information received by a Contracting Party shall be treated as secret in the same manner as information obtained under the domestic laws of that Party and shall be disclosed only to persons or authorities (including courts and administrative bodies) concerned with the assessment or collection of, the enforcement or prosecution in respect of, or the determination of appeals in relation to, the taxes covered by this Agreement. Such persons or authorities shall use the information only for such purposes. They may disclose the information in public court proceedings, or in judicial decisions, including, in the case of the Hong Kong Special Administrative Region, the decisions of the Board of Review. Information shall not be disclosed to any third jurisdiction for any purpose without the consent of the Contracting Party originally furnishing the information.
2. In no case shall the provisions of paragraph 1 be construed so as to impose on a Contracting Party the obligation:
    (a) To carry out administrative measures at variance with the laws and the administrative practice of that or of the other Contracting Party;
    (b) To supply information which is not obtainable under the laws or in the normal course of the administration of that or of the other Contracting Party;
    (c) To supply information, which would disclose any trade, business, industrial, commercial or professional secret or trade process, or information, the disclosure of which would be contrary to public policy.

Article 26 – Members of Government Missions

Nothing in this Agreement shall affect the fiscal privileges of members of government missions, including consular posts, under the general rules of international law or under the provisions of special agreements.

Article 27 – Miscellaneous Rules

Nothing in this Agreement shall prejudice the right of each Contracting Party to apply its domestic laws and measures concerning tax avoidance, whether or not described as such.

Article 28 – Entry into Force

1. Each of the Contracting Parties shall notify the other in writing of the completion of the procedures required by its laws for the bringing into force of this Agreement. This Agreement shall enter into force on the date of the later of these notifications.
2. The provisions of this Agreement shall have effect:
   (a) In the Hong Kong Special Administrative Region:
   in respect of Hong Kong Special Administrative Region tax, for any year of assessment beginning on or after 1 April in the calendar year next following that in which this Agreement enters into force;
   (b) In Vietnam:
   (i) with regard to taxes withheld at source, in respect of amounts paid or credited on or after 1 January in the calendar year next following that in which this Agreement enters into force; and
   (ii) with regard to other taxes, in respect of taxable years beginning on or after 1 January in the calendar year next following that in which this Agreement enters into force.

Article 29 – Termination

This Agreement shall remain in force until terminated by a Contracting Party. Either Contracting Party may terminate this Agreement by giving the other Contracting Party written notice of termination on or before 30 June in any calendar year beginning after the expiration of a period of five years from the date of its entry into force.

In such event, this Agreement shall cease to have effect:

(a) In the Hong Kong Special Administrative Region:
in respect of Hong Kong Special Administrative Region tax, for any year of assessment beginning on or after 1 April in the calendar year next following that in which the notice is given;
(b) In Vietnam:
   (i) in respect of taxes withheld at source, in relation to taxable amount paid or credited on or after 1 January following the calendar year in which the notice of termination is given, and in any subsequent calendar years; and
   (ii) in respect of other taxes, in relation to income, profits or gains arising in the calendar year following the calendar year in which the notice of termination is given, and in any subsequent calendar years.

Protocol

1. For the purposes of Article 3 paragraph 2 and in the case of the Hong Kong Special Administrative Region, the term "penalty or interest" includes, without limitation, any sum added to Hong Kong Special Administrative Region tax by reason of default and recovered therewith, and additional tax assessed for infringement of or failure to comply with its tax laws.
2. For the purposes of Article 7 paragraph 3, the term "banking enterprise" means, in the case of the Hong Kong Special Administrative Region, a financial institution as defined under the Inland Revenue Ordinance, Chapter 112 of the Laws of Hong Kong.
3. For the purposes of Article 13 paragraph 4, the term "assets" shall be read as the value of the assets, and the term "mainly" shall be read as "not less than 50 per cent".

Chapter 9
European Area Treaties

9.1 Vietnam–European Union Bilateral Agreement's History and Evolution

Despite the fact that the European Union's (EU) relationship with Vietnam has evolved from a parental to a competitive one, Europe has continued to extend generous support to Vietnam in exchange for bilateral trade cooperation; the EU member states and the European Commission are the second largest bilateral ODA donor and largest non-refundable aid provider to Vietnam, with commitments worth over US$13 billion between 1996 and 2012. An integral part of the EU–Vietnam cooperation entails cross-cutting themes such as environmental protection and human rights.

Realizing that Vietnam has undergone radical economic transformation over the past two decades and holds potential for European investment in the future, in June 2012, the EU Trade Commissioner Karel De Gucht launched negotiations for a comprehensive Free Trade Agreement (FTA) with Vu Huy Hoang, Vietnam's Minister for Industry and Trade. Under the agreement, which is currently under negotiation, the focus is on a comprehensive agreement covering tariffs, non-tariff barriers, and commitment on procurement, regulatory issues, services, competition, and sustainable development. As of 2012, Vietnam was EU's fifth largest trading partner from ASEAN (after Singapore and Malaysia), whereas the EU was Vietnam's third largest trading partner. Thus, in regard to the FTA, negotiating better access for EU exporters to the ASEAN markets is a priority for EU.

Apart from the FTA, Vietnam and EU also signed a new Partnership and Cooperation Agreement in June 2012, which replaced the Framework Cooperation Agreement of 1995 (to mark this, both parties also signed a €150 million European Investment Bank-funded climate change contract). The new PCA, which enables both parties to harness their comparative advantages and supplement their economic structures, aims to broaden cooperation between the EU and Vietnam in areas such as trade, environment, energy, governance, science and technology, tourism, culture, migration, as well as initiatives against organized crime and

Table 9.1 EU's exports to Vietnam and imports from Vietnam

SITC codes	SITC sections	Value (millions of euro)	Share of total (%)	Share of total EU exports (%)
European Union, exports to… Vietnam				
	Total	5,209	100.0	0.3
SITC 7	Machinery and transport equipment	2,461	47.3	0.4
SITC 5	Chemicals and related prod, n.e.s.	832	16.0	0.3
SITC 6	Manufactured goods classified chiefly by material	638	12.3	0.3
SITC 0	Food and live animals	493	9.5	0.8
SITC 2	Crude materials, inedible, except fuels	299	5.7	0.7
SITC 8	Miscellaneous manufactured articles	280	5.4	0.2
SITC 1	Beverages and tobacco	92	1.8	0.4
SITC 9	Commodities and transactions n.c.e.	43	0.8	0.1
SITC 3	Mineral fuels, lubricants and related materials	7	0.1	0.0
SITC 4	Animal and vegetable oils, fats and waxes	3	0.1	0.1

SITC codes	SITC sections	Value (millions of euro)	Share of total (%)	Share of total EU imports (%)
European Union, imports from… Vietnam				
	Total	12,838	100.0	0.7
SITC 8	Miscellaneous manufactured articles	5,270	41.0	2.5
SITC 7	Machinery and transport equipment	3,738	29.1	0.9
SITC 0	Food and live animals	2,398	18.7	2.9
SITC 6	Manufactured goods classified chiefly by material	914	7.1	0.5
SITC 2	Crude materials, inedible, except fuels	296	2.3	0.4
SITC 5	Chemicals and related prod, n.e.s.	110	0.9	0.1
SITC 9	Commodities and transactions n.c.e.	19	0.2	0.0
SITC 1	Beverages and tobacco	4	0.0	0.1
SITC 4	Animal and vegetable oils, fats and waxes	3	0.0	0.0
SITC 3	Mineral fuels, lubricants and related materials	0	0.0	0.0

corruption. It also allows both states to increase cooperation in areas such as non-proliferation of weapons of mass destruction and counter-terrorism. While EU can continue to supply advanced technologies and high value-added services to Vietnam, which lacks enough of those resources, Vietnam can meet EU's demand for rubber, latex, coffee, footwear, and tea since it has a competitive advantage in producing those commodities (Table 9.1).

Diplomatic ties between Vietnam and the European Union were first established in 1990, and the Delegation of the European Union to Vietnam was officially opened on 1996. Vietnam is a founding member of the Asia-Europe Meeting (ASEM), which attempts to bring together the 27 nations of the EU with the ASEAN nations including China.

Vietnamese exports to EU benefit from the EU's Generalized System of Preferences (GSP) that grants tariff reductions to developing nations such as Vietnam. The GSP is an important factor in Vietnam's impressive export performance to the EU (during the signing of the PCA and FTA in 2012, Vietnamese officials requested the European Council's President to continue maintaining GSP for Vietnam); in 2011, Vietnam's trade surplus with EU was as large as its global trade deficit. However, certain remaining market access obstacles in Vietnam, which have hindered bilateral trade, remain a cause of concern for EU (Figs. 9.1 and 9.2).

9.2 Italy–Vietnam Treaty

The Government of the Socialist Republic of Vietnam and the Government of the Italian Republic, desiring to conclude an Agreement to avoid double taxation with respect to taxes on income and to prevent fiscal evasion, have agreed upon the following measures:

Article 1 – Personal Scope

This Agreement shall apply to persons who are residents of one or both of the Contracting States.

Article 2 – Taxes Covered

1. This Agreement shall apply to taxes on income imposed on behalf of each Contracting State or of its political or administrative subdivisions or local authorities, irrespective of the manner in which they are levied.
2. There shall be regarded as taxes on income all taxes imposed on total income or on elements of income, including taxes on gains from the alienation of movable or immovable property, taxes on the total amounts of wages or salaries paid by enterprises, as well as taxes on capital appreciation.
3. The existing taxes to which the Agreement shall apply are in particular:

    a. In the case of Vietnam:

    (i) the personal income tax;
    (ii) the profit tax; and
    (iii) the profit remittance tax;
    whether or not they are collected by withholding at source,
    (hereinafter referred to as "Vietnamese tax");

EU'S TRADE BALANCE WITH VIETNAM

European Union, Trade with Vietnam — millions of euro, %

Period	Imports	Variation (%, y-o-y)	Share of total EU Imports (%)	Exports	Variation (%, y-o-y)	Share of total EU Exports (%)	Balance	Trade
2007	7,868	13.9	0.5	3,588	50.9	0.3	-4,280	11,456
2008	8,586	9.1	0.5	3,378	-5.9	0.3	-5,207	11,964
2009	7,813	-9.0	0.6	3,762	11.4	0.3	-4,051	11,576
2010	9,586	22.7	0.6	4,675	24.3	0.3	-4,911	14,261
2011	12,930	34.9	0.8	5,186	10.9	0.3	-7,745	18,116
2011Q1	3,125	-	0.7	970	-	0.3	-2,154	4,095
2011Q2	2,688	-	0.6	1,295	-	0.3	-1,394	3,983
2011Q3	3,463	-	0.8	1,272	-	0.3	-2,191	4,735
2011Q4	3,654	-	0.8	1,648	-	0.4	-2,006	5,303
2012Q1	4,151	32.8	0.9	1,138	17.2	0.3	-3,013	5,289
2012Q2	4,069	51.4	0.9	1,185	-8.5	0.3	-2,884	5,254
2012Q3	5,203	50.2	1.2	1,323	4.0	0.3	-3,879	6,526
2012Q4	.	.	.	.	.	.	.	.
Average annual growth (2007-2011)		13.2			9.6			12.1

Fig. 9.1 EU's trade balance with Vietnam (in millions of €). *Source*: European Trade Commission

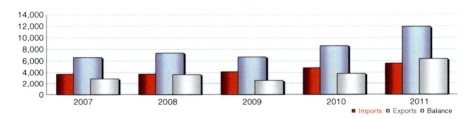

Fig. 9.2 EU's trade balance with Vietnam. *Source*: European Trade Commission

  b. In the case of Italy:

   (i) the personal income tax;
   (ii) the corporate income tax; and
   (iii) the local income tax;

   whether or not they are collected by withholding at source,

   (hereinafter referred to as "Italian tax").

4. This Agreement shall also apply to any identical or substantially similar taxes, which are imposed after the date of signature of this Agreement in addition to, or in place of, the existing taxes. The competent authorities of the Contracting States shall notify each other of any important changes, which have been made in their respective taxation laws.

Article 3 – General Definitions

1. In this Agreement, unless the context otherwise requires:
   a. The term "Vietnam" means the Socialist Republic of Vietnam; when used in a geographical sense, it means all its national territory, including its territorial sea and any area beyond and adjacent to its territorial sea, within which Vietnam, by Vietnamese legislation and in accordance with international law, has sovereign rights of exploration for and exploitation of natural resources of the sea-bed and its sub-soil and superjacent waters;
   b. The term "Italy" means the Italian Republic and includes any area beyond the territorial waters of Italy which, in accordance with the laws of Italy and international

law concerning the exploration and exploitation of natural resources, may be designated as an area within which the rights of Italy, with respect to the seabed and subsoil and natural resources, may be exercised;
c. The terms "a Contracting State" and "the other Contracting State" mean Vietnam or Italy as the context requires;
d. The term "person" includes an individual, a company and any other body of persons;
e. The term "company" means any body corporate or any entity which is treated as a body corporate for tax purposes;
f. The terms "enterprise of a Contracting State" and "enterprise of the other Contracting State" mean respectively an enterprise carried on by a resident of a Contracting State and an enterprise carried on by a resident of the other Contracting State;
g. The term "international traffic" means any transport by a ship or aircraft operated by an enterprise which has its place of effective management in a Contracting State, except when the ship or aircraft is operated solely between places in the other Contracting State;
h. The term "nationals" means:

   (i) all individuals possessing the nationality of a Contracting State;
   (ii) all legal persons, partnerships and associations deriving their status as such from the laws in force in a Contracting State;

i. The term "competent authority" means:

   (i) in the case of Vietnam, the Ministry of Finance;
   (ii) in the case of Italy, the Ministry of Finance.

2. As regards the application of this Agreement by a Contracting State any term not defined therein shall, unless the context otherwise requires, have the meaning which it has under the laws of that State concerning the taxes to which the Agreement applies.

Article 4 – Resident

1. For the purposes of this Agreement, the term "resident of a Contracting State" means any person who, under the law of that State, is liable to tax therein by reason of his domicile, residence, place of management, place of registration or any other criterion of a similar nature. But this term does not include any person who is liable to tax in that State in respect only of income from sources situated in that State.
2. Where by reason of the provisions of paragraph 1 an individual is a resident of both Contracting States, then his status shall be determined as follows:

   a. He shall be deemed to be a resident of the Contracting State in which he has a permanent home available to him. If he has a permanent home available to him in both Contracting States, he shall be deemed to be a resident of the Contracting State with which his personal and economic relations are closer (centre of vital interests);
   b. If the Contracting State in which he has his centre of vital interests cannot be determined, or if he has no permanent home available to him in either Contracting State, he shall be deemed to be a resident of the Contracting State in which he has an habitual abode;
   c. If he has an habitual abode in both Contracting States or in neither of them, he shall be deemed to be a resident of the Contracting State of which he is a national;
   d. If he is a national of both Contracting States or of neither of them, the competent authorities of the Contracting States shall settle the question by mutual agreement.

3. Where by reason of the provisions of paragraph 1, a person other than an individual is a resident of both Contracting States, then it shall be deemed to be a resident of the State in which its place of effective management is situated.

Article 5 – Permanent Establishment

1. For the purposes of this Agreement, the term "permanent establishment" means a fixed place of business in which the business of the enterprise is wholly or partly carried on.
2. The term "permanent establishment" includes especially:
    a. A place of management;
    b. A branch;
    c. An office;
    d. A factory;
    e. A workshop;
    f. A mine, an oil or gas well, a quarry or other place of extraction of natural resources;
    g. A building site, construction, assembly or installation project or supervisory activities in connection there with, but only where such site, project or activities continue for a period of more than six months;
    h. The furnishing of services, including consultancy services, by an enterprise through employees or other personnel engaged by the enterprise for such purpose, but only where activities of that nature continue (for the same or a connected project) within the country for a period or periods aggregating more than six months within any 12-month period.
3. Notwithstanding the preceding provisions of this Article, the term "permanent establishment" shall be deemed not to include:
    a. The use of facilities solely for the purpose of storage or display of goods or merchandise belonging to the enterprise;
    b. The maintenance of a stock of goods or merchandise belonging to the enterprise solely for the purpose of storage or display;
    c. The maintenance of a stock of goods or merchandise belonging to the enterprise solely for the purpose of processing by another enterprise;
    d. The maintenance of a fixed place of business solely for the purpose of purchasing goods or merchandise, or of collecting information for the enterprise;
    e. The maintenance of a fixed place of business solely for the purpose of carrying on, for the enterprise, any other activity of a preparatory or auxiliary character.
4. Notwithstanding the provisions of paragraphs 1 and 2, where a person - other than an agent of an independent status to whom paragraph 5 applies - is acting in a Contracting State on behalf of an enterprise of the other Contracting State, that enterprise shall be deemed to have a permanent establishment in the first-mentioned Contracting State in respect of any activity which that person undertakes for the enterprise, if such a person:
    a. Has and habitually exercises in that Contracting State an authority to conclude contracts in the name of the enterprise, unless the activities of such person are limited to those mentioned in paragraph 3 which, if exercised through a fixed place of business, would not make this fixed place of business a permanent establishment under the provisions of that paragraph; or
    b. Has no such authority, but habitually maintains in the first-mentioned State a stock of goods or merchandise from which he regularly delivers goods or merchandise on behalf of the enterprise.
5. An enterprise of a Contracting State shall not be deemed to have a permanent establishment in the other Contracting State merely because it carries on business in that other State through a broker, general commission agent or any other agent of an independent status, where such persons are acting in the ordinary course of their business.
6. The fact that a company which is a resident of a Contracting State controls or is controlled by a company which is a resident of the other Contracting State, or which carries on business in that other State (whether through a permanent establishment or

otherwise), shall not of itself constitute either company a permanent establishment of the other.

Article 6 – Income from Immovable Property

1. Income derived by a resident of a Contracting State from immovable property (including income from agriculture or forestry) situated in the other Contracting State may be taxed in that other State.
2. The term "immovable property" shall be defined in accordance with the law of the Contracting State in which the property in question is situated. The term shall in any case include property accessory to immovable property, livestock and equipment used in agriculture and forestry, rights to which the provisions of general law respecting landed property apply. Usufruct of immovable property and rights to variable or fixed payments as consideration for the working of, or the right to work, mineral deposits, sources and other natural resources shall also be considered as "immovable property". Ships, boats and aircraft shall not be regarded as immovable property.
3. The provisions of paragraph 1 shall apply to income derived from the direct use, letting, or use in any other form of immovable property.
4. The provisions of paragraphs 1 and 3 shall also apply to the income from immovable property of an enterprise and to income from immovable property used for the performance of independent personal services.

Article 7 – Business Profits

1. The profits of an enterprise of a Contracting State shall be taxable only in that State unless the enterprise carries on business in the other Contracting State through a permanent establishment situated therein. If the enterprise carries on business as aforesaid, the profits of the enterprise may be taxed in the other State but only so much of them as is attributable to that permanent establishment.
2. Subject to the provisions of paragraph 3, where an enterprise of a Contracting State carries on business in the other Contracting State through a permanent establishment situated therein, there shall in each Contracting State be attributed to that permanent establishment the profits which it might be expected to make if it were a distinct and separate enterprise engaged in the same or similar activities under the same or similar conditions and dealing wholly independently with the enterprise of which it is a permanent establishment.
3. In determination of the profits of a permanent establishment, there shall be allowed as deductions expenses which are incurred for the purposes of the permanent establishment including executive and general administrative expenses so incurred, whether in the State in which the permanent establishment is situated or elsewhere.
4. Insofar as it has been customary in a Contracting State to determine the profits to be attributed to a permanent establishment on the basis of an apportionment of the total profits of the enterprise to its various parts, nothing in paragraph 2 shall preclude that Contracting State from determining the profits to be taxed by such an apportionment as may be customary. The method of apportionment adopted shall, however, be such that the result shall be in accordance with the principles embodied in this Article.
5. No profits shall be attributed to a permanent establishment by reason of the mere purchase by that permanent establishment of goods or merchandise for the enterprise.
6. For the purposes of the preceding paragraphs, the profits to be attributed to the permanent establishment shall be determined by the same method year by year unless there is good and sufficient reason to the contrary.
7. Where profits include items of income, which are dealt with separately in other Articles of this Agreement, then the provisions of those Articles shall not be affected by the provisions of this Article.

Article 8 – Shipping and Air Transport

1. Profits from the operation of ship or aircraft in international traffic shall be taxable only in the Contracting State in which the place of effective management of the enterprise is situated.
2. If the place of effective management of a shipping enterprise is aboard a ship, then it shall be deemed to be situated in the Contracting State in which the home harbor of the ship is situated or if there is no such home harbor in the Contracting State of which the operator of the ship is a resident.
3. The provisions of paragraph 1 shall also apply to profits derived from the participation in a pool, a joint business or in an international operating agency.

Article 9 – Associated Enterprises

1. Where
    a. An enterprise of a Contracting State participates directly or indirectly in the management, control or capital of an enterprise of the other Contracting State, or
    b. The same persons participate directly or indirectly in the management, control or capital of an enterprise of a Contracting State and an enterprise of the other Contracting State, and in either case conditions are made or imposed between the two enterprises in their commercial or financial relations which differ from those which would be made between independent enterprises, then any profits which would, but for those conditions, have accrued to one of the enterprises, but, by reason of those conditions, have not so accrued, may be included in the profits of that enterprise and taxed accordingly.
2. Where a Contracting State includes in the profits of an enterprise of that State - and taxes accordingly - profits on which an enterprise of the other Contracting State has been charged to tax in that other State and the profits so included are profits which would have been accrued to the enterprise of the first mentioned State if the conditions made between the two enterprises had been those which would have been made between independent enterprises, then that other State shall make an appropriate adjustment to the amount of the tax charged therein on those profits. Any such adjustment shall be made only in accordance with the mutual agreement procedure provided for by Article 25 of this Agreement and with paragraph (d) of the Additional Protocol to the Agreement.

Article 10 – Dividends

1. Dividends paid by a company, which is a resident of a Contracting State to a resident of the other Contracting State, may be taxed in that other State.
2. However such dividends may also be taxed in the Contracting State of which the company paying the dividends is a resident and according to the laws of that State, but if the recipient is the beneficial owner of the dividends the tax so charged shall not exceed:
    a. 5 percent of the gross amount of the dividends if the recipient is a company (excluding partnerships) which owns directly at least 70 percent of the capital of the company paying the dividends;
    b. 10 percent of the gross amount of the dividends of the recipient is a company (excluding partnerships) which owns directly at least 25 percent up to 70 percent of the capital of the company paying the dividends;
    c. 15 percent of the gross amount of the dividends in all other cases.
    The competent authorities of the Contracting States shall by mutual agreement settle the mode of application of this limitation.

This paragraph shall not affect the taxation of the company in respect of the profits out of which the dividends are paid.

3. The term "dividends" as used in this Article means income from shares, "jouissance" shares or "jouissance" rights, mining shares, founders' shares or other rights not being debt-claims, participating in profits, as well as income from other corporate rights which is subjected to the same taxation treatment as income from shares by the taxation laws of the State of which the company making the distribution is a resident.
4. The provisions of paragraphs 1 and 2 shall not apply if the beneficial owner of the dividends, being a resident of a Contracting State, carries on business in the other Contracting State of which the company paying the dividends is a resident through a permanent establishment situated therein, or performs in that other State independent personal services from a fixed base situated therein, and the holding in respect of which the dividends are paid is effectively connected with such permanent establishment or fixed base. In such a case the dividends are taxable in that other Contracting State according to its own law.
5. Where a company which is a resident of a Contracting State derives profits or income from the other Contracting State, that other State may not impose any tax on the dividends paid by the company, except insofar as such dividends are paid to a resident of that other State or insofar as the holding in respect of which the dividends are paid is effectively connected with a permanent establishment or a fixed base situated in that other State, nor subject the company's undistributed profits to a tax on the company's undistributed profits, even if the dividends paid or the undistributed profits consist wholly or partly of profits or income arising in such other State.

Article 11 – Interest

1. Interest arising in a Contracting State and paid to a resident of the other Contracting State may be taxed in that other State.
2. However, such interest may also be taxed in the Contracting State in which it arises, and according to the laws of that State, but if the recipient is the beneficial owner of the interest the tax so charged shall not exceed 10 percent of the gross amount of the interest. The competent authorities of the Contracting States shall by mutual agreement settle the mode of application of this limitation.
3. Notwithstanding the provisions of paragraph 2, interest arising in a Contracting State shall be exempt from tax in that State if:

   a. The payer of the interest is the Government of that Contracting State or a local authority thereof; or
   b. The interest is paid to the Government of the other Contracting State or local authority thereof or any agency or instrumentality (including a financial institution) wholly owned by that other Contracting State or local authority thereof; or
   c. The interest is paid to any other agency or instrumentality (including a financial institution) in relation to loans made in application of an agreement concluded between the Governments of the Contracting States.

4. The term "interest" as used in this Article means income from Government securities, bonds or debentures, whether or not secured by mortgage, and whether or not carrying a right to participate in the profits, and debt-claims of every kind as well as all other income assimilated to income from money lent by the taxation law of the State in which the income arises.
5. The provisions of paragraphs from 1 to 3 shall not apply if the beneficial owner of the interest, being a resident of a Contracting State, carries on business in the other Contracting State in which the interest arises, through a permanent establishment situated therein, or performs in that other State independent personal services from a fixed base situated therein and the debt-claim in respect of which the interest is paid is

effectively connected with such permanent establishment or fixed base. In such a case, the interest is taxable in that other Contracting State according to its own law.
6. Interest shall be deemed to arise in a Contracting State when the payer is that State itself, a political or administrative subdivision, a local authority or a resident of that State. Where, however, the person paying the interest, whether he is a resident of a Contracting State or not, has in a Contracting State a permanent establishment or a fixed base in connection with which the indebtedness on which the interest is paid was incurred, and such interest is borne by such permanent establishment or fixed base, then such interest shall be deemed to arise in the Contracting State in which the permanent establishment or a fixed base is situated.
7. Where, by reason of a special relationship between the payer and the beneficial owner or between both of them and some other person, the amount of the interest, having regard to the debt-claim for which it is paid, exceeds the amount which would have been agreed upon by the payer and the beneficial owner in the absence of such relationship, the provisions of this Article shall apply only to the last-mentioned amount. In such case, the excess part of the payments shall remain taxable according to the laws of each Contracting State, due regard being had to the other provisions of this Agreement.

Article 12 – Royalties and Fees for Technical Services

1. Royalties and fees for technical services arising in a Contracting State and paid to a resident of the other Contracting State may be taxed in that other State.
2. However, such royalties and fees for technical services may also be taxed in the Contracting State in which they arise, and according to the laws of that State, but if the recipient is the beneficial owner of the royalties or of fees for technical services, the tax so charged shall not exceed:
    a. In the case of royalties 10 percent of the gross amount of such royalties;
    b. In the case of fees for technical services 7.5 percent of the gross amount of such fees.
3. The term "royalties" as used in this Article means payments of any kind received as a consideration for the use of, or the right to use, any copyright of literary, artistic or scientific work including cinematograph films, or films or tapes used for radio or television broadcasting, any patent, trade mark, design or model, plan, secret formula or process or for the use of, or the right to use, industrial, commercial or scientific equipment or for information concerning industrial, commercial or scientific experience.
4. The term "fees for technical services" as used in this Article means payments of any kind to any person, other than payments to an employee of the person making the payment, in consideration for any services of a managerial, technical or consultancy nature rendered in the Contracting State of which the payer is a resident.
5. The provisions of paragraphs 1 and 2 shall not apply if the beneficial owner of the royalties or fees for technical services, being a resident of a Contracting State, carries on business in the other Contracting State in which the royalties or fees for technical services arise, through a permanent establishment situated therein, or performs in that other State independent personal services from a fixed base situated therein, and the right or property in respect of which the royalties or fees for technical services are paid is effectively connected with such permanent establishment or fixed base. In such case, the royalties or fees for technical services are taxable in that other Contracting State according to its own law.
6. Royalties and fees for technical services shall be deemed to arise in a Contracting State when the payer is that State itself, a political or administrative subdivision, or a local authority or a resident of that State. Where, however, the person paying the royalties or fees for technical services, whether he is a resident of a Contracting State or not, has in a Contracting State a permanent establishment or fixed base in connection with which the

obligation to make the payments was incurred and the payments are borne by that permanent establishment or fixed base, then the royalties or fees for technical services shall be deemed to arise in the Contracting State in which the permanent establishment or fixed base is situated.
7. Where, by reason of a special relationship between the payer and the beneficial owner or between both of them and some other person, the amount of the royalties or fees for technical services, having regard to the use, right or information for which they are paid, exceeds the amount which would have been agreed upon by the payer and the beneficial owner in the absence of such relationship, the provisions of this Article shall apply only to the last-mentioned amount. In that case, the excess part of the payments shall remain taxable according to the laws of each Contracting State, due regard being had to the other provisions of this Agreement.

Article 13 – Gains from the Alienation of Property

1. Gains from the alienation of immovable property, as defined in paragraph 2 of Article 6, may be taxed in the Contracting State in which such property is situated.
2. Gains from the alienation of movable property forming part of the business property of a permanent establishment which an enterprise of a Contracting State has in the other Contracting State or of movable property pertaining to a fixed base available to a resident of a Contracting State in the other Contracting State for the purpose of performing independent personal services, including such gains from the alienation of such a permanent establishment (alone or with the whole enterprise) or of such fixed base, may be taxed in that other State.
3. Gains from the alienation of ships or aircraft operated in international traffic or movable property pertaining to the operation of such ships or aircraft shall be taxable only in the Contracting State in which the place of effective management of the enterprise is situated.
4. Gains from the alienation of shares representing a participation of at least 25 percent in the stock capital of a company, which is a resident of a Contracting State, may be tax in that State.
5. Gains from the alienation of any property other than that referred to in paragraphs 1, 2, 3 and 4 shall be taxable only in the Contracting State of which the alienator is a resident.

Article 14 – Independent Personal Services

1. Income derived by a resident of a Contracting State in respect of professional services or other activities of a similar character shall be taxable only in that State unless he has a fixed base regularly available to him in the other Contracting State for the purpose of performing his activities. If he has such a fixed base, the income may be taxed in the other Contracting State but only so much of it as is attributable to that fixed base.
2. The term "professional services" includes, especially, independent scientific, literary, artistic, educational or teaching activities as well as the independent activities of physicians, lawyers, engineers, architects, dentists and accountants.

Article 15 – Dependent Personal Services

1. Subject to the provisions of Articles 16, 18, 19, 20 and 21 salaries, wages and other similar remuneration derived by a resident of a Contracting State in respect of an employment shall be taxable only in that State unless the employment is exercised in the other Contracting State. If the employment is so exercised, such remuneration as is derived therefrom may be taxed in that other State.
2. Notwithstanding the provisions of paragraph 1, remuneration derived by a resident of a Contracting State in respect of an employment exercised in the other Contracting State shall be taxable only in the first-mentioned State if:

a. The recipient is present in the other State for a period or periods not exceeding in the aggregate 183 days in the fiscal year concerned, and
   b. The remuneration is paid by, or on behalf of, an employer who is not a resident of the other State, and
   c. The remuneration is not borne by a permanent establishment or a fixed base, which the employer has in the other State.
3. Notwithstanding the preceding provisions of this Article, remuneration derived in respect of an employment exercised aboard a ship or aircraft operated in international traffic, may be taxed in the Contracting State in which the place of effective management of the enterprise is situated

Article 16 – Directors' Fees

Directors' fees and other similar payments derived by a resident of a Contracting State in his capacity as a member of the board of directors of a company which is a resident of the other Contracting State may be taxed in that other State.

Article 17 – Artistes and Sportsmen

1. Notwithstanding the provisions of Articles 14 and 15, income derived by a resident of a Contracting State as an entertainer, such as a theater, motion picture, radio or television artiste, or a musician, or as a sportsman, from his personal activities as such exercised in the other Contracting State, may be taxed in that other State.
2. Where income in respect of personal activities exercised by an entertainer or a sportsman in his capacity as such accrues not to the entertainer or sportsman himself but to another person, that income may, notwithstanding the provisions of Articles 7, 14 and 15, be taxed in the Contracting State in which the activities of the entertainer or sportsman are exercised.

Article 18 – Pensions

Subject to the provisions of paragraph 2 of Article 19, pensions and other similar remuneration paid to a resident of a Contracting State in consideration of past employment shall be taxable only in that State.

Article 19 – Government Service

1. a. Remuneration, other than a pension, paid by a Contracting State or a political subdivision or a local authority thereof to an individual in respect of services rendered to that State or subdivision or authority shall be taxable only in that State
   b. However, such remuneration shall be taxable only in the other Contracting State if the services are rendered in that State and the individual is a resident of that State, who:
      (i) is a national of that State; or
      (ii) did not become a resident of that State solely for the purpose of rendering the services.

2. a. Any pension paid by, or out of funds created by, a Contracting State or a political or administrative subdivision or a local authority thereof to an individual in respect of services rendered to that State or subdivision or authority shall be taxable only in that State.
   b. However, such pension shall be taxable only in the other Contracting State if the individual is a resident of, and a national of, that other State.

3. The provisions of Articles 15, 16 and 18 shall apply to remuneration and pensions in respect of services rendered in connection with a business carried on by a Contracting State or a political subdivision or a local authority thereof.

Article 20 – Professors and Teachers

A professor or teacher who makes a temporary visit to a Contracting State for a period not exceeding two years for the purpose of teaching or conducting research at a university, college, school or other educational institution, and who is, or immediately before such visit was, a resident of the other Contracting State shall be exempt from tax in the first-mentioned Contracting State in respect of remuneration for such teaching or research.

Article 21 – Students

1. Payments which a student or business apprentice who is or was immediately before visiting a Contracting State a resident of the other Contracting State and who is present in the first-mentioned Contracting State solely for the purpose of his education or training receives for the purpose of his maintenance, education or training shall not be taxed in that State, provided that such payments arise from sources outside that State.
2. Income derived by a student, an apprentice or business trainee in respect of activities exercised in a Contracting State in which he is present solely for the purpose of his education or training, shall not be taxable in that State, during a reasonable period of time for such an education or training unless it exceeds the amount necessary for his maintenance, education or training.

Article 22 – Other Income

1. Items of income of a resident of a Contracting State, wherever arising, not dealt with in the foregoing Articles of this Agreement shall be taxable only in that State.
2. The provisions of paragraph 1 shall not apply to the income, other than income from immovable property as defined in paragraph 2 of Article 6, if the recipient of such income, being a resident of a Contracting State, carries on business in the other Contracting State through a permanent establishment situated therein, or performs in that other State independent personal services from a fixed base situated therein, and the right or property in respect of which the income is paid is effectively connected with such permanent establishment or fixed base. In such case the items of income are taxable in that other Contracting State according to its own law.
3. Where, by reason of a special relationship between the persons who have carried on activities from which income referred to in paragraph 1 is derived, the payment for such activities exceeds the amount which would have been agreed upon by independent persons, the provisions of paragraph 1 shall apply only to the last mentioned amount. In such case, the excess part of the payment shall remain taxable according to the laws of each Contracting State, due regard being had to the other provisions of this Agreement.

Article 23 – Elimination of Double Taxation

1. It is agreed that double taxation shall be avoided in accordance with the following paragraphs of this Article.
2. In the case of Vietnam:
Where a resident of Vietnam derives income, profits or gains which under the law of Italy and in accordance with this Agreement may be taxed in Italy, Vietnam shall allow as a credit against its tax on the income, profits or gains an amount equal to the tax paid

in Italy. The amount of credit, however, shall not exceed the amount of the Vietnamese tax on that income, profits or gains computed in accordance with the taxation laws and regulations of Vietnam.

3. In the case of Italy:

If a resident of Italy owns items of income which are taxable in Vietnam, Italy, in determining its income taxes specified in Article 2 of this Agreement, may include in the basic upon which such taxes are imposed the said items of income, unless specific provisions of this Agreement otherwise provide.

In such a case, Italy shall deduct from the taxes so calculated the income tax paid in Vietnam but in an amount not exceeding that proportion of the aforesaid Italian tax which such items of income bear to the entire income.

However, no deduction will be granted if the item of income is subjected in Italy to a final withholding tax by request of the recipient of the said income in accordance with the Italian law.

4. For the purposes of credit as referred to in paragraphs 2 and 3 of this Article where tax on business profit, dividends, interest or royalties arising in a Contracting State is exempted or reduced for a limited period of time in accordance with the laws and regulations of that State to promote foreign investments for economic development purposes, such tax which has been exempted or reduced shall be deemed to have been paid at an amount of:

   a. 32.5 per cent of the business profits referred to under Article 7;
   b. 10 per cent of the gross amount of the dividends referred to under Article 10;
   c. 10 per cent of the gross amount of the interest referred to under Article 11;
   d. 10 per cent of the gross amount of the royalties referred to under Article 12.

   The provisions of this paragraph shall apply for the first 10 years for which this Agreement is effective.

Article 24 – Non-discrimination

1. Nationals of a Contracting State shall not be subjected in the other Contracting State to any taxation or any requirement connected therewith which is other or more burdensome than the taxation and connected requirements to which nationals of that other State in the same circumstances are or may be subjected. This provision shall, notwithstanding the provision of Article 1, also apply to persons who are not residents of one or both of the Contracting State.

2. The taxation on a permanent establishment which an enterprise of a Contracting State has in the other Contracting State shall not be less favorably levied in that other State than the taxation levied on enterprises of that other State carrying on the same activities, provided that this paragraph shall not prevent that other Contracting State from imposing on the profits attributable to a permanent establishment in that State of a company which is a resident of the first-mentioned Contracting State further tax not exceeding 10 percent of those profit.

   This provision shall not be construed as obliging a Contracting State to grant to residents of the other Contracting State any personal allowances, reliefs and reductions for taxation purposes on account of civil status or family responsibilities which it grants to its own residents.

3. Except where the provisions of paragraph 1 of Article 9, paragraph 7 of Article 11, or paragraph 7 of Article 12, apply, interest, royalties and other disbursements paid by an enterprise of a Contracting State to a residents of the other Contracting State shall, for the purpose of determining the taxable profits of such enterprise, be deductible under the same conditions as if they had been paid to a resident of the first-mentioned State.

4. Enterprises of a Contracting State, the capital of which is wholly or partly owned or controlled, directly or indirectly by one or more residents of the other Contracting State, shall not be subjected in the first-mentioned Contracting State to any taxation or any requirement connected therewith which is other or more burdensome than the taxation and connected requirements to which other similar enterprises of the first-mentioned State are or may be subjected.
5. However, the provisions mentioned in the previous paragraph of this Article shall not affect the domestic provisions for the prevention of fiscal evasion and tax avoidance. In particular, the expression "domestic provisions" shall include in any case the provisions for the limitation of the deduction of expenses and other similar deductible burdens deriving from transaction between enterprises of a Contracting State and enterprises situated in the other Contracting State.
6. The provisions of this Article shall apply only to taxes, which are the subject of this Agreement.

Article 25 – Mutual Agreement Disclosure

1. Where a person considers that the actions of one or both of the Contracting States result or will result for him in taxation not in accordance with the provisions of this Agreement, he may, irrespective of the remedies provided by the domestic law of those States, present his case to the competent authority of the Contracting State of which the person is a resident or, if his case come under paragraph 1 of Article 24, to that of the Contracting State of which he is a national. The case must be presented within two years from the first notification of the action resulting in taxation not in accordance with the provisions of the Agreement.
2. The competent authority shall endeavor, if the objection appears to it to be justified and if it is not itself able to arrive at a satisfactory solution, to resolve the case by mutual agreement with the competent authority of the other Contracting State, with a view to the avoidance of taxation not in accordance with the Agreement.
3. The competent authorities of the Contracting States shall endeavor to resolve by mutual agreement any difficulties or doubts arising as to the interpretation or application of the Agreement.
4. The competent authorities of the Contracting States may communicate with each other directly for the purpose of reaching an agreement in the sense of the preceding paragraphs. When it seem advisable in order to reach agreement to have an oral exchange of opinions, such exchange may take place through a Commission consisting of representatives of the competent authorities of the Contracting States.

Article 26 – Exchange of Information

1. The competent authorities of the Contracting States shall exchange such information as is necessary for carrying out the provisions of this Agreement or of the domestic laws of the Contracting States concerning taxes covered by the Agreement insofar as the taxation thereunder is not contrary to the Agreement as well as to prevent fiscal evasion. The exchange of information is not restricted by Article 1. Any information received by a Contracting State shall be treated as secret in the same manner as information obtained under the domestic laws of that State and shall be disclosed only to persons or authorities (including courts and administrative bodies) involved in the assessment or collection of, the enforcement or prosecution in respect of, or the determination of appeals in relation to, the taxes covered by the Agreement. Such persons or authorities shall use the information only for such purposes. They may disclose the information in public court proceedings or in judicial decisions.
2. In no case shall the provisions of paragraph 1 be construed so as to impose on a Contracting State the obligation:

a. To carry out administrative measures at variance with the laws and administrative practice of that or of the other Contracting State;
b. To supply information which is not obtainable under the laws or in the normal course of the administration of that or of the other Contracting State;
c. To supply information, which would disclose any trade, business, industrial, commercial or professional secret or trade process, or information, the disclosure of which would be contrary to public policy (ordre public).

Article 27 – Diplomatic Agents and Consular Officers

Nothing in this Agreement shall affect the fiscal privileges of diplomatic agents or consular officers under the general rules of international law or under the provisions of special agreements.

Article 28 – Refunds

1. Taxes withheld at the source in a Contracting State will be refunded by request of the taxpayer or of the State of which he is a resident if the right to collect the said taxes is affected by the provisions of this Agreement.
2. Claims for the refund, that shall be produced within the time limit fixed by the law of the Contracting State which is obliged to carry out the refund, shall be accompanied by an official certificate of the Contracting State of which the taxpayer is a resident certifying the existence of the conditions required for being entitled to the application of the allowances provided for by this Agreement.
3. The competent authorities of the Contracting States shall by mutual agreement settle the mode of application of this Article, in accordance with the provisions of Article 25 of this Agreement.

Article 29 – Entry into Force

1. Each of the Contracting States shall notify to the other in writing through the diplomatic channel the completion of the procedures required by its legislation for the entry into force of this Agreement. This Agreement shall enter into force on the date of the later of these notifications.
2. This Agreement shall have effect:

    a. In respect of taxes withheld at source, to amounts derived on or after 1st January 1996;
    b. In respect of other taxes on income, to taxes chargeable for any taxable period beginning on or after 1st January 1996.

3. Claims for refund or credits arising in accordance with this Agreement in respect of any tax payable by residents of either of the Contracting States referring to the periods beginning on or after 1st January 1996 and until the entry into force of this Agreement shall be lodged within two years from the date of entry into force of this Agreement or from the date the tax was charged, whichever is later.

Article 30 – Termination

This Agreement shall remain in force until terminated by one of the Contracting States. Either Contracting State may terminate the Agreement, through diplomatic channels, by giving notice of termination at least six months before the end of any calendar year after the period of five years from the date on which the Agreement enters into force. In such event, the Agreement shall cease to have effect:

a. In respect of taxes withheld at source, to amounts derived on or after 1st January following the calendar year in which the notice of termination is given;

b. In respect of other taxes, in relation to income, to taxes chargeable for any taxable period beginning on or after 1st January in the calendar year next following that in which the notice is given.

DONE in duplicate at Hanoi the 26th day of November of the year one thousand nine hundred and ninety-six, in the Vietnamese, Italian and English languages, all texts being equally authoritative, except in the case of doubt, when the English text shall prevail.

Additional Protocol

At the signing of the Agreement concluded today between the Government of the Socialist Republic of Vietnam and the Government of the Italian Republic for the avoidance of double taxation with respect to taxes on income and the prevention of fiscal evasion the undersigned have agreed upon the following additional provisions which shall form an integral part of the said Agreement.

It is understood that:

a. With reference to Article 7, nothing in this Article shall affect the application of any law of a Contracting State relating to the determination of the tax liability of a person in cases where the information available to the competent authority of that State is inadequate to determine the profits to be attributed to a permanent establishment, provided that that law shall be applied, so far as the information available to the competent authority permits, consistently with the principles of this Article;
b. With reference to Article 7, paragraph 3, the expression "expenses which are incurred for the purpose of the permanent establishment" means the expenses directly connected with the activity of the permanent establishment;
c. With reference to paragraph 4 of Article 10, paragraph 5 of Article 11, paragraph 4 of Article 12, paragraph 2 of Article 22, the last sentence contained therein shall not be construed as being contrary to the principles embodied in Articles 7 and 14 of this Agreement;
d. With reference to paragraph 1 of Article 25, the expression "irrespective of the remedies provided by the domestic law" means that the mutual agreement procedure is not alternative with the national contentious proceedings which shall be, in any case, preventively initiated, when the claim is related with an assessment of the taxes not in accordance with this Agreement;
e. The provision of paragraph 3 of Article 28, shall not affect the competent authorities of the Contracting States from the carrying out, by mutual agreement, of other practices for the allowance of the reductions for taxation purposes provided for in this Agreement.
f. With reference to Articles 10, 11 and 12, if in any Agreement for the avoidance of double taxation concluded by Vietnam with a third State which is a member of the European Union after the date of signature of this Agreement, Vietnam after that date would agree to fix lower rates of taxes than those provided in paragraphs 2 of the said Articles 10, 11 and 12 or exempt royalties arising in Vietnam from Vietnamese tax on royalties, such lower rates of taxes or exemption shall automatically apply as if it had been specified in the relating paragraphs of the above Articles of this Agreement.

DONE in duplicate at Hanoi the 26th day of November of the year one thousand nine hundred and ninety-six, in the Vietnamese, Italian and English languages, all texts being equally authoritative, except in the case of doubt, when the English text shall prevail.

9.3 Sweden–Vietnam Treaty

The Government of the Socialist Republic of Vietnam and the Government of the Kingdom of Sweden, desiring to conclude an Agreement for the avoidance of double taxation and the prevention of fiscal evasion with respect to taxes on income, have agreed as follows:

Article 1 – Personal Scope

This Agreement shall apply to persons who are residents of one or both of the Contracting States.

Article 2 – Taxes Covered

1. This Agreement shall apply to taxes on income imposed on behalf of a Contracting State or of its political subdivisions or local authorities, irrespective of the manner in which they are levied.
2. There shall be regarded as taxes on income all taxes imposed on total income, or on elements of income, including taxes on gains from the alienation of movable or immovable property, taxes on the total amounts of wages or salaries paid by enterprises as well as taxes on capital appreciation.
3. The existing taxes to which the Agreement shall apply are:

    a. In Vietnam:

    (i) the personal income tax;
    (ii) the profit tax; and
    (iii) the profit remittance tax;

    (hereinafter referred to as "Vietnamese tax");

    b. In Sweden:

    (i) the national income tax, including the tax for employees at sea and the with holding tax on dividends;
    (ii) the income tax for non-residents;
    (iii) the income tax for non-resident artistes and athletes; and
    (iv) the municipal income tax;

    (hereinafter referred to as "Swedish tax").

4. The Agreement shall also apply to any identical or substantially similar taxes, which are imposed after the date of signature of this Agreement in addition to, or in place of the existing taxes. The competent authorities of the Contracting States shall notify each other of important changes, which have been made in their respective taxation laws.

Article 3 – General Definitions

1. For the purposes of this Agreement, unless the context otherwise requires:

    a. The term "Vietnam" means the Socialist Republic of Vietnam; when used in a geographical sense, it means all its national territory, including its territorial sea and any area beyond its territorial sea, within which Vietnam by Vietnamese legislation and in accordance with international law, has sovereign right of exploration for and exploitation of natural resources of the seabed and its subsoil and superjacent water mass;

b. The term "Sweden" means the Kingdom of Sweden and, when used in a geographical sense, includes the national territory, the territorial sea of Sweden as well as other maritime areas over which Sweden in accordance with international law exercises sovereign rights or jurisdiction;
c. The terms "a Contracting State" and "the other Contracting State" mean Vietnam or Sweden as the context requires;
d. The term "person" includes an individual, a company and any other body of persons;
e. The term "company" means any body corporate or any entity which is treated as a body corporate for tax purposes;
f. The terms "enterprise of a Contracting State" and "enterprise of the other Contracting State" mean respectively an enterprise carried on by a resident of a Contracting State and an enterprise carried on by a resident of the other Contracting State;
g. The term "national" means:

   (i) any individual possessing the nationality of a Contracting State;
   (ii) any legal person, partnership and association deriving its status as such from the laws in force in a Contracting State;

h. The term "international traffic" means any transport by a ship or aircraft operated by an enterprise of a Contracting State, except when the ship or aircraft is operated solely between places in the other Contracting State; and
i. The term "competent authority" means:

   (i) in the case of Vietnam, the Minister of Finance or his authorized representative; and
   (ii) in the case of Sweden, the Minister of Finance, his authorized representative or the authority which is designated as a competent authority for the purposes of this Agreement.

2. As regards the application of the Agreement by a Contracting State, any term not defined therein shall, unless the context otherwise requires, have the meaning which it has under the law of that State concerning the taxes to which the Agreement applies.

Article 4 – Resident

1. For the purposes of this Agreement, the term "resident of a Contracting State" means any person who, under the laws of that State, is liable to tax therein by reason of his domicile, residence, nationality, place of management or any other criterion of a similar nature.
2. Where by reason of the provisions of paragraph 1 an individual is a resident of both Contracting States, then his status shall be determined as follows:

   a. He shall be deemed to be a resident of the State in which he has a permanent home available to him. If he has a permanent home available to him in both States, he shall be deemed to be a resident of the State with which his personal and economic relations are closer (center of vital interests);
   b. If the Contracting State in which he has his centre of vital interests cannot be determined, or if he has no permanent home available to him in either State, he shall be deemed to be a resident of the State in which he has an habitual abode;
   c. If he has an habitual abode in both States or in neither of them, he shall be deemed to be a resident of the State of which he is a national;
   d. If he is a national of both States or of neither of them, the competent authorities of the Contracting States shall settle the question by mutual agreement.

3. Where by reason of the provisions of paragraph 1, a person other than an individual is a resident of both Contracting States, then it shall be deemed to be a resident of the State in which its place of effective management is situated.

Article 5 – Permanent Establishment

1. For the purposes of this Agreement, the term "permanent establishment" means a fixed place of business through which the business of an enterprise is wholly or partly carried on.
2. The term "permanent establishment" includes especially:
   a. A place of management;
   b. A branch;
   c. An office;
   d. A factory;
   e. A workshop; and
   f. A mine, an oil or gas well, a quarry or any other place of extraction of natural resources.
3. A building site, construction, assembly or installation project or supervisory activities in connection therewith constitutes a permanent establishment, only where such site, project or activities continue for a period of more than six months.
4. Notwithstanding paragraphs 1 and 2 the furnishing of services, including consultancy services, by an enterprise through employees or other personnel engaged by the enterprise for such purpose, always constitutes a permanent establishment where activities of that nature continue (for the same or a connected project) within the country for a period or periods aggregating more than six months within any twelve month period.
5. Notwithstanding the preceding provisions of this Article, the term "permanent establishment" shall be deemed not to include:
   a. The use of facilities solely for the purpose of storage or display of goods or merchandise belonging to the enterprise;
   b. The maintenance of a stock of goods or merchandise belonging to the enterprise solely for the purpose of storage or display;
   c. The maintenance of a stock of goods or merchandise belonging to the enterprise solely for the purpose of processing by another enterprise;
   d. The maintenance of a fixed place of business solely for the purpose of purchasing goods or merchandise or of collecting information, for the enterprise;
   e. The maintenance of a fixed place of business solely for the purpose of carrying on, for the enterprise, any other activity of a preparatory or auxiliary character;
   f. The maintenance of a fixed place of business solely for any combination of activities mentioned in sub-paragraphs a) to e), provided that the overall activity of the fixed place of business resulting from this combination is of a preparatory or auxiliary character.
6. Notwithstanding the provisions of paragraphs 1 and 2, where a person-other than an agent of an independent status to whom paragraph 8 applies - is acting in a Contracting State on behalf of an enterprise of the other Contracting State, that enterprise shall be deemed to have a permanent establishment in the first-mentioned Contracting State in respect of any activities which that person undertakes for the enterprise, if such a person:
   a. Has and habitually exercises in that State an authority to conclude contracts in the name of the enterprise, unless the activities of such person are limited to those mentioned in paragraph 5 which, if exercised through a fixed place of business, would not make this fixed place of business a permanent establishment under the provisions of that paragraph; or

b. Has no such authority, but habitually maintains in the first-mentioned State a stock of goods or merchandise from which he regularly delivers goods or merchandise on behalf of the enterprise.
7. Notwithstanding the preceding provisions of this Article, an insurance enterprise of a Contracting State shall, except in regard to re-insurance, be deemed to have a permanent establishment in the other Contracting State if it collects premiums in the territory of that other State or insures risks situated therein through a person other than an agent of an independent status to whom paragraph 8 applies.
8. An enterprise of a Contracting State shall not be deemed to have a permanent establishment in the other Contracting State merely because it carries on business in that State through a broker, general commission agent or any other agent of an independent status, provided that such persons are acting in the ordinary course of their business.
9. The fact that a company which is a resident of a Contracting State controls or is controlled by a company which is a resident of the other Contracting State, or which carries on business in that other State (whether through a permanent establishment or otherwise), shall not of itself constitute either company a permanent establishment of the other.

Article 6 – Income from Immovable Property

1. Income derived by a resident of a Contracting State from immovable property (including income from agriculture or forestry) situated in the other Contracting State may be taxed in that other State.
2. The term "immovable property" shall have the meaning, which it has under the law of the Contracting State in which the property in question is situated. The term shall in any case include property accessory to immovable property, livestock and equipment used in agriculture and forestry, rights to which the provisions of general law respecting landed property apply, buildings, usufruct of immovable property and rights to variable or fixed payments as consideration for the working of, or the right to work, mineral deposits, sources and other natural resources; ships and aircraft shall not be regarded as immovable property.
3. The provisions of paragraph 1 shall apply to income derived from the direct use, letting, or use in any other form of immovable property.
4. The provisions of paragraphs 1 and 3 shall also apply to the income from immovable property of an enterprise and to income from immovable property used for the performance of independent personal services.

Article 7 – Business Profits

1. The profits of an enterprise of a Contracting State shall be taxable only in that State unless the enterprise carries on business in the other Contracting State through a permanent establishment situated therein. If the enterprise carries on business as aforesaid, the profits of the enterprise may be taxed in the other State but only so much of them as is attributable to that permanent establishment.
2. Subject to the provisions of paragraph 3, where an enterprise of a Contracting State carries on business in the other Contracting State through a permanent establishment situated therein, there shall in each Contracting State be attributed to that permanent establishment the profits which it might be expected to make if it were a distinct and separate enterprise engaged in the same or similar activities under the same or similar conditions and dealing wholly independently with the enterprise of which it is a permanent establishment.
3. In determining the profits of a permanent establishment, there shall be allowed as deductions expenses which are incurred for the purposes of the business of the

permanent establishment, including executive and general administrative expenses so incurred, whether in the State in which the permanent establishment is situated or elsewhere. However, no such deduction shall be allowed in respect of amounts, if any, paid (otherwise than towards reimbursement of actual expenses) by the permanent establishment to the head office of the enterprise or any of its other offices, by way of royalties, fees or other similar payments in return for the use of patents or other rights, or by way of commission, for specific services performed or for management, or, except in the case of a banking enterprise, by way of interest on moneys lent to the permanent establishment. Likewise, no account shall be taken, in the determination of the profits of a permanent establishment, for amounts charged (otherwise than towards reimbursement of actual expenses), by the permanent establishment to the head office of the enterprise or any of its other offices, by way of royalties, fees or other similar payments in return for the use of patents or other rights, or by way of commission for specific services performed or for management, or, except in the case of banking enterprise by way of interest on moneys lent to the head office of the enterprise of any of its other offices.
4. Nothing in this Article shall affect the application of any law of a Contracting State relating to the determination of the tax liability of a person in cases where the information available to the competent authority of that State is inadequate to determine the profits to be attributed to a permanent establishment, provided that law shall be applied, so far as the information available to the competent authority permits, consistently with the principles of this Article.
5. Insofar as it has been customary in a Contracting State to determine the profits to be attributed to a permanent establishment on the basis of an apportionment of the total profits of the enterprise to its various parts, nothing in paragraph 2 shall preclude such Contracting State from determining the profits to be taxed by such an apportionment as may be customary; the method of apportionment adopted shall, however, be such that the result shall be in accordance with the principles contained in this Article.
6. For the purposes of the preceding paragraphs, the profits to be attributed to the permanent establishment shall be determined by the same method year by year unless there is good and sufficient reason to the contrary.
7. Where profits include items of income, which are dealt with separately in other Articles of this Agreement, then the provisions of those Articles shall not be affected by the provisions of this Article.

Article 8 – Shipping and Air Transport

1. Profits derived by an enterprise of a Contracting State from the operation of aircraft or ships in international traffic shall be taxable only in that Contracting State.
2. With respect to profits derived by the air transport consortium Scandinavian Airlines System (SAS) the provisions of paragraph 1 shall apply only to such part of the profits as corresponds to the participation held in that consortium by AB Aerotransport (ABA), the Swedish partner of Scandinavian Airlines System (SAS).
3. The provisions of paragraph 1 shall also apply to profits from the participation in a pool, a joint business or an international operating agency.

Article 9 – Associated Enterprises

1. Where
    a. An enterprise of a Contracting State participates directly or indirectly in the management, control or capital of an enterprise of the other Contracting State, or
    b. The same persons participate directly or indirectly in the management, control or capital of an enterprise of a Contracting State and an enterprise of the other

Contracting State, and in either case conditions are made or imposed between the two enterprises in their commercial or financial relations which differ from those which would be made between independent enterprises, then any profits which would, but for those conditions, have accrued to one of the enterprises, but, by reason of those conditions, have not so accrued, may be included in the profits of that enterprise and taxed accordingly.

2. Nothing in this Article shall affect the application of any law of a Contracting State relating to the determination of the tax liability of a person, including determinations in cases where the information available to the competent authority of that State is inadequate to determine the income to be attributed to an enterprise, provided that law shall be applied, so far as it is practicable to do so, consistently with the principles of this Article.

Article 10 – Dividends

1. Dividends paid by a company, which is a resident of a Contracting State to a resident of the other Contracting State, may be taxed in that other State.
2. However, such dividends may also be taxed in the Contracting State of which the company paying the dividends is a resident and according to the laws of that State, but if the recipient is the beneficial owner of the dividends the tax so charged shall not exceed:
   a. 5 per cent of the gross amount of the dividends if the beneficial owner is a company (other than a partnership) which holds directly at least 70 per cent or has invested at least twelve millions US dollar in the capital of the company paying the dividends;
   b. 10 per cent of the gross amount of the dividends if the beneficial owner is a company (other than a partnership) which holds less than 70 per cent but at least 25 per cent of the capital of the company paying the dividends;
   c. 15 per cent of the gross amount of the dividends in all other cases.

   This paragraph shall not affect the taxation of the company in respect of the profits out of which the dividends are paid.
3. The term "dividends" as used in this Article means income from shares, mining shares, founders' shares or other rights, not being debt-claims, participating in profits, as well as income from other corporate rights, which is subjected to the same taxation treatment as income from shares by the laws of the State of which the company making the distribution is a resident.
4. The provisions of paragraphs 1 and 2 shall not apply if the beneficial owner of the dividends, being a resident of a Contracting State, carries on business in the other Contracting State of which the company paying the dividends is a resident through a permanent establishment situated therein, or performs in that other State independent personal services from a fixed base situated therein, and the holding in respect of which the dividends are paid is effectively connected with such permanent establishment or fixed base. In such case, the provisions of Article 7 or Article 14, as the case may be, shall apply.
5. Where a company which is a resident of a Contracting State derives profits or income from the other Contracting State, that other State may not impose any tax on the dividends paid by the company, except insofar as such dividends are paid to a resident of that other Contracting State or insofar as the holding in respect of which the dividends are paid is effectively connected with a permanent establishment or a fixed base situated in that other State, nor subject the company's undistributed profits to a tax on the company's undistributed profits, even if the dividends paid or the undistributed profits consist wholly or partly of profits or income arising in such other State.

Article 11 – Interest

1. Interest arising in a Contracting State and paid to a resident of the other Contracting State may be taxed in that other State.
2. However, such interest may also be taxed in the Contracting State in which it arises and according to the laws of that State, but if the recipient is the beneficial owner of the interest the tax so charged shall not exceed 10 per cent of the gross amount of the interest.
3. Notwithstanding the provisions of paragraph 2, interest arising in a Contracting State and paid to the Government of the other Contracting State shall be exempt from tax in the first-mentioned Contracting State.

   For the purposes of this paragraph, the term "Government":

   a. In the case of Vietnam, means the Government of the Socialist Republic of Vietnam and shall include:
      (i) the State Bank of Vietnam;
      (ii) the local authorities; and
      (iii) such institutions, the capital of which is wholly owned by the Government of the Socialist Republic of Vietnam or any local authorities as may be agreed from time to time between the competent authorities of the two Contracting States;

   b. In the case of Sweden, means the Government of the Kingdom of Sweden and shall include:
      (i) the Central Bank;
      (ii) a political subdivision or local authority;
      (iii) SWEDECORP (Styrelsen for internationellt naringslivsbistand) and Swedfund International AB or any other Swedish institution that may be founded by the Swedish Government to fulfill the same purposes as the said institutions as may be agreed from time to time between the competent authorities of the two Contracting States.

4. The term "interest" as used in this Article means income from debt-claims of every kind, whether or not secured by mortgage and whether or not carrying a right to participate in the debtor's profits, and in particular, income from government securities and income from bonds or debentures, including premiums and prizes attaching to such securities, bonds or debentures. Penalty charges for late payment shall not be regarded as interest for the purpose of this Article.
5. The provisions of paragraphs 1, 2 and 3 shall not apply if the beneficial owner of the interest, being a resident of a Contracting State, carries on business in the other Contracting State in which the interest arises, through a permanent establishment situated therein, or performs in that other State independent personal services from a fixed base situated therein, and the debt-claim in respect of which the interest is paid is effectively connected with such permanent establishment or fixed base. In such case the provisions of Article 7 or Article 14, as the case may be, shall apply.
6. Interest shall be deemed to arise in a Contracting State when the payer is that State itself, a political subdivision, a local authority or a resident of that State. Where, however, the person paying the interest, whether he is a resident of a Contracting State or not, has in a Contracting State a permanent establishment or a fixed base in connection with which the indebtedness on which the interest is paid was incurred, and such interest is borne by such permanent establishment or fixed base, then such interest shall be deemed to arise in the State in which the permanent establishment or fixed base is situated.
7. Where, by reason of a special relationship between the payer and the beneficial owner or between both of them and some other person, the amount of the interest, having regard

to the debt-claim for which it is paid, exceeds the amount which would have been agreed upon by the payer and the beneficial owner in the absence of such relationship, the provisions of this Article shall apply only to the last-mentioned amount. In such case, the excess part of the payments shall remain taxable according to the laws of each Contracting State, due regard being had to the other provisions of this Agreement.

Article 12 – Royalties

1. Royalties arising in a Contracting State and paid to a resident of the other Contracting State may be taxed in that other Contracting State.
2. However, such royalties may also be taxed in the Contracting State in which they arise and according to the laws of that State, but if the recipient is the beneficial owner of the royalties the tax so charged shall not exceed 15 per cent of the gross amount of the royalties. Notwithstanding the preceding sentence, if the royalties are paid with respect to any patent, design or model, secret formula or process, or for information concerning industrial or scientific experience or for the use of or the right to use industrial, commercial or scientific equipment involving a transfer of know how, the tax so charged shall not exceed 5 per cent of the gross amount of the royalties.
3. The term "royalties" as used in this Article means payments of any kind received as a consideration for the use of, or the right to use, any copyright of literary, artistic or scientific work including cinematograph films, or films or tapes used for radio or television broadcasting, any patent, trade mark, design or model, plan, secret formula or process, or for the use of, or the right to use, industrial, commercial or scientific equipment, or for information concerning industrial, commercial or scientific experience.
4. The provisions of paragraphs 1 and 2 shall not apply if the beneficial owner of the royalties, being a resident of a Contracting State, carries on business in the other Contracting State in which the royalties arise, through a permanent establishment situated therein, or performs in that other State independent personal services from a fixed base situated therein, and the right or property in respect of which the royalties are paid is effectively connected with such permanent establishment or fixed base. In such case, the provisions of Article 7 or Article 14, as the case may be, shall apply.
5. Royalties shall be deemed to arise in a Contracting State when the payer is that State itself, a political subdivision, or a local authority or a resident of that State. Where, however, the person paying the royalties, whether he is a resident of a Contracting State or not, has in a Contracting State a permanent establishment or fixed base in connection with which the liability to pay the royalties was incurred, and such royalties are borne by such permanent establishment or fixed base, then such royalties shall be deemed to arise in the State in which the permanent establishment or fixed base is situated.
6. Where, by reason of a special relationship between the payer and the beneficial owner or between both of them and some other person, the amount of the royalties, having regard to the use, right or information for which they are paid, exceeds the amount which would have been agreed upon by the payer and the beneficial owner in the absence of such relationship, the provisions of this Article shall apply only to the last-mentioned amount. In such case, the excess part of the payments shall remain taxable according to the laws of each Contracting State, due regard being had to the other provisions of this Agreement.

Article 13 – Gains from the Alienation of Property

1. Gains from the alienation of immovable property, as defined in paragraph 2 of Article 6, may be taxed in the Contracting State in which such property is situated. Gains derived by a resident of a Contracting State from the alienation of shares or comparable

interests in a company, the assets of which consist wholly or principally of immovable property situated in the other Contracting State, may be taxed in that other State.
2. Gains from the alienation of movable property forming part of the business property of a permanent establishment which an enterprise of a Contracting State has in the other Contracting State or of movable property pertaining to a fixed base available to a resident of a Contracting State in the other Contracting State for the purpose of performing independent personal services, including such gains from the alienation of such a permanent establishment (alone or with the whole enterprise) or of such fixed base, may be taxed in that other State.
3. Gains from the alienation of any property other than that referred to in paragraphs 1 and 2, shall be taxable only in the Contracting State of which the alienator is a resident. However, gains derived by a resident of a Contracting State from the alienation of shares or comparable interests in a company which is a resident of the other Contracting State and which primarily is or has been making passive investments in the form of acquiring shares, bonds or debentures or other securities or is or has been doing other purely financial transactions, may be taxed in that other State.
4. Notwithstanding the provisions of paragraph 3, gains from the alienation of shares or other corporate rights derived by an individual who has been a resident of a Contracting State and who has become a resident of the other Contracting State, may be taxed in the first-mentioned State if the alienation of the shares or other corporate rights occur at any time during the five years next following the date on which the individual has ceased to be a resident of the first-mentioned State.

Article 14 – Independent Personal Services

1. Income derived by a resident of a Contracting State in respect of professional services or other activities of an independent character shall be taxable only in that State. However, when the activities are performed or exercised in the other Contracting State, the income may also be taxed in that other State:
    a. If he has a fixed base regularly available to him in the other Contracting State for the purpose of performing his activities; in that case, only so much of the income as is attributable to that fixed base may be taxed in that other Contracting State; or
    b. If his stay in the other Contracting State is for a period or periods amounting to or exceeding in the aggregate 183 days in any twelve month period; in that case, only so much of the income as is derived from his activities performed in that other State may be taxed in that State; or
    c. If the remuneration for his activities in the other Contracting State is paid by a resident of that Contracting State or is borne by a permanent establishment or a fixed base situated in that Contracting State and exceeds in that fiscal year 40.000 US dollar.
2. The term "professional services" includes especially independent scientific, literary, artistic, educational or teaching activities as well as the independent activities of physicians, lawyers, engineers, architects, dentists and accountants.

Article 15 – Dependent Personal Services

1. Subject to the provisions of Articles 16, 18 and 19, salaries, wages and other similar remuneration derived by a resident of a Contracting State in respect of an employment shall be taxable only in that State unless the employment is exercised in the other Contracting State. If the employment is so exercised, such remuneration as is derived therefrom may be taxed in that other State.

2. Notwithstanding the provisions of paragraph 1, remuneration derived by a resident of a Contracting State in respect of an employment exercised in the other Contracting State shall be taxable only in the first-mentioned State if:
   a. The recipient is present in the other State for a period or periods not exceeding in the aggregate 183 days in any twelve month period, and
   b. The remuneration is paid by, or on behalf of, an employer who is not a resident of the other State, and
   c. The remuneration is not borne by a permanent establishment or a fixed base, which the employer has in the other State.
3. Notwithstanding the preceding provisions of this Article, remuneration derived in respect of an employment exercised aboard a ship or aircraft operated in international traffic by an enterprise of a Contracting State may be taxed in that State.

Article 16 – Directors' Fees

Directors' fees and other similar payments derived by a resident of a Contracting State in his capacity as a member of the board of directors of a company which is a resident of the other Contracting State may be taxed in that other State.

Article 17 – Artistes and Athletes

1. Notwithstanding the provisions of Articles 14 and 15, income derived by a resident of a Contracting State as an entertainer, such as a theatre, motion picture, radio or television artiste or a musician, or as an athlete, from his personal activities as such exercised in the other Contracting State, may be taxed in that other State.
2. Where income in respect of personal activities exercised by an entertainer or an athlete in his capacity as such accrues not to the entertainer or athlete himself but to another person, that income may, notwithstanding the provisions of Articles 7, 14 and 15, be taxed in the Contracting State in which the activities of the entertainer or athlete are exercised.
3. The provisions of paragraphs 1 and 2 shall not apply to remuneration or profits derived from activities exercised in a Contracting State if the visit to that State is directly supported wholly from the public funds of the other Contracting State according to the cultural exchange program between the two Contracting States.

Article 18 – Pensions, Annuities and Similar Payments

1. Subject to the provisions of paragraph 2 of Article 19, pensions and other similar remuneration, disbursements under the Social Security legislation and annuities arising in a Contracting State and paid to a resident of the other Contracting State may be taxed in the first-mentioned Contracting State.
2. The term "annuity" means a stated sum payable periodically at stated times during life or during a specified or ascertainable period of time under an obligation to make the payments in return for adequate and full consideration in money or money's worth.

Article 19 – Government Service

1. a. Remuneration, other than a pension, paid by a Contracting State or a political subdivision or a local authority thereof to an individual in respect of services rendered to that State or subdivision or authority shall be taxable only in that State.

b. However, such remuneration shall be taxable only in the other Contracting State if the services are rendered in that State and the individual is a resident of that State who:

   (i) is a national of that State; or
   (ii) did not become a resident of that State solely for the purpose of rendering the services.

2. a. Any pension (except for pension paid under the Social Security legislation) paid by, or out of funds created by, a Contracting State or a political subdivision or a local authority thereof to an individual in respect of services rendered to that State or subdivision or authority shall be taxable only in that State.
   b. However, such pension shall be taxable only in the other Contracting State if the individual is a resident of, and a national of, that other State.

3. The provisions of Articles 15, 16 and 18 shall apply to remuneration and pensions in respect of services rendered in connection with a business carried on by a Contracting State or a political subdivision or a local authority thereof.

Article 20 – Students and Apprentices

Payments which a student or business apprentice who is or was immediately before visiting a Contracting State a resident of the other Contracting State and who is present in the first mentioned State solely for the purpose of his education or training receives for the purpose of his maintenance, education or training shall not be taxed in that State, provided that such payments arise from sources outside that State.

Article 21 – Other Income

1. Items of income of a resident of a Contracting State, wherever arising, not dealt with in the foregoing Articles of this Agreement shall be taxable only in that State.
2. However, any such income derived by a resident of a Contracting State from sources in the other Contracting State may be taxed in that other State.
3. The provisions of paragraph 1 shall not apply to the income, other than income from immovable property as defined in paragraph 2 of Article 6, if the recipient of such income, being a resident of a Contracting State, carries on business in the other Contracting State through a permanent establishment situated therein, or performs in that other State independent personal services from a fixed base situated therein, and the right or property in respect of which the income is paid is effectively connected with such permanent establishment or fixed base. In such case the provisions of Article 7 or Article 14, as the case may be, shall apply.

Article 22 – Elimination of Double Taxation

1. In the case of Vietnam, double taxation shall be avoided as follows:

   Where a resident of Vietnam derives income, profits or gains which under the law of Sweden and in accordance with this Agreement may be taxed in Sweden, Vietnam shall allow as a credit against its tax on the income, profits or gains an amount equal to the tax paid in Sweden. The amount of credit, however, shall not exceed the amount of the Vietnamese tax on that income, profits or gains computed in accordance with the taxation laws and regulations of Vietnam.

2. In the case of Sweden, double taxation shall be avoided as follows:
   a. Where a resident of Sweden derives income which under the laws of Vietnam and in accordance with the provisions of this Agreement may be taxed in Vietnam, Sweden shall allow - subject to the provisions of the law of Sweden concerning credit for foreign tax (as it may be amended from time to time without changing the general principle hereof) - as a deduction from the tax on such income, an amount equal to the Vietnamese tax paid in respect of such income.
   b. Where a resident of Sweden derives income, which, in accordance with the provisions of this Agreement, shall be taxable only in Vietnam, Sweden may, when determining the graduated rate of Swedish tax, take into account the income, which shall be taxable only in Vietnam.
   c. Notwithstanding the provisions of sub-paragraph a. of this paragraph, dividends paid by a company, which is a resident of Vietnam to a company, which is a resident of Sweden, shall be exempt from Swedish tax according to the provisions of Swedish law governing the exemption of tax on dividends paid to Swedish companies by subsidiaries abroad.
   d. For the purposes of sub-paragraph a. of this paragraph the term "Vietnamese tax paid" shall be deemed to include the Vietnamese tax which would have been paid but for any time-limited exemption or reduction of tax granted under incentive provisions contained in Vietnamese laws designed to promote economic development to the extent that such exemption or reduction is granted for profits from industrial and manufacturing activities as well as agriculture (including cattle raising), forestry, fishing, tourism (including restaurants and hotels), mining and quarrying, provided that the activities have been carried out in Vietnam. For the purposes of subparagraph c. of this paragraph a tax of 15 per cent calculated on a Swedish tax base should be considered to have been paid for such activities under those conditions mentioned in the previous sentence.
   e. For the purpose of sub-paragraph a. of this paragraph the Vietnamese tax paid in respect of royalties received (which can not according to paragraph 2 of Article 12 exceed 5 per cent of the gross amount of such royalty) as a consideration for the use of any patent, design or model, plan, secret formula or process, or for information concerning industrial, commercial or scientific experience shall where it has been used in such an activity as specified in sub-paragraph (d) under the conditions specified in that sub-paragraph, be deemed to always have been paid at a rate of 10 per cent, of the gross amount of the royalties.
   f. The provisions of paragraphs d. and e. shall apply only for the first ten years during which this Agreement is effective. This period may be extended by a mutual agreement between the competent authorities.

Article 23 – Limitation of Benefits

Where any person derives income other than dividends mentioned in Article 10 from a source situated outside Vietnam and such income is exempt from tax under the laws of Vietnam and also exempt from tax in Sweden under this Agreement, Sweden may tax such income under its own laws notwithstanding the provisions of this Agreement.

Article 24 – Non-discrimination

1. Nationals of a Contracting State shall not be subjected in the other Contracting State to any taxation or any requirement connected therewith, which is other or more burdensome than the taxation and connected requirements to which nationals of that other State in the same circumstances are or may be subjected.

2. The taxation on a permanent establishment, which an enterprise of a Contracting State has in the other Contracting State, shall not be less favorably levied in that other State than the taxation levied on enterprises of that other State carrying on the same activities. This provision shall not be construed as obliging a Contracting State to grant to residents of the other Contracting State any personal allowances, relief and reductions for taxation purposes on account of civil status or family responsibilities which it grants to its own residents.
3. Except where the provisions of paragraph 1 of Article 9, paragraph 7 of Article 11 or paragraph 6 of Article 12 of this Agreement apply, interest, royalties and other disbursements paid by an enterprise of a Contracting State to a resident of the other Contracting State shall, for the purpose of determining the taxable profits of such enterprise, be deductible under the same conditions as if they had been paid to a resident of the first-mentioned State.
4. Enterprises of a Contracting State, the capital of which is wholly or partly owned or controlled, directly or indirectly, by one or more residents of the other Contracting State, shall not be subjected in the first-mentioned State to any taxation or any requirement connected therewith which is other or more burdensome than the taxation and connected requirements to which other similar enterprises of the first-mentioned State are or may be subjected.
5. The provisions of paragraphs 2 and 4 of this Article shall not apply to the Vietnamese profit remittance tax, which in any case shall not exceed 10 per cent of the gross amount of profits remitted, and the Vietnamese taxation in respect of oil exploration or production activities or in respect of agricultural production activities.
6. Nothing contained in this Article shall be construed as obliging either Contracting State to grant to individuals not resident in that State any of the personal allowances, relieves and reductions for tax purposes, which are granted to individuals so resident.
7. The provisions of this Article shall apply only to the taxes, which are the subject of this Agreement.

Article 25 – Mutual Agreement Procedure

1. When a person who is a resident of a Contracting State considers that the actions of the competent authority of one or both of the Contracting States result or will result for him in taxation not in accordance with the provisions of this Agreement, he may, irrespective of the remedies provided by the domestic law of those State, present his case to the competent authority of the Contracting State of which the person is a resident. The case must be presented within three years from the first notification of the action resulting in taxation not in accordance with the provisions of the Agreement.
2. The competent authority shall endeavor, if the objection appears to it to be justified and if it is not itself able to arrive at a satisfactory solution, to resolve the case by mutual agreement with the competent authority of the other Contracting State, with a view to the avoidance of taxation, which is not in accordance with this Agreement. Any agreement reached shall be implemented notwithstanding any time limits in the domestic law of the Contracting States.
3. The competent authorities of the Contracting State shall jointly endeavor to resolve any difficulties or doubts arising as to the application of the Agreement. They may also consult together for the elimination of double taxation in cases not provided for in the Agreement.
4. The competent authorities of the Contracting States may communicate with each other directly for the purpose of reaching an agreement in the sense of the preceding paragraphs. The competent authorities, through consultations, shall develop appropriate bilateral procedures, conditions, methods and techniques for the implementation of the mutual agreement procedure provided for in this Article.

Article 26 – Exchange of Information

1. The competent authorities of the Contracting States shall exchange such information as is necessary for carrying out the provisions of this Agreement or of the domestic laws of the Contracting States concerning taxes covered by the Agreement, insofar as the taxation thereunder is not contrary to the Agreement, in particular for the prevention of fraud or evasion of such taxes. The exchange of information is not restricted by Article 1. Any information received by a Contracting State shall be treated as secret in the same manner as information obtained under the domestic laws of that State. However, if the information is originally regarded as secret in the transmitting State it shall be disclosed only to persons or authorities (including courts and administrative bodies) involved in the assessment or collection of, the enforcement or prosecution in respect of, or the determination of appeals in relation to, the taxes which are the subject of the Agreement. Such persons or authorities shall use the information only for such purposes. They may disclose the information in public court proceedings or in judicial decision. The competent authorities shall, through consultation, develop appropriate conditions, methods and techniques concerning the matters in respect of which such exchanges of information shall be made, including, where appropriate, exchanges of information regarding tax avoidance.
2. In no case shall the provisions of paragraph 1 be construed so as to impose on a Contracting State the obligation:
   a. To carry out administrative measures at variance with the laws and the administrative practice of that or of the other Contracting State;
   b. To supply information which is not obtainable under the laws or in the normal course of the administration of that or of the other Contracting State;
   c. To supply information, which would disclose any trade, business, industrial commercial or professional secret or trade process, or information, the disclosure of which would be contrary to public policy.

Article 27 – Diplomatic Agents and Consular Officers

Nothing in this Agreement shall affect the fiscal privileges of diplomatic agents or consular officers under the general rules of international law or under the provisions of special agreements.

Article 28 – Entry into Force

1. Each Contracting State shall notify the other in writing that the procedures required by its legislation for the entry into force of this Agreement have been complied with. The Agreement enters into force with the reception of the last notification.
2. The Agreement shall have effect:

   a. In Vietnam:
      (i) in respect of taxes withheld at source, in relation to taxable amounts paid on or after 1 January following the calendar year in which the Agreement enters into force;
      (ii) in respect of other Vietnamese taxes, in relation to income, profits or gains arising in the calendar year following the calendar year in which the Agreement enters into force, and in subsequent calendar year.

   b. In Sweden:
      on income derived on or after the first day of January of the year next following that of the entry into force of the Agreement.

Article 29 – Termination

This Agreement shall remain in force until terminated by a Contracting State. Either Contracting State may terminate the Agreement, through the diplomatic channel, by giving to the other Contracting State, written notice of termination at least six months before the end of any calendar year after the expiration of a period of five years from the date of its entry into force. In such event the Agreement shall cease to have effect:

a. In Vietnam:
   (i) in respect of taxes withheld at source, in relation to taxable amounts paid on or after 1 January following the calendar year in which the notice of termination is given;
   (ii) in respect of other Vietnamese taxes, in relation to income, profits or gains arising in the calendar year following the calendar year in which the notice of termination is given, and in subsequent calendar years.

b. In Sweden:
on income derived on or after the first day of January of the year next following that in which the notice of termination is given.

DONE in duplicate at Stockholm this 24th day of March of the year one thousand nine hundred and ninety-four in the Vietnamese, English and Swedish languages, all texts being equally authoritative. In case of divergence the English text shall prevail.

Protocol

At the moment of signing the Agreement between the Government of the Socialist Republic of Vietnam and the Government of the Kingdom of Sweden for the avoidance of double taxation and the prevention of fiscal evasion with respect to taxes on income, the undersigned have agreed that the following provision shall form an integral part of the Agreement.

I. **Ad Article 2**
It is agreed that social security fees, including the Swedish General Salary-fee, are not covered by this Agreement even though they may be calculated on the total amounts of wages or salaries paid by enterprises.

II. **Ad Article 24**
For so long as Vietnam continues to grant to investors licenses under the Law on Foreign Investment in Vietnam, which specify the taxation to which the investor shall be subject, the imposition of such taxation shall not be regarded as breaching the terms of paragraphs 2 and 4 of Article 24.

DONE in duplicate at Stockholm this 24th day of March of the year one thousand nine hundred and ninety-four in the Vietnamese, English and Swedish languages, all texts being equally authoritative. In case of divergence the English text shall prevail.

9.4 Denmark–Vietnam Treaty

The Government of the Socialist Republic of Vietnam and the Government of the Kingdom of Denmark, desiring to conclude an Agreement for the avoidance of double taxation and the prevention of fiscal evasion with respect to taxes on income, have agreed as follows:

Article 1 – Personal Scope

This Agreement shall apply to persons who are residents of one or both of the Contracting States.

Article 2 – Taxes Covered

1. Tax Agreement shall apply to taxes on income imposed on behalf of a Contracting State or of its political subdivisions or local authorities, irrespective of the manner in which they are levied.
2. There shall be regarded as taxes on income all taxes imposed on total income, or on elements of income, including taxes on gains from the alienation of movable or immovable property, taxes on the total amounts of wages or salaries paid by enterprises, as well as taxes on capital appreciation.
3. The existing taxes to which the Agreement shall apply are:

    a. In Vietnam:

    (i) the personal income tax;
    (ii) the profit tax; and
    (iii) the profit remittance tax;
    (hereinafter referred to as "Vietnamese tax");

    b. In Denmark:

    (i) the income tax to the State;
    (ii) the municipal income tax;
    (iii) the income tax to the country municipalities; and
    (iv) taxes imposed under the Hydrocarbon Tax Act;
    (hereinafter referred to as "Danish tax").

4. The Agreement shall also apply to any identical or substantially similar taxes, which are imposed after the date of signature of this Agreement in addition to, or in place of, the existing taxes. The competent authorities of the Contracting State shall notify each other of substantial changes, which have been made in their respective taxation laws.

Article 3 – General Definitions

1. For the purposes of this Agreement, unless the context otherwise requires;

    a. The term "Vietnam" means the Socialist Republic of Vietnam; when used in a geographical sense, it means all its national territory, including its territorial sea and any area beyond and adjacent to its territorial sea, within which Vietnam, by Vietnamese legislation and in accordance with international law, has sovereign rights of exploration for and exploitation of natural resources of the seabed and its subsoil and superjacent water mass;

    b. The term "Denmark" means the Kingdom of Denmark including any area outside the territorial sea of Denmark which in accordance with international law has been or may hereafter be designated under Danish laws as an area within which Denmark may exercise sovereign rights with respect to the exploration and exploitation of the natural resources of the seabed or its subsoil and superjacent waters and with regard to other activities for the economic exploitation and exploration of the said area; the term does not comprise the Faroe Islands and Greenland;

    c. The term "a Contracting State" and "the other Contracting State" mean Vietnam or Denmark as the context requires;

d. The term "person" includes an individual, a company and any other body of persons;
e. The term "company" means any body corporate or any entity which is treated as a body corporate for tax purposes;
f. The term "enterprise of a Contracting State" and "enterprise of the other Contracting State" mean respectively an enterprise carried on by a resident of a Contracting State and a enterprise carried on by a resident of the other Contracting State;
g. The term "nationals" means:

   (i) all individuals possessing the nationality of a Contracting State;
   (ii) all legal persons, partnerships and associations deriving their status as such from the laws in force in a Contracting State;

h. The term "international traffic" means any transport by a ship or aircraft operated by an enterprise of a Contracting State, except when the ship or aircraft is operated solely between places in the other Contracting State; and
i. The term "competent authority" means:

   (i) in the case of Vietnam, the Minister of Finance or his authorized representative; and
   (ii) in the case of Denmark, the Minister for Taxation or his authorized representative.

2. As regards the application of the Agreement by a Contracting State any term not defined therein shall, unless the context otherwise requires, have the meaning which it has under the law of that State concerning the taxes to which the Agreement applies.

Article 4 – Resident

1. For the purposes of this Agreement, the term "resident of a Contracting State" means any person who, under the laws of that State, is liable to tax therein by reason of his domicile, residence, place of management, place of registration or any other criterion of a similar nature.
2. Where by reason of the provisions of paragraph 1 an individual is a resident of both Contracting State, then his status shall be determined as follows:

   a. He shall be deemed to be a resident of the State in which he has a permanent home available to him; if he has a permanent home available to him in both States, he shall be deemed to be a resident of the State with which his personal and economic relations are closer (centre of vital interests);
   b. If the State in which he has his centre of vital interests cannot be determined, or if he has no permanent home available to him in either State, he shall be deemed to be a resident of the State in which he has an habitual abode;
   c. If he has a habitual abode in both States or in neither of them, he shall be deemed to be a resident of the State of which he is a national.
   d. If he is a national of both States or of neither of them, the competent authorities of the Contracting States shall settle the question by mutual agreement.

3. Where by reason of the provision of paragraph 1, a person other than an individual is a resident of both Contracting State, then it shall be deemed to be a resident of the State in which its place of registration is situated. However, where such person has its place of registration in one of the States and its place of effective management in the other State, then the competent authorities of the Contracting State shall determine by mutual agreement the State of which the person shall be deemed to be a resident for the purposes of this Agreement. In the absence of such mutual agreement for the purposes of this Agreement, the person shall in each Contracting State be deemed not to be a resident of the other Contracting State.

Article 5 – Permanent Establishment

1. For the purposes of this Agreement, the term "permanent establishment" means a fixed place of business through which the business of the enterprise is wholly or partly carried on.
2. The term "permanent establishment" includes especially:
   a. A place of management;
   b. A branch;
   c. An office;
   d. A factory;
   e. A workshop; and
   f. A mine, an oil or gas well, a quarry or any other place of extraction of natural resources.
3. The term "permanent establishment" likewise encompasses:
   a. A building site, construction, assembly or installation project or supervisory activities in connection therewith, but only where such site, project or activities continue for a period of more than six months;
   b. The furnishing of services, including consultancy services, by an enterprise through employees or other personnel engaged by the enterprise for such purpose, but only where activities of that nature continue (for the same or a connected project) within the country for a period or periods aggregating more than six months within any 12-month period.
4. Notwithstanding the preceding provisions of this Article, the term "permanent establishment" shall be deemed not to include:
   a. The use of facilities solely for the purpose of storage or display of goods or merchandise belonging to the enterprise;
   b. The maintenance of a stock of goods or merchandise belonging to the enterprise solely for the purpose of storage or display;
   c. The maintenance of a stock of goods or merchandise belonging to the enterprise solely for the purpose of processing by another enterprise;
   d. The maintenance of a fixed place of business solely for the purpose of purchasing goods or merchandise or of collecting information for the enterprise;
   e. The maintenance of a fixed place of business solely for the purpose of carrying on, for the enterprise, any other activity of a preparatory or auxiliary character;
   f. The maintenance of a fixed place of business solely for any combination of activities mentioned in subparagraphs (a.) to (e.) provided that the overall activity of the fixed place of business resulting from this combination is of a preparatory or auxiliary character.
5. Notwithstanding the provisions of paragraphs 1 and 2, where a person - other than an agent of an independent status to whom paragraph 6 applies - is acting in a Contracting State on behalf of an enterprise of the other Contracting State, that enterprise shall be deemed to have a permanent establishment in the first-mentioned Contracting State in respect of any activities which that person undertakes for the enterprise, if such a person.
   a. Has and habitually exercises in that State an authority to conclude contracts in the name of the enterprise, unless the activities of such person are limited to those mentioned in paragraph 4 which, if exercised through a fixed place of business, would not make this fixed place of business a permanent establishment under the provisions of that paragraph; or

b. Has no such authority, but habitually maintains in the first-mentioned State a stock of goods or merchandise from which he regularly delivers goods or merchandise on behalf of the enterprise.

6. An enterprise shall not be deemed to have a permanent establishment in a Contracting State merely because it carries on business in that State through a broker, general commission agent or any other agent of an independent status, provided that such persons are acting in the ordinary course of their business. However, when the activities of such an agent are devoted wholly or almost wholly on behalf of that enterprise, he will not be considered an agent of an independent status within the meaning of this paragraph.
7. The fact that a company which is a resident of a Contracting State controls or is controlled by a company which is a resident of the other Contracting State, or which carries on business in that other State (whether through a permanent establishment or otherwise), shall not of itself constitute either company a permanent establishment of the other.

Article 6 – Income from Immovable Property

1. Income derived by a resident of a Contracting State from immovable property (including income from agriculture or forestry) situated in the other Contracting State may be taxed in that other State.
2. The term "immovable property" shall have the meaning which is has under the law of the Contracting State in which the property in question is situated and shall include any option or similar right in respect thereof. The term shall in any case include property accessory to immovable property, livestock and equipment used in agriculture and forestry, rights to which the provision of general law respecting landed property apply, usufruct of immovable property, rights to explore for or to exploit mineral deposits, sources and other natural resources and rights to amounts computed by reference to the amount or value of production from such resources; ships, boats and aircraft shall not be regarded as immovable property.
3. The provisions of paragraph 1 shall apply to income derived from the direct use, letting, or use in any other form of immovable property.
4. The provisions of paragraphs 1 and 3 shall also apply to the income from immovable property of an enterprise and to income from immovable property used for the performance of independent personal services.

Article 7 – Business Profits

1. The profits of an enterprise of a Contracting State shall be taxable only in that State unless the enterprise carries on business in the other Contracting State through a permanent establishment situated therein. If the enterprise carries on business as aforesaid, the profits of the enterprise may be taxed in the other State but only so much of them as is attributable to:

    a. That permanent establishment; or
    b. Sales in that other State of goods or merchandise of the same or similar kind as those sold through that permanent establishment; or
    c. Other business activities carried on in that other State of the same or similar kind as those effected through that permanent establishment.

    The provisions of subparagraphs (b) and (c) shall not apply if the enterprise shows that such sales or activities could not reasonably have been undertaken by that permanent establishment.

2. Subject to the provisions of paragraph 3, where an enterprise of a Contracting State carries on business in the other Contracting State through a permanent establishment situated therein, there shall be attributed in each Contracting State to that permanent establishment the profits which it might be expected to make if it were a distinct and separate enterprise engaged in the same or similar activities under the same or similar conditions and dealing wholly independently with the enterprise of which it is a permanent establishment.
3. In determining the profits of a permanent establishment, there shall be allowed as deductions expenses which are incurred for the purposes of the business of the permanent establishment, including executive and general administrative expenses so incurred, whether in the State in which the permanent establishment is situated or elsewhere. However, no such deduction shall be allowed in respect of amounts, if any, paid (otherwise than towards reimbursement of actual expenses) by the permanent establishment to the head office of the enterprise or any of its other offices, by way of royalties, fees or other similar payments in return for the use of patents or other rights, or by way of commission, for specific services performed or for management, or, except in the case of a banking enterprise, by way of interest on moneys lent to the permanent establishment. Likewise, no account shall be taken, in the determination of the profits of a permanent establishment, for amounts charged (otherwise than towards reimbursement of actual expenses), by the permanent establishment to the head office of the enterprise or any of its other offices, by way of royalties, fees or other similar payments in return for the use of patents or other rights, or by way of commission for specific services performed or for management, or, except in the case of banking enterprise by way of interest on moneys lent to the head office of the enterprise or any of its other offices.
4. Nothing in this Article shall affect the application of any law of a Contracting State relating to the determination of the tax liability of a person in cases where the information available to the competent authority of that State is inadequate to determine the profits to be attributed to a permanent establishment, provided that such law shall be applied, so far as the information available to the competent authority permits, consistently with the principles of this Article.
5. Insofar as it has been customary in a Contracting State to determine the profits to be attributed to a permanent establishment on the basis of an apportionment of the total profits of the enterprise to its various parts, nothing in paragraph 2 shall preclude that Contracting State from determining the profits to be taxed by such an apportionment as may be customary; the method of apportionment adopted shall, however, be such that the result shall be in accordance with the principles contained in this Article.
6. No profits shall be attributed to a permanent establishment by reason of the mere purchase by that permanent establishment of goods or merchandise for the enterprise.
7. For the purposes of the preceding paragraphs, the profits to be attributed to the permanent establishment shall be determined by the same method year by year unless there is good and sufficient reason to the contrary.
8. Where profits include items of income, which are dealt with separately in other Article of this Agreement, then the provisions of those Articles shall not be affected by the provisions of this Article.

Article 8 – Shipping and Air Transport

1. Profits derived by an enterprise of a Contracting State from the operation of aircraft or ships in international traffic shall be taxable only in that Contracting State.
2. For the purposes of this Article, profits from the operation of ships or aircraft in international traffic include:

a. Income from rental on a bareboat basis of ships or aircraft; and
   b. Profits from the use, maintenance or rental of containers (including trailers and related equipment for transport of containers) used for transport of goods or merchandise, where such rental or such use, maintenance or rental, as the case may be, is incidental to the operation of ships or aircraft in international traffic.
3. The provisions of paragraph 1 shall also apply to profits from the participation in a pool, a joint business or an international operating agency.
4. With respect to profits derived by the Danish, Norwegian and Swedish air transport consortium, known as the Scandinavian Airlines System (SAS), the provisions of paragraphs 1 and 3 shall apply only to such proportion of the profits as corresponds to the participation in that consortium held by Det Danske Luftfartsselskab (DDL), the Danish partner of Scandinavian Airlines System (SAS).

Article 9 – Associated Enterprises

1. Where
   a. An enterprise of a Contracting State participates directly or indirectly in the management, control or capital of an enterprise of the other Contracting State, or
   b. The same persons participate directly or indirectly in the management, control or capital of an enterprise of a Contracting State and an enterprise of the other Contracting State, and in either case conditions are made or imposed between the two enterprises in their commercial or financial relations which differ from those which would be made between independent enterprises, the any profits which would, but for those conditions, have accrued to one of the enterprises, but, by the reason of those conditions, have not so accrued, may be included in the profits of that enterprise and taxed accordingly.
2. Nothing in this Article shall affect the application of any law of a Contracting State relating to the determination of the tax liability of a person, including determinations in cases where the information available to the competent authority of that State is inadequate to determine the income to be attributed to an enterprise, provided, that such law shall be applied, so far as it is practicable to do so, consistently with the principles of this Article.
3. Where a Contracting State includes in the profits of an enterprise of that State - and taxes accordingly - profits on which an enterprise of the other Contracting state has been charged to tax in that other State and the profits so included are profits which would have accrued to the enterprise of the first-mentioned State if the conditions made between the two enterprises had been those which would have been made between independent enterprises, then that other State shall make an appropriate adjustment to the amount of the tax charged therein on those profits. In determining such adjustment, due regard shall be had to the other provisions of this Agreement and the competent authorities of the Contracting State shall, if necessary, consult each other.

Article 10 – Dividends

1. Dividends paid by a company, which is a resident of a Contracting State to a resident of the other Contracting State, may be taxed in that other State.
2. However, such dividends may also be taxed in the Contracting State of which the company paying the dividends is a resident and according to the laws of that State, but if the recipient is the beneficial owner of the dividends the tax so charged shall not exceed:

a. 5 per cent of the gross amount of the dividends if the beneficial owner is a company (other than a partnership) which holds directly at least 70 per cent or has invested at least twelve millions USD of the capital of the company paying the dividends;
b. 10 per cent of the gross amount of the dividends if the beneficial owner is a company (other than a partnership) which holds less than 70 per cent but at least 25 per cent of the capital of the company paying the dividends;
c. 15 per cent of the gross amount of the dividends in all other cases.

This paragraph shall not affect the taxation of the company in respect of the profits out of which the dividends are paid.

3. The term "dividends" as used in this Article means income from shares or other rights, not being debt-claims, participating in profits, and income from other corporate rights which is subjected to the same taxation treatment as income from shares by the laws of the State of which the company making the distribution is a resident.
4. The provisions of paragraphs 1 and 2 shall not apply if the beneficial owner of the dividends, being a resident of a Contracting State, carries on business in the other Contracting State of which the company paying the dividends is a resident through a permanent establishment situated therein, or performs in that other State independent personal services from a fixed base situated therein, and the holding in respect of which the dividends are paid is effectively connected with such permanent establishment or fixed base. In such case the provisions of Article 7 or Article 14, as the case may be, shall apply.
5. Where a company which is a resident of a Contracting State derives profits or income from the other Contracting State, that other State may not impose any tax on the dividends paid by the company, except insofar as such dividends are paid to a resident of that other Contracting State or insofar as the holding in respect of which the dividends are paid is effectively connected with a permanent establishment or a fixed base situated in that other State, not subject the company's undistributed profits to a tax on the company's undistributed profits, even if the dividends paid or the undistributed profits consist wholly or partly of profits or income arising in such other State.

Article 11 – Interest

1. Interest arising in a Contracting State and paid to a resident of the other Contracting State may be taxed in that other State.
2. However, such interest may also be taxed in the Contracting State in which it arises, and according to the laws of that State, but if the recipient is the beneficial owner of the interest the tax so charged shall not exceed 10 per cent of the gross amount of the interest.
3. Notwithstanding the provisions of paragraphs 1 and 2,
    a. Interest arising in Vietnam shall be exempt from Vietnamese tax if the interest is paid to:
        (i) the State of Denmark, a political subdivision, a local authority or statutory body thereof:
        (ii) the National Bank of Denmark;
        (iii) any other institution the capital of which is wholly or mainly owned by the government of Denmark, as may be agreed from time to time between the competent authorities of the Contracting States;
    b. Interest arising in Denmark shall be exempt from Danish tax if the interest is paid to:
        (i) The Government of Vietnam, a political subdivision, a local authority or statutory body thereof;

(ii) The State Bank of Vietnam;
   (iii) a statutory body, or any other institution the capital of which is wholly or mainly owned by the Government of Vietnam, as may be agreed from time to time between the competent authorities of the Contracting States.
4. The term "interest" as used in this Article means income from debt-claims of every kind, whether or not secured by mortgage, but not carrying a right to participate in the debtor's profits, and in particular, income from government securities and income from bonds or debentures, including premiums and prizes attaching to such securities, bonds or debentures. Penalty charges for late payment shall not be regarded as interest for the purpose of this Article.
5. The provisions of paragraphs 1, 2 and 3 shall not apply if the beneficial owner of the interest, being a resident of a Contracting State, carries on business in the other Contracting State in which the interest arises, through a permanent establishment situated therein, or performs in that other State independent personal services from a fixed base situated therein and the debt-claim in respect of which the interest is paid is effectively connected with (a) such permanent establishment or fixed base, or with (b) business activities referred to under (c) of paragraph 1 of Article 7. In such case the provisions of Article 7 or Article 14, as the case may be, shall apply.
6. Interest shall be deemed to arise in a Contracting State when the payer is that State itself, a political subdivision, a local authority or a resident of that State. Where, however, the person paying the interest, whether he is a resident of a Contracting State or not, has in a Contracting State a permanent establishment or a fixed base in connection with which the indebtedness in which the interest is paid was incurred, and such interest is borne by such permanent establishment or fixed base, then such interest shall be deemed to arise in the State in which the permanent establishment or fixed base is situated.
7. Where, by reason of a special relationship between the payer and the beneficial owner or between both of them and some other person, the amount of the interest, having regard to the debt-claim for which it is paid, exceeds the amount which would have been agreed upon by the payer and the beneficial owner in the absence of such relationship, the provisions of this Article shall apply only to the last-mentioned amount. In such case, the excess part of the payments shall remain taxable according to the laws of each Contracting State, due regard being had to the other provisions of this Agreement.

Article 12 – Royalties

1. Royalties arising in a Contracting State and paid to a resident of the other Contracting State may be taxed in that other Contracting State.
2. However, such royalties may also be taxed in the Contracting State in which they arise and according to the laws of that State, but if the recipient is the beneficial owner of the royalties the tax so charged shall not exceed 15 per cent of the gross amount of the royalties. Notwithstanding the preceding sentence, if the royalties are paid with respect to any patent, design or model, plan, secret formula or process, or for information concerning industrial or scientific experience or for the use of or the right to use industrial, commercial or scientific equipment involving a transfer of know-how, the tax so charged shall not exceed 5 per cent of the gross amount of the royalties.
3. The term "royalties" as used in this Article means payments of any kind received as a consideration for the use of, or the right to use, any copyright of literary, artistic or scientific work including cinematograph films, or films or tapes used for radio or television broadcasting, any patent, trade mark, design or model, plan, secret formula or process, or for the use of, or the right to use, industrial, commercial or scientific equipment or for information concerning industrial, commercial or scientific experience.

4. The provisions of paragraphs 1 and 2 shall not apply if the beneficial owner of the royalties, being a resident of a Contracting State, carries on business in the other Contracting State in which the royalties arise, through a permanent establishment situated therein, or performs in that other State independent personal services from a fixed base situated therein, and the right or property in respect of which the royalties are paid is effectively connected with (a) such permanent establishment or fixed base or with (b) business activities referred to under (c) of paragraph 1 of Article 7. In such cases the provisions of Article 7 or Article 14, as the case may be, shall apply.
5. Royalties shall be deemed to arise in a Contracting State when the payer is that State itself, a political subdivision, or a local authority or a resident of that State. Where, however, the person paying the royalties, whether he is a resident of a Contracting State or not, has in a Contracting State a permanent establishment or fixed base in connection with which the liability to pay the royalties was incurred, and such royalties are borne by such permanent establishment or fixed base, the such royalties shall be deemed to arise in the State in which the permanent establishment or fixed base is situated.
6. Where, by reason of a special relationship between the payer and the beneficial owner or between both of them and some other person, the amount of the royalties, having regard to the use, right or information for which they are paid, exceeds the amount which would have been agreed upon by the payer and the beneficial owner in the absence of such relationship, the provisions of this Article shall apply only to the last-mentioned amount. In such case, the excess part of the payments shall remain taxable according to the laws of each Contracting State, due regard being had to the other provisions of this Agreement.

Article 13 – *Gains from the Alienation of Property*

1. Gains derived by a resident of a Contracting State from the alienation of immovable property referred to in Article 6 and situated in the other Contracting State may be taxed in that other State.
2. Gains from the alienation of movable property forming part of the business property of a permanent establishment which an enterprise of a Contracting State has in the other Contracting State or of movable property pertaining to a fixed base available to a resident of a Contracting State in the other Contracting State for the purpose of performing independent personal services, including such gains from the alienation of such a permanent establishment (alone or with the whole enterprise) or of such fixed base, may be taxed in that other State.
3. Gains derived by a resident of a Contracting State from the alienation of shares or comparable interests in a company, the assets of which consist wholly or principally of immovable property situated in the other Contracting State, may be taxed in that other State.
4. Gains derived by an enterprise of a Contracting State from the alienation of ships or aircraft operated in international traffic or movable property pertaining to the operation of such ships or aircraft, or containers (including trailers and related equipment for transport of containers), the use of which is incidental to the operation of such ships or aircraft, shall be taxable only in that Contracting State. The provisions of this paragraph, however, shall not apply if the containers or trailers and related equipment are used for transport solely between places within the other Contracting State.
5. With respect to gains derived by the Danish, Norwegian and Swedish air transport consortium Scandinavian Airlines System (SAS), the provisions of paragraph 4 shall apply only to such proportions of the gains as corresponds to the participation in that consortium held by Det Danske Luftfartsselskab (DDL), the Danish partner of Scandinavian Airlines System (SAS).

6. Gains from the alienation of shares other than those mentioned in paragraph 3 representing a participation of at least 10 per cent in a company, which is a resident of a Contracting State, may be taxed in that State.
7. Gains from the alienation of any property other than that referred to in paragraphs 1, 2, 3, 4, 5 and 6 shall be taxable only in the Contracting State of which the alienator is a resident.
8. In the case of an individual who was a resident of a Contracting State and has become a resident of the other Contracting State, paragraphs 6 and 7 of this Article shall not affect the right of the first-mentioned State under its national laws to tax the individual on a capital appreciation up to the change of residence in respect of shares.

Where the shares are subsequently alienated and the gains from such alienation are taxed in the other Contracting State in accordance with this Article, that other State shall allow as a deduction from the tax on the income, an amount equal to the income tax, which was paid in the first-mentioned State.

Such deduction shall not, however, exceed that part of the income tax as computed before the deduction is given which is attributable to the income which may be taxed in the first-mentioned State in accordance with the first sentence of this paragraph.

Article 14 – Independent Personal Services

1. Income derived by a resident of a Contracting State in respect of professional services or other activities of an independent character shall be taxable only in that State except in the following circumstances, where such income may also be taxed in the other Contracting State:
    a. If he has a fixed base regularly available to him in the other Contracting State for the purpose of performing his activities; in that case, only so much of the income as is attributable to that fixed base may be taxed in that other Contracting State; or
    b. If his stay in the other Contracting State is for a period or periods amounting to or exceeding in the aggregate 183 days in the fiscal year concerned; in that case, only so much of the income as is derived from his activities performed in that other State may be taxed in that State.
2. The term "professional services" included especially independent scientific, literary, artistic, educational or teaching activities as well as the independent activities of physician, lawyers, engineers, architects, dentists and accountants.

Article 15 – Dependent Personal Services

1. Subject to the provisions of Articles 16, 18, 19 and 21, salaries, wages and other similar remuneration derived by a resident of a Contracting State in respect of an employment shall be taxable only in that State unless the employment is exercised in the other Contracting State. If the employment is so exercised, such remuneration as is derived therefrom may be taxed in that other State.
2. Notwithstanding the provisions of paragraph 1, remuneration derived by a resident of a Contracting State in respect of an employment exercised in the other Contracting State shall be taxable only in the first-mentioned State if:
    a. The recipient is present in the other State for a period or periods not exceeding in the aggregate 183 days in any twelve month period commencing or ending in the fiscal year concerned, and
    b. The remuneration is paid by, or on behalf of, an employer who is not a resident of the other State, and
    c. The remuneration is not borne by a permanent establishment or a fixed base, which the employer has in the other State.

3. Notwithstanding the preceding provisions of this Article, remuneration derived in respect of an employment exercised aboard a ship or aircraft operated in international traffic by an enterprise of a Contracting State shall be taxable only in that State.
4. Where a resident of Denmark derives remuneration in respect of an employment exercised aboard an aircraft operated in international traffic by the Scandinavian Airlines System (SAS) consortium, such remuneration shall be taxable only in Denmark.

Article 16 – Directors' Fees

Directors' fees and other similar payments derived by a resident of a Contracting State in his capacity as a member of the board of directors of a company which is a resident of the other Contracting State may be taxed in that other State.

Article 17 – Artistes and Sportsmen

1. Notwithstanding the provisions of Articles 14 and 15, income derived by an resident of a Contracting State as an entertainer, such as a theatre, motion picture, radio or television artiste, or a musician, or as a sportsmen, from his personal activities as such exercised in the other Contracting State, may be taxed in that other State.
2. Where income in respect of personal activities exercised by an entertainer or a sportsman in his capacity as such accrues not to the entertainer or sportsman himself but to another person, that income may, notwithstanding the provisions of Articles 7, 14 and 15, be taxed in the Contracting State in which the activities of the entertainer or sportsman are exercised.
3. Notwithstanding the provisions of paragraphs 1 and 2, income derived by entertainers or sportsmen who are residents of a Contracting State from activities in the other Contracting State under a plan of cultural exchange between the Governments of both Contracting States shall be exempt from tax in that other Contracting State.

Article 18 – Pensions and Similar Payments

1. Subject to the provisions of paragraph 2 of Article 19, pensions and other similar remuneration paid to a resident of a Contracting State in consideration of past employment shall be taxable only in that State.
2. In the case of an individual who was a resident of a Contracting State and has become a resident of the other Contracting State, paragraph 1 of this Article shall not affect the right of the first State under its national laws to tax pensions, other similar remuneration and annuities accruing to such individual from the first State.
3. The term "annuities" means stated sums payable periodically at stated times, during life or during a specified or ascertainable period of time, under an obligation to make the payments in return for adequate and full consideration in money or money's worth.

Article 19 – Government Service

1. a. Remuneration, other than a pension, paid by a Contracting State or a political subdivision or a local authority thereof to an individual in respect of services rendered to that State or subdivision or authority shall be taxable only in that State.

b. However, such remuneration shall be taxable only in the other Contracting State if the services are rendered in that State and the individual is a resident of that State who:

   (i) is a national of that State; or
   (ii) did not become a resident of that State solely for the purpose of rendering the services.

2. a. Any pension paid by, or out of funds created by, a Contracting State or a political subdivision or a local authority thereof to an individual in respect of services rendered to that State or subdivision or authority may be taxed in that State.
   b. However, such pension shall be taxable only in the other Contracting State if the individual is a resident of, and a national of, that other State.

3. The provisions of Articles 15, 16 and 18 shall apply to remuneration and pensions in respect of services rendered in connection with a business carried on by a Contracting State or a political subdivision or a local authority thereof.

Article 20 – Students and Apprentices

1. Payments which a student or business apprentice who is or was immediately before visiting a Contracting State a resident of the other Contracting State and who is present in the first-mentioned State solely for the purpose of his education or training receives for the purpose of his maintenance, education or training shall not be taxed in that State, provided that such payments arise from sources outside that State.

2. Notwithstanding the provisions of paragraph 1, remuneration which a student or a business apprentice who is a or was formerly a resident of a Contracting State and who is present in the other Contracting State solely for the purpose of his education or training derives from services rendered in that other State shall not be taxed in that other State provided that such services are in connection with his education or training and that the remuneration for such services is necessary to supplement the resources available to him for the purpose of his maintenance.

Article 21 – Teachers, Professors and Researchers

An individual who is, or immediately before visiting a Contracting State was, a resident of the other Contracting State and is present in the first-mentioned Contracting State for the primary purpose of teaching, giving lectures or conducting research at a university, college, school or educational institution or scientific research institution accredited by the Government of the first-mentioned Contracting State shall be exempt from tax in the first mentioned Contracting State, for a period of two years from the date of his arrival in the first-mentioned Contracting State, in respect of remuneration for such teaching, lectures or research.

Article 22 – Other Income

1. Items of income of a resident of a Contracting State, wherever arising, not dealt with in the foregoing Articles of this Agreement shall be taxable only in that State.

2. However, any such income derived by a resident of a Contracting State from sources in the other Contracting State may also be taxed in that other State.

3. The provisions of paragraph 1 shall not apply to the income, other than income from immovable property as defined in paragraph 2 of Article 6, if the recipient of such income, being a resident of a Contracting State, carries on business in the other Contracting State through a permanent establishment situated therein, or performs in

that other State independent personal services from a fixed base situated therein, and the right or property in respect of which the income is paid is effectively connected with such permanent establishment or fixed base. In such case the provisions of Article 7 or Article 14, as the case may be, shall apply.

Article 23 – Activities in Connection with Preliminary Surveys, Exploration or Extraction of Hydrocarbons

Notwithstanding the provisions of Article 5 and Article 14, a person who is a resident of a Contracting State and carries on activities in connection with preliminary surveys, exploration or extraction of hydrocarbons situated in the other Contracting State shall be deemed to be carrying on in respect of those activities a business in that other Contracting State through a permanent establishment or fixed base situated therein.

Article 24 – Elimination of Double Taxation

1. In Vietnam double taxation shall be eliminated as follows:
   Where a resident of Vietnam derives income, which, in accordance with this Agreement, may be taxed in Denmark, Vietnam shall allow as a deduction from the tax on the income of that resident, an amount equal to the income tax paid thereon in Denmark. Such deduction shall not, however, exceed that part of the income tax in Vietnam as computed before the deduction is given, which is attributable to the income which may be taxed in Denmark.
2. In Denmark double taxation shall be eliminated as follows:
   a. Subject to the provisions of subparagraph (c.), where a resident of Denmark derived income, which, in accordance with the provisions of this Agreement, may be taxed in Vietnam, Denmark shall allow as a deduction from the tax on the income of that resident, an amount equal to the income tax paid in Vietnam.
   b. Such deduction shall not, however, exceed that part of the income tax, as computed before the deduction is given, which is attributable to the income which may be taxed in Vietnam.
   c. Where a resident of Denmark derives income, which, in accordance with the provisions of the Agreement, shall be taxable only in Vietnam, Denmark may include this income in the tax base, but shall allow as a deduction from the income tax that part of the income tax, which is attributable to the income derived from Vietnam.
   d. For the purposes of subparagraphs (a.) and (b.) of this paragraph the Vietnamese tax paid in respect of royalties received (which can not according to paragraph 2 of Article 12 exceed 5 per cent of the gross amount of such royalty) as a consideration for the use of any patent, design or model, plan, secret formula or process, or for information concerning industrial, commercial or scientific experience shall, where it has been used in an activity (other than business activities in the financial sector) which has been carried out in Vietnam, be deemed to have been paid at a rate of 12,5 per cent of the gross amount of the royalties.
   This provision shall not apply where royalties are paid in respect of assets, as mentioned in this subparagraph, which are sold by the payer and leased back by the recipient to the payer (or an associated enterprise within the meaning of Article 9) of the royalties.
   e. Where exemption from or reduction of Vietnamese tax, payable in accordance with the provisions of Article 7 in respect of profits derived by a Danish enterprise from a permanent establishment situated in Vietnam, has been granted under Vietnamese

law, then, for the purposes of subparagraphs (a.) and (b.), deduction from Danish tax for Vietnamese tax shall be allowed as if no such exemption or reduction had been granted, provided that the permanent establishment is engaged in business activities (other than business) activities in the financial sector) and that no more than 25 per cent of such profits consist of interest and gains from the alienation of shares and bonds or consist of profits derived from third State.
  f. Where dividends are paid by a company which is a resident of Vietnam to a person (being a Company) which is a resident of Denmark, and which owns directly or indirectly not less than 25 per cent of the share capital of the first-mentioned company, then such dividends shall be exempt from tax in Denmark, provided that the company paying the dividends is engaged in business activities (other than business activities in the financial sector) and that no more than 25 per cent of the company's profits consist of interest and gains from the alienation of shares and bonds or consist of profits derived from third States.
  g. In the case of a dividend paid by a company which is a resident of Vietnam to a company which is a resident of Denmark and which owns at least 10 per cent of the share capital of the company paying the dividends, if the dividend is not exempt from Danish tax in accordance with subparagraph (f), the credit for the purposes of subparagraphs (a.) and (b.) of this paragraph shall take into account the Vietnamese tax payable by the company paying the dividend in respect of the profits out of which such dividend is paid.
  h. The provisions in subparagraphs (d.), (e.) and (f.) shall apply for the first ten years for which the Agreement is effective. The competent authorities shall consult each other in order to determine whether this period shall be extended. Any such extension shall take effect from such date and subject to such modifications and conditions, including conditions as to termination, as may be specified and agreed between the Contracting State in notes to be exchanged through diplomatic channels or in any other manner in accordance with their constitutional procedures.

Article 25 – Limitation of Benefits

Without prejudice to subparagraph (f.) of paragraph 1 of Article 24, where any person derives income from a source situated outside Vietnam and such income is exempt from tax under the laws of Vietnam and also exempt from tax in Denmark under this Agreement, Denmark may tax such income under its own laws notwithstanding the provisions of this Agreement.

Article 26 – Non-discrimination

1. Nationals of a Contracting State shall not be subjected in the other Contracting State to any taxation or any requirement connected therewith which is other or more burdensome than the taxation and connected requirements to which nationals of that other State in the same circumstances are or may be subjected.
2. The taxation on a permanent establishment, which an enterprise of a Contracting State has in the other Contracting State, shall not be less favorably levied in that other State than the taxation levied on enterprises of that other State carrying on the same activities.

This provision shall not be construed as obliging a Contracting State to grant to residents of the other Contracting State any personal allowances, reliefs and reductions for taxation purposes on account of civil status or family responsibilities which it grants to its own residents.

3. Except where the provisions of paragraph 1 of Article 9, paragraph 7 of Article 11, or paragraph 6 of Article 12, apply, interest, royalties and other disbursements paid by an enterprise of a Contracting State to a resident of the other Contracting State shall, for the purpose of determining the taxable profits of such enterprise, be deductible under the same conditions as if they had been paid to a resident of the first-mentioned State.
4. Enterprises of a Contracting State, the capital of which is wholly or partly owned or controlled, directly or indirectly by one or more residents of the other Contracting State, shall not be subjected in the first-mentioned Contracting State to any taxation or any requirement connected therewith which is other or more burdensome than the taxation and connected requirements to which other similar enterprises of the first-mentioned State are or may be subjected.
5. The provisions of paragraphs 2 and 4 of this Article shall not apply to the Vietnamese profit remittance tax, which in any case shall not exceed 10 per cent of the gross amount of profits remitted, and the Vietnamese taxation in respect of agricultural production activities.
6. Nothing contained in this Article shall be construed as obliging either Contracting State to grant to individuals not resident in that State any of the personal allowances, reliefs and reductions for tax purposes, which are granted to individuals so resident.
7. The provisions of this Article shall apply only to the taxes, which are the subject of this Agreement.
8. Notwithstanding the provisions of this Article, for so long as Vietnam continues to grant to investors licenses under the Law on Foreign Investment in Vietnam, which specify the taxation to which the investor shall be subjected, the imposition of such taxation shall not be regarded as breaching the terms of paragraphs 2 and 4 of this Article.

Article 27 – Mutual Agreement Procedure

1. Where a person who is a resident of a Contracting State considers that the actions of the competent authority of one or both of the Contracting States result or will result for him in taxation not in accordance with the provisions of this Agreement, he may, irrespective of the remedies provided by the domestic law of those States, present his case to the competent authority of the Contracting State of which that person is a resident, or if his case comes under paragraph 1 of Article 26, to that of the Contracting State of which he is a national. The case must be presented within three years from the first notification of the action resulting in taxation not in accordance with the provisions of the Agreement.
2. The competent authority shall endeavor, if the objection appears to it to be justified and if it is not itself able to arrive at a satisfactory solution, to resolve the case by mutual agreement with the competent authority of the other Contracting State, with a view to the avoidance of taxation which is not in accordance of taxation which is not in accordance with this Agreement. Any agreement reached shall be implemented notwithstanding any time limits in the domestic law of the Contracting States.
3. The competent authorities of the Contracting States shall jointly endeavor to resolve any difficulties or doubts arising as to the application of the Agreement. They may also consult together for the elimination of double taxation in cases not provided for in the Agreement.
4. The competent authorities of the Contracting States may communicate with each other directly for the purpose of reaching an agreement in the sense of the preceding paragraphs. The competent authorities, through consultations, shall develop appropriate bilateral procedures, conditions, methods and techniques for the implementation of the mutual agreement procedure provided for in this Article. In addition, a competent authority may devise appropriate unilateral procedures, conditions, methods and techniques to facilitate the above-mentioned bilateral actions and the implementation of mutual agreement procedures.

Article 28 – Exchange of Information

1. The competent authorities of the Contracting States shall exchange such information as is necessary for carrying out the provisions of this Agreement or of the domestic laws of the Contracting States concerning taxes covered by the Agreement insofar as the taxation thereunder is not contrary to the Agreement. The exchange of information is not restricted by Article 1. Any information received by a Contracting State shall be treated as secret in the same manner as only to persons or authorities (including courts and administrative bodies) involved in the assessment or collection of, the enforcement or prosecution in respect of, or the determination of appeals in relation to, the taxes covered by the Agreement. Such persons or authorities shall use the information only for such purposes. They may disclose the information in public court proceedings or in judicial decisions.
2. In no case shall the provisions of paragraph 1 be construed so as to impose on a Contracting State the obligation:

    a. To carry out administrative measures at variance with the laws and administrative practice of that or of the other Contracting State;
    b. To supply information which is not obtainable under the laws or in the normal course of the administration of that or of the other Contracting State;
    c. To supply information, which would disclose any trade, business, industrial, commercial or professional secret or trade process, or information, the disclosure of which would be contrary to public policy.

Article 29 – Diplomatic Agents and Consular Officers

Nothing in this Agreement shall affect the fiscal privileges of diplomatic agents or consular officers under the general rules of international law or under the provisions of special agreements.

Article 30 – Territorial Extension

1. This Agreement may be extended, either in its entirety or with any necessary modifications to the territories under Denmark's sovereignty which are specifically excluded from the application of the agreement or to any territory for whose international relations Denmark is responsible, and which imposes taxes substantially similar in character to those to which the Agreement applies. Any such extension shall take effect from such date and subject to such modifications and conditions, including conditions as to termination, as may be specified and agreed between the Contracting States in notes to be exchanged through diplomatic channels or in any other manner in accordance with their constitutional procedures.
2. Unless otherwise agreed by both Contracting States, the termination of the agreement by one of them under Article 32 shall also terminate, in the manner provided for in that Article, the application of the Agreement to any territory to which it has been extended under this Article.

Article 31 – Entry into Force

1. The Governments of the Contracting States shall notify to each other that the constitutional requirements for the entry into force of this Agreement have been complied with. This Agreement shall enter into force on the date of the later of these notifications.
2. This Agreement shall have effect:

a. In Vietnam:

   (i) in respect of taxes withheld at source, in relation to taxable amounts paid on or after 1 January following the calendar year in which the Agreement inters into force;
   (ii) in respect of other Vietnamese taxes, in relation to income, profits or gains arising in the calendar year following the calendar year in which the Agreement enters into force;

b. In Denmark:

   (i) in respect of taxes withheld at source, in relation to taxable amounts paid on or after 1 January following the calendar year in which the Agreement enters into force;
   (ii) in respect of other Danish taxes, in relation to income, profits or gains arising in the tax year beginning on or after 1 January in the calendar year following the year in which the Agreement enters into force.

Article 32 – Termination

This Agreement shall remain in force until terminated by one of the Contracting States. Either Contracting State may terminate the Agreement, through diplomatic channels, by giving to the other Contracting State written notice of termination at least six months before the end of any calendar year after the expiry of five years from the date of entry into force of the Agreement. In such event the Agreement shall cease to have effect:

a. In Vietnam:

   (i) in respect of taxes withheld at source, in relation to taxable amounts paid on or after 1 January following the calendar year in which the notice of termination is given;
   (ii) in respect of other Vietnamese taxes, in relation to income, profits or gains arising in the calendar year following the calendar year in which the notice of termination is given, and in subsequent calendar years;

b. In Denmark:

   (i) in respect of taxes withheld at source, in relation to taxable amounts paid on or after 1 January following the calendar year in which the notice of termination is given;
   (ii) in respect of other Danish taxes, in relation to income, profits or gains arising in the tax year beginning on or after 1 January in the calendar year following the year in which the notice of termination is given, and in subsequent calendar years.

DONE in duplicate at Copenhagen this 31st day of May of the year one thousand nine hundred and ninety-five in the Vietnamese, Danish and English languages, all three texts being equally authentic. In case of divergence of interpretation, the English text shall prevail.

Protocol

At the moment of signing the Agreement between the Government of the Socialist Republic of Vietnam and the Government of the Kingdom of Denmark for the on income the undersigned have agreed upon the following provisions which shall constitute an integral part of the Agreement.

With respect to Article 5, paragraphs 4 and 5

In respect of subparagraphs (a.) and (b.) of paragraph 4 of Article 5, it is understood that the maintenance of a stock of goods or merchandise solely for the purpose of future delivery or facilities used solely for the purpose of future delivery of goods or merchandise of an enterprise of a Contracting State in the other Contracting State shall not constitute a permanent establishment in the other Contracting State as long as the conditions of subparagraph (b.) of paragraph 5 of the same Article are not fulfilled.

With respect to Article 13, paragraph 8

The competent authorities of a Contracting State shall upon request of the other Contracting State inform the competent authorities of that other State in cases where tax is levied in accordance with the provisions of this paragraph. Details shall be given about the calculation of the tax and about the tax base.

DONE in duplicate at Copenhagen this 31st day of May of the year one thousand nine hundred and ninety-five in the Vietnamese, Danish and English languages, all three texts being equally authentic. In case of divergence of interpretation, the English text shall prevail.

9.5 Germany–Vietnam Treaty

The Socialist Republic of Vietnam and the Federal Republic of Germany, desiring to conclude an Agreement for the avoidance of double taxation and the prevention of fiscal evasion with respect to taxes on income and on capital, have agreed as follows:

Article 1 – Personal Scope

This Agreement shall apply to persons who are residents of one or both of the Contracting States.

Article 2 – Taxes Covered

1. This Agreement shall apply to taxes on income and on capital imposed on behalf of a Contracting State, of a Land or its political subdivisions or local authorities, irrespective of the manner in which they are levied.
2. There shall be regarded as taxes on income and on capital all taxes imposed on total income, on total capital, or on elements of income or of capital, including taxes on gains from the alienation of movable or immovable property, taxes on the total amounts of wages or salaries paid by enterprises as well as taxes on capital appreciation.
3. The existing taxes to which this Agreement shall apply are:

    (a) In Vietnam:

    (i) the personal income tax;
    (ii) the profit tax; and
    (iii) the profit remittance tax;
    (hereinafter referred to as "Vietnamese tax");

    (b) In the Federal Republic of Germany:

    (i) the Income tax;
    (ii) the corporation tax;
    (iii) the capital tax; and
    (iv) the trade tax;
    (hereinafter referred to as "German tax");

4. The Agreement shall also apply to any identical or substantially similar taxes which are imposed after the date of signature of this Agreement in addition to, or in place of, the existing taxes The competent authorities of the Contracting States shall notify each other of important changes which have been made in their respective taxation laws.

Article 3 – General Definitions

1. For the purpose of this Agreement, unless the context otherwise requires:

    (a) The term "Vietnam" means the Socialist Republic of Vietnam; when used in a geographical sense, it means all its national territory, including its territorial sea and any area beyond its territorial sea, within which Vietnam by Vietnamese legislation and in accordance with international law, has sovereign rights of exploration for and exploitation of natural resources of the sea-bed and its sub-soil and superjacent water mass;

    (b) The term "Federal Republic of Germany" means the area in which the tax law of the Federal Republic of Germany is in force, including the area of the sea-bed, its sub-soil and the superjacent water column adjacent to the territorial sea, insofar as the Federal Republic of Germany exercises there sovereign rights and jurisdiction in conformity with international law and its national legislation;

    (c) The terms "a Contracting State" and "the other Contracting State" mean Vietnam or the Federal Republic of Germany as the context requires;

    (d) The term "person" means an individual or a company;

    (e) The term "company" means any body corporate or any entity which is treated as a body corporate for tax purposes;

    (f) The terms "enterprise of a Contracting State" and "enterprise of the other Contracting State" mean respectively and enterprise carried on by a resident of a Contracting State and an enterprise carried on by a resident of the other Contracting State;

    (g) The term "national" means:

      (i) in respect of Vietnam any individual possessing the nationality of Vietnam and any legal person, partnership and association deriving its status as such from the laws in force in Vietnam;

      (ii) in respect of the Federal Republic of Germany any German within the meaning of Article 116, paragraph (1), of the Basic Law for the Federal Republic of Germany and any legal person, partnership and association deriving its status as such from the law in force in the Federal Republic of Germany;

    (h) The term "international traffic" means any transport by a ship or aircraft operated by an enterprise which has its place of effective management in a Contracting State, except when the ship or aircraft is operated solely between places in the other Contracting State; and

    (i) the term "competent authority" means:

      (i) in the case of Vietnam, the Minister of Finance or his authorised representative; and

      (ii) in the case of the Federal Republic of Germany, the Federal Ministry of Finance.

2. As regards the application of the Agreement by a Contracting State, any term not defined therein shall, unless the context otherwise requires, have the meaning which it has under the law of that State concerning the taxes to which the Agreement applies.

Article 4 – Resident

1. For the purpose of this Agreement, the term "resident of a Contracting State" means any person who, under the laws of that State, is liable to tax therein by reason of his domicile, residence, place of management or any other criterion of a similar nature.
2. Where by reason of the provisions of paragraph 1 an individual is a resident of both Contracting States, then his status shall be determined as follows:

    (a) He shall be deemed to be as resident of the State in which he has a permanent home available to him. If he has a permanent home available to him in both States, he shall be deemed to be a resident of the State with which his personal and economic relation are closer (center of vital interests);
    (b) If the State in which he has his center of vital interests cannot be determined, or if he has no permanent home available to him in either State, he shall be deemed to be a resident of the State in which he has an habitual abode;
    (c) If he has an habitual abode in both States or in neither of them, he shall be deemed to be a resident of the State of which he is a national;
    (d) If he is a national of both States or of neither of them, the competent authorities of the Contracting States shall settle the question by mutual agreement.

3. Where by reason of the provision of paragraph 1, a company is a resident of both Contracting State, then it shall be deemed to be a resident of the State in which its place of effective management is situated.

Article 5 – Permanent Establishment

1. For the purpose of this Agreement, the term "permanent establishment" means a fixed place of business through which the business of an enterprise is wholly or partly carried on.
2. The term "permanent establishment" include especially

    (a) A place of management;
    (b) A branch;
    (c) An office;
    (d) A factory;
    (e) A workshop; and
    (f) A mine, an oil or gas well, a quarry or any other place of extraction of natural resources.

3. A building site or construction or installation project constitutes a permanent establishment only if it lasts more than six months.
4. Notwithstanding the preceding provisions of this Article, the term "permanent establishment" shall be deemed not to include:

    (a) The use of facilities solely for the purpose of storage, display or delivery of goods or merchandise belonging to the enterprise;
    (b) The maintenance of a stock of goods or merchandise belonging to the enterprise solely for the purpose of storage, display or delivery;
    (c) The maintenance of a stock of goods or merchandise belonging to the enterprise solely for the purpose of processing by another enterprise;
    (d) The maintenance of a fixed place of business solely for the purpose of purchasing goods or merchandise or of collection information, for the enterprise;
    (e) The maintenance of a fixed place of business solely for the purpose of carrying on, for the enterprise, any other activity of a preparatory or auxiliary character;
    (f) The maintenance of a fixed place of business solely for any combination of activities mentioned in sub-paragraphs (a) to (e), provided that the overall activity of the fixed place of business resulting from this combination is of a preparatory or auxiliary character.

5. Notwithstanding the provisions of paragraphs 1 and 2, where a person - other than an agent of an independent status to whom paragraph 6 applies - is acting on behalf of an enterprise and has, and habitually exercises, in a Contracting State an authority to concludes contracts in the name of the enterprise, that enterprise shall be deemed to have a permanent establishment in the State in respect of any activities which that person undertakes for the enterprise, unless the activities of such person are limited to those mentioned in paragraph 4 which, if exercised through a fixed place of business, would not make this fixed place of business a permanent establishment under the provision of that paragraph.
6. An enterprise shall not be deemed to have a permanent establishment in a Contracting State merely because it carries on business in that State through a broker, general commission agent or any other agent of an independent status, provided that such persons are acting in the ordinary course of their business.
7. The fact that a company which is a resident of a Contracting State controls or is controlled by a company which is a resident of the other Contracting State, or which carries on business in that other State (whether through a permanent establishment or otherwise), shall not of itself constitute either company a permanent establishment of the other.

Article 6 – Income from Immovable Property

1. Income derived by a resident of a Contracting State from immovable property (including income from agriculture or forestry) situated in the other Contracting State may be taxed in that other State.
2. The term "immovable property" shall have the meaning, which it has under the law of the Contracting State in which the property in question is situated. The term shall in any case include property accessory to immovable property, livestock and equipment used in agriculture and forestry, rights to which the provisions of general law respecting landed property apply, usufruct of immovable property and rights to variable or fixed payments as consideration for the working of, or the right to work, mineral deposits, sources and other natural resources; ships and aircraft shall not be regarded as immovable property.
3. The provisions of paragraph 1 shall apply to income derived from the direct use, letting, or use in any other form of immovable property.
4. The provisions of paragraphs 1 and 3 shall also apply to the income from immovable property of an enterprise and to income from immovable property used for the performance of independent personal services.

Article 7 – Business Profits

1. The profits of an enterprise of a Contracting State shall be taxable only in that State unless the enterprise carries on business in the other Contracting State through a permanent establishment situated therein. If the enterprise carries on business as aforesaid, the profits of the enterprise may be taxed in the other State but only so much of them as is attributable to that permanent establishment.
2. Subject to the provisions of paragraph 3, where an enterprise of a Contracting State carries on business in the other Contracting State through a permanent establishment situated therein, there shall in each Contracting State be attributed to the permanent establishment the profits which it might be expected to make if it were a distinct and separate enterprise engaged in the same or similar activities under the same or similar conditions and dealing wholly independently with the enterprise of which it is a permanent establishment.
3. In determining the profits of a permanent establishment, there shall be allowed as deductions expenses which are incurred for the purpose of the business of the permanent

establishment, including executive and general administrative expenses so incurred, whether in the State in which the permanent establishment is situated or elsewhere.
4. Insofar as it has been customary in a Contracting State to determine the profits to be attributed to a permanent establishment on the basis of an apportionment of the total profits of the enterprise to its various parts, nothing in paragraph 2 shall preclude such Contracting State from determining the profits to be taxed by such an apportionment as may be customary; the method of apportionment adopted shall, however, be such that the result shall be in accordance with the principle contained in this Article.
5. No profits shall be attributed to a permanent establishment by reason of the mere purchase by that permanent establishment of goods or merchandise for the enterprise.
6. For the purpose of the preceding paragraphs, the profits to be attributed to the permanent establishment shall be determined by the same method year by year unless there is goods and sufficient reason to the contrary.
7. Where profits include items of income, which are dealt with separately in other Articles of this Agreement, then the provisions of those Articles shall not be affected by the provisions of this Article.

Article 8 – Shipping and Air Transport

1. Profits from the operation of ships or aircraft in international traffic shall be taxable only in the Contracting State in which the place of effective management of the enterprise is situated.
2. The provisions of paragraph 1 shall also apply to profits from the participation in a pool, a joint business or an international operating agency.

Article 9 – Associated Enterprises

Where

(a) An enterprise of a Contracting State participates directly or indirectly in the management, control or capital of an enterprise of the other Contracting State, or
(b) The same person participate directly or indirectly in the management, control or capital of an enterprise of a Contracting State and an enterprise of the other Contracting State, and in either case conditions are made or imposed between the two enterprises in their commercial or financial relations which differ from those which would be made between independent enterprise, then any profits which would, but for those conditions, have accrued to one of the enterprises, but, by reason of those conditions, have not so accrued, may be included in the profits of that enterprise and taxed accordingly.

Article 10 – Dividends

1. Dividends paid by a company, which is a resident of a Contracting State to a resident of the other Contracting State, may be taxed in that other State.
2. However, such dividends may also be taxed in the Contracting State of which the company paying the dividends is a resident and according to the laws of that State, but if the recipient is the beneficial owner of the dividends the tax so charged shall not exceed:

    (a) 5 per cent of the gross amount of the dividends if the recipient is a company (excluding partnerships) which owns directly at least 70 per cent of the capital of the company paying the dividends;

(b) 10 per cent of the gross amount of the dividends if the recipient is a company (excluding partnership) which owns directly at least 25 per cent of the capital of the company paying the dividends;
(c) 15 per cent of the gross amount of the dividends in all other cases.

3. The term "dividends" as used in this Article means dividends on shares including income from shares, "jouissance" shares or "jouissance" rights, mining shares, founders' shares or other rights, not being debt-claims, participating in profits, as well as other income which is subjected to the same taxation treatment as income from shares by the laws of the State of which the company making the distribution is a resident.
4. The provisions of paragraphs 1 and 2 shall not apply if the beneficial owner of the dividends, being a resident of a Contracting State, carries on business in the other Contracting State of which the company paying the dividends is a resident through a permanent establishment situated therein, or performs in that other State independent personal services from a fixed base situated therein, and the holding in respect of which the dividends are paid is effectively connected with such permanent establishment or fixed base. In such case the provisions of Article 7 or Article 14, as the case may be, shall apply.
5. Where a company which is a resident of a Contracting State derives profits or income from the other Contracting State, that other State may not impose any tax on the dividends paid by the company, except insofar as such dividends are paid to a resident of that other State or insofar as the holding in respect of which the dividends are paid is effectively connected with a permanent establishment or a fixed base situated in that other State, nor subject the company's undistributed profits to a tax on the company's undistributed profits, even if the dividends paid or the undistributed profits consist wholly or partly of profits or income arising in that other State.

Article 11 – Interest

1. Interest arising in a Contracting State and paid to resident of the other Contracting State may be taxed in that other State.
2. However, such interest may also be taxed in the Contracting State in which it arises, and according to the laws of the State, but if the recipient is the beneficial owner of the interest, the tax so charged shall not exceed 10 per cent of the gross amount of the interest.
3. Notwithstanding the provisions of paragraph 2,
   (a) Interest arising in Vietnam and paid to the Government of the Federal Republic of Germany, the Deutsche Bundesbank, fthe Kreditanstalt für Wiederaufbau or the Deutsche Investitionsund Entwicklungsgesellschaft (DEG) and interest paid in consideration of a loan guaranteed by HERMES-Deckung shall be exempt from Vietnamese tax;
   (b) Interest arising in the Federal Republic of Germany and paid to the Government of Vietnam, the State Bank of Vietnam or the local authorities of Vietnam shall be exempt from German tax.
4. The term "interest" as used in this Article means income from debt-claims of every kind, whether or not secured by mortgage, and whether or not carrying a right to participate in the debtor's profits, and in particular, income from government securities and income from bonds or debentures, including premiums and prizes attaching to such securities, bonds or debentures. Penalty charges for late payment shall not be regarded as interest for the purpose of this Article.
5. The provisions of paragraph 1, 2 and 3 shall not apply if the beneficial owner of the interest, being a resident of a Contracting State, carries on business in the other Contracting State in which the interest arises, through a permanent establishment

situated therein, or performs in that other State independent personal services from a fixed base situated therein and the debt-claim in respect of which the interest is paid is effectively connected with such permanent establishment or fixed base. In such case the provisions of Article 7 or Article 14, as the case may be, shall apply.
6. Interest shall be deemed to arise in a Contracting State when the payer is that State itself, a Land, a political subdivision, a local authority or a resident of that State. Where, however, the person paying the interest, whether he is a resident of a Contracting State or not, has in a Contracting State a permanent establishment or a fixed base in connection with which the indebtedness on which the interest is paid was incurred, and such interest is borne by such permanent establishment or fixed base, then such interest shall be deemed to arise in the State in which the permanent establishment or fixed base is situated.
7. Where, by reason of a special relationship between the payer and the beneficial owner or between both of them and some other person, the amount of the interest, having regard to the debt-claim for which it is paid, exceeds the amount which would have been agreed upon by the payer and the beneficial owner in the absence of such relationship, the provisions of this Article shall apply only to the last-mentioned amount. In such case, the excess part of payments shall remain taxable according to the laws of each Contracting State, due regard being had to the other provisions of this Agreement.

Article 12 – Royalties and Fees for Technical Services

1. Royalties and fees for technical services arising in a Contracting State and paid to a resident of the other Contracting State may be taxed in the Contracting State in which they arise and according to the laws of that State, but if the recipient is the beneficial owner of the royalties or of the fees for technical services the tax so charged shall not exceed:
   (a) In the case of royalties 10 per cent of the gross amount of such royalties,
   (b) In the case of fees for technical services 7.5 per cent of the gross amount of such fees.
2. The term "royalties" as used in this Article means payments of any kind received as a consideration for the use of, or the right to use, any copyright of literary, artistic or scientific work (including cinematographic films and films or tapes for radio or television broadcasting), any patent, trade mark, design or model, plan, secret formula or process, or for the use of, or the right to use, industrial, commercial, or scientific equipment, or for information concerning industrial, commercial or scientific experience.
3. The term "fees for technical services" as used in this Article means payments of any kind to any person, other than payments to an employee of the person making the payments, in consideration for any services of a managerial, technical or consultancy nature rendered in the Contracting State of which the payer is a residence.
4. The provisions of paragraph 1 of this Article shall not apply if the beneficial owner of the royalties or fees for technical services, being a resident of a Contracting State, carries on business in the other Contracting State in which the royalties or fees for technical services arise through a permanent establishment situated therein, or performs in that other State independent personal services from a fixed base situated therein, and the right, property or contract in respect of which the royalties or fees for technical services are paid is effectively connected with such permanent establishment or fixed base. In such case, the provisions of Article 7 or Article 14, as the case may be, shall apply.
5. Royalties and fees for technical services shall be deemed to arise in a Contracting State when the payer is that State itself, a Land, a political subdivision, a local authority or a resident of that State. Where, however, the person paying the royalties or fees for

technical services, whether he is a resident of a Contracting State or not, has in a Contracting State a permanent establishment or a fixed base in connection with which the obligation to make the payment was incurred, and the payments are borne by that permanent establishment or fixed base, then the royalties or fees for technical services shall be deemed to arise in the Contracting State in which the permanent establishment or fixed base is situated.
6. Where, by reason of a special relationship between the payer and the beneficial owner of between both of them and some other person, the amount of the royalties or fees for technical paid exceeds, for whatever reason, the amount which would have been agreed upon by the payer and the beneficial owner in the absence of such relationship, the provisions of this Article shall apply only to the least-mentioned amount. In such case, the excess part of the payments shall remain taxable according to the laws of each Contracting State, due regard being had to the other provisions of this Agreement.

Article 13 – Gains from the Alienation of Property

1. Gains derived by a resident of a Contracting State from the alienation of immovable property referred to in Article 6 and situated in the other Contracting State may be taxed in that other State.
2. Gains from the alienation of movable property forming part of the business property of a permanent establishment which an enterprise of a Contracting State has in the other Contracting State or of movable property pertaining to a fixed base available to a resident of a Contracting State in the other Contracting State for the purpose of performing independent personal services, including such gains from the alienation of such a permanent establishment (alone or with the whole enterprise) or of such fixed base, may be taxed in that other State.
3. Gains from the alienation of ships or aircraft operated in international traffic or movable property pertaining to the operation of such ships or aircraft shall be taxable only tin the Contracting State in which the place of effective management of the enterprise is situated.
4. Gains from the alienation of shares of the capital stock of a company the property of which consists directly or indirectly principally of immovable property situated in a Contracting State may be taxed in that State.
5. Gains from the alienation of any property other than that referred to in paragraphs 1, 2, 3 and 4 shall be taxable only in the State of which the alienator is a resident.

Article 14 – Independent Personal Services

1. Income derived by a resident of a Contracting State in respect of professional services or other activities of an independent character shall be taxable only in that State unless he has a fixed base regularly available to him in the other Contracting State for the purpose of performing his activities. If he has such a fixed base, the income may be taxed in the other State but only so much of it as is attributable to that fixed base.
2. The term "professional services" includes especially independent scientific, literary, artistic, educational or teaching activities as well as the independent activities of physicians, lawyers, engineers, architects, dentists and accountants.

Article 15 – Dependent Personal Services

1. Subject to the provisions of Article 16, 18 and 19, salaries, wages and other similar remuneration derived by a resident of a Contracting State in respect of an employment shall be taxable only in that State unless the employment is exercised in the other

Contracting State. If the employment is so exercised, such remuneration as is derived therefrom may be taxed in that other State.
2. Notwithstanding the provisions of paragraph 1, remuneration derived by a resident of a Contracting State in respect of an employment exercised in the other Contracting State shall be taxable only in the first-mentioned State if:

   (a) The recipient is present in the other State for a period or periods not exceeding in the aggregate 183 days in the calendar year concerned, and
   (b) The remuneration is paid by, or on behalf of, an employer who is not a resident of the other State, and
   (c) The remuneration is not borne by a permanent establishment or a fixed base, which the employer has in the other State.

3. Notwithstanding the preceding provisions of this Article, remuneration derived in respect of an employment exercised aboard a ship or aircraft operated in international traffic by an enterprise of a Contracting State shall be taxable only in that State.

Article 16 – Directors' Fees

Directors' fees and other similar payments derived by a resident of a Contracting State in his capacity as a member of the board of directors of a company which is a resident of the other Contracting State may be taxed in that other State.

Article 17 – Artistes and Athletes

1. Notwithstanding the provisions of Article 14 and 15, income derived by a resident of a Contracting State as an entertainer, such as a theatre, motion picture, radio or television artiste, or a musician, or as an athlete, from his personal activities as such exercised in the other Contracting State, may be taxed in that other State.
2. Where income in respect of personal activities exercised by an entertainer or an athlete in his capacity as such accrues not to the entertainer or athlete himself but to another person, the income may, notwithstanding the provisions of Article 7, 14 and 15, be taxed in the Contracting State in which the activities of the entertainer or athlete are exercised.
3. Notwithstanding the provisions of paragraph 1 and 2 of the Article, income derived in respect of activities referred to in paragraph 1 of this Article within the framework of any cultural or sports exchange programmed agreed to by both Contracting States shall be exempted from tax in the Contracting State in which these activities are exercised.

Article 18 – Pensions

Subject to the provisions of paragraph 2 of Article 19, pensions and other similar remuneration paid to a resident of a Contracting State in consideration of past employment shall be taxable only in that State.

Article 19 – Government Service

1. (a) Remuneration other than a pension, paid by a Contracting State, a Land, a political subdivision or a local authority thereof to an individual in respect of services rendered to that State, Land, subdivision or authority shall be taxable only in that State.
   (b) However, such remuneration shall be taxable only in the other Contracting State, if the services are rendered in that State and the individual is a resident of that State who:

(i) is a national of that State; or
(ii) did not become a resident of that State solely for the purpose of rendering the services.

2. (a) Any pension paid by a Contracting State, a Land, a political subdivision or a local authority thereof to an individual in respect of services rendered to that State, Land, subdivision or authority shall be taxable only in that State.
   (b) However, such pension shall be taxable only in the other Contracting State if the individual is a resident of, and a national of, that other State.
3. The provisions of Article 15, 16 and 18 shall apply to remuneration and pensions in respect of services rendered in connection with a business carried on by a Contracting State, a Land, a political subdivision or a local authority thereof.
4. The provisions of paragraph 1 shall likewise apply in respect of remuneration paid, under a development assistance programme of a Contracting State, a Land, a political subdivision or a local authority thereof, out of funds exclusively supplied by that State, Land, political subdivision or local authority, to a specialist or volunteer seconded to the other Contracting State with the consent of that other State.

Article 20 – Teachers, Students and Trainees

1. An individual who visit a Contracting State at the invitation of that State or of a university, college, school, museum or other cultural institution of that State or under an official programme of cultural exchange for a period not exceeding two years solely for the purpose of teaching, giving lectures or carrying out research at such institution and who is, or was immediately before that visit, a resident of the other Contracting State shall be exempted from tax in the first-mentioned State on his remuneration for such activity, provided that such remuneration is derived by him from outside that State.
2. Payments which a student or business apprentice who is or was immediately before visiting a Contracting State a resident of the other Contracting State and who is present in the first-mentioned State solely for the purpose of his education or training receives for the purpose of his maintenance, education or training shall not be taxed in that State, provided that such payments arise from sources outside that State.
3. Notwithstanding the provisions of Article 15, remuneration for services rendered by a student or a business apprentice (including in the case of the Federal Republic of Germany a "Volontär" or a "Praktikant") in a Contracting State shall not be taxed in that State, provided that such services are in connection with his studies or training, and the total amount of such remuneration does not exceed DM 9,000 or the equivalent in Vietnamese currency in a calendar year.

Article 21 – Other Income

1. Items of income of a resident of a Contracting State, wherever arising, not dealt with in the foregoing Articles of this Agreement shall be taxable only in that State.
2. The provisions of paragraph 1 shall not apply to income, other than income from immovable property as defined in paragraph 2 of Article 6, if the recipient of such income, being a resident of a Contracting State, carries on business in the other Contracting State through a permanent establishment situated therein, or performs in that other State independent personal services from a fixed base situated therein, and the right or property in respect of which the income is paid is effectively connected with such permanent establishment or fixed base. In such case the provisions of Article 7 or Article 14, as the case may be, shall apply.

Article 22 – Capital

1. Capital represented by immovable property referred to in Article 6, owned by a resident of a Contracting State and situated in the other Contracting State, may be taxed in that other State.
2. Capital represented by movable property forming part of the business property of a permanent establishment which an enterprise of a Contracting State has in the other Contracting State or by movable property pertaining to a fixed base available to a resident of a Contracting State in the other Contracting State for the purpose of performing independent personal services, may be taxed in that other State.
3. Capital represented by ships and aircraft operated in international traffic and by movable property pertaining to the operation of such ships or aircraft, shall be taxable only in the Contracting State in which the place of effective management of the enterprise is situated.
4. All other elements of capital of a resident of a Contracting State shall be taxable only in that State.

Article 23 – Methods for Elimination of Double Taxation

1. In Vietnam the double taxation shall be eliminated as follows:
   Where a resident of Vietnam derives income or owns elements of capital, which, in accordance with the provisions of this Agreement, may be taxed in the Federal Republic of Germany, Vietnam shall allow:

   (a) As a deduction from the tax on the income of that resident an amount equal to the income tax paid in the Federal Republic of Germany;
   (b) As a deduction from the tax on the capital of that resident, an amount equal to the capital tax paid in the Federal Republic of Germany.

   Such deduction in either case shall not, however, exceed that part of Vietnamese income tax or capital tax, as computed before the deduction is given, on the income or the capital, in accordance with the taxation laws and regulations of Vietnam.
2. Tax shall be determined in the case of a resident of the Federal Republic of Germany as follows:

   (a) Unless foreign tax credit is to be allowed under sub-paragraph (b), there shall be exempted from German tax any item of income arising in Vietnam and any item of capital situated within Vietnam which, according to this Agreement, may be taxed in Vietnam. The Federal Republic of Germany, however, retains the right to take into account in the determination of its rate of tax the items of income and capital so exempted.
   (b) Subject to the provisions of German tax law regarding credit for foreign tax, there shall be allowed as a credit against German income, corporation and capital tax payable in the respect of the following items of income arising in Vietnam and the items of capital situated therein the Vietnamese tax paid under the laws of Vietnam and in accordance with this Agreement on:

   aa) dividends not dealt with in sub-paragraph (a);
   bb) interest;
   cc) royalties;
   dd) fees for technical services;
   ee) income in the meaning of Article 13 paragraph 4;
   ff) directors' fees;
   gg) income of artistes and athletes.

(c) For the purpose of credit referred to in sub-paragraph (b) the Vietnamese tax shall, irrespective of the amount of tax actually paid, be deemed to be, in the case of

   aa) dividends not mentioned in sub-paragraph (a), 10 per cent of the gross amount of the dividends;
   bb) interest, 10 per cent of the gross amount of the interest but 5 per cent as long as paragraph 5 of the Protocol is applicable; and
   cc) royalties, 10 per cent of the gross amount of the royalties;

   provided that such dividends, interest or royalties are paid before the end of the tenth year after the entry into force of this Agreement.

(d) Notwithstanding the provisions of sub-paragraph (a) items of income dealt with in Article 7 and Article 10 and gains derived from the alienation of the business property of a permanent establishment as well as the items of capital underlying such income shall be exempted from German tax only if the resident of the Federal Republic of Germany can prove that the receipts of the permanent establishment or company are derived exclusively or almost exclusively from active operations.
In the case of items of income dealt with in Article 10 and the items of capital underlying such income the exemption shall apply even when the dividends are derived from holdings in other companies being residents of Vietnam which carry on active operations and in which the company which last made a distribution has a holding of more than 25 per cent.
Active operations are the following: producing or selling goods or merchandise, giving technical advice or rendering engineering services, or doing banking or insurance business, within Vietnam.
If this is not proved, only the credit procedure as per sub-paragraph (b) shall apply, except for the fictitious credit as per sub-paragraph (c).

Article 24 – Non-Discrimination

1. Nationals of a Contracting State shall not be subjected in the other Contracting State to any taxation or any requirement connected therewith which is other or more burdensome than the taxation and connected requirements to which nationals of that other State in the same circumstances are or may be subjected. This provision shall, notwithstanding the provisions of Article 1, also apply to persons who are not residents of one or both of the Contracting States.
2. The taxation on a permanent establishment which an enterprise of a Contracting State has in the other Contracting State shall not be less favorably levied in that other State than the taxation levied on enterprise of that other State carrying on the same activities, provided that this paragraph shall not prevent that other State from imposing on the profits attributable to a permanent establishment in that State of a company which is a resident of the first-mentioned State further tax not exceeding 10 per cent on such profits as far as they are remitted from the permanent establishment to the head office. Moreover, this paragraph shall not apply to the taxation of permanent establishments in Vietnam of enterprises in respect of oil exploration or production activities or in respect of activities, which in the case of Vietnamese enterprises are subject to tax under the Law on Agriculture Land Using Tax.
3. Nothing contained in this Article shall be construed as obliging either Contracting State to grant to individuals not resident in that State any of the personal allowances, reliefs and reductions for tax purposes, which are granted to individuals so resident.

4. Except where the provisions of Article 9, paragraph 7 of Article 11, or paragraph 6 of Article 12 apply, interest, royalties and other disbursements paid by an enterprise of a Contracting State to a resident of the other Contracting State shall, for the purpose of determining the taxable profits of such enterprise, be deductible under the same conditions as if they had been paid to a resident of the first-mentioned State. Similarly, any debts of an enterprise of a Contracting State to a resident of the other Contracting State shall, for the purpose of determining the taxable capital of such enterprise, be deductible under the same conditions as if they had been contracted to a resident of the first-mentioned State.
5. Enterprises of a Contracting State, the capital of which is a wholly or partly owned or controlled, directly or indirectly, by one or more residents of the other Contracting State, shall not be subjected in the first-mentioned State to any taxation or any requirement connected therewith which is other or more burdensome than the taxation and connected requirements to which other similar enterprises of the first-mentioned State are or may be subjected.

Article 25 – Mutual Agreement Procedure

1. Where a person who is a resident of a Contracting State considers that the actions of the competent authority of one or both of the Contracting States result or will result for him in taxation not in accordance with the provisions of this Agreement, he may, irrespective of the remedies provided by the domestic law of those States, present his case to the competent authority of the Contracting State of which the person is a resident. The case must be presented within three years from the first notification of the action resulting in taxation not in accordance with the provisions of the Agreement.
2. The competent authority shall endeavor, if the objection appears to it to be justified and if it is not itself able to arrive at a satisfactory solution, to resolve the case by mutual agreement with the competent authority of the other Contracting State, with a view to the avoidance of taxation, which is not in accordance with the Agreement. Any agreement reached shall be implemented notwithstanding any time limits in the domestic laws of the Contracting States.
3. The competent authorities of the Contracting States shall jointly endeavor to resolve any difficulties or doubts arising as to the interpretation or application of the Agreement. They may also consult together for the elimination of double taxation in cases not provided for in the Agreement.
4. If the taxation of income in a Contracting State is effected by way of withholding tax at source, and if this taxation is limited by the provisions of this Agreement, the application of this tax reduction or exemption shall be governed by the national law of that State in conjunction with the procedures agreed upon for this purpose between the competent authorities of the two Contracting States.
5. The competent authorities of the Contracting States may communicate with each other directly for the purpose of reaching an agreement in the sense of the preceding paragraphs.

Article 26 – Exchange of Information

1. The competent authorities of the Contracting States shall exchange such information as is necessary for carrying out the provisions of this Agreement. Any information received by a Contracting State shall be treated as secret in the same manner as information obtained under the domestic laws of that State and shall be disclosed only to persons or authorities (including courts and administrative bodies) involved in the assessment or collection of, the enforcement or prosecution in respect of, or the determination of appeals in relation to, the taxes covered by the Agreement. Such persons or authorities

shall use the information only for such purposes. They may disclose the information in public court proceedings or in judicial decisions.
2. In no case shall the provisions of paragraph 1 be construed so as to impose on a Contracting State the obligation:

   (a) To carry out administrative measures at variance with the laws and administrative practice of that or of the other Contracting State;
   (b) To supply information which is not obtained under the laws or in the normal course of the administration of that or of the other Contracting State;
   (c) To supply information, which would disclose any trade, business, industrial, commercial or professional secret or trade process, or information, the disclosure of which would be contrary to public policy (ordre public).

Article 27 – Diplomatic Agents and Consular Officers

Nothing in this Agreement shall affect the fiscal privileges of members of a diplomatic mission, a consular post or an international organization under the general rules of international law or under the provisions of special agreements.

Article 28 – Entry into Force

The Governments of the Contracting States shall notify each other of the completion of the procedures required by its law for the entry into force of this Agreement. This Agreement shall enter into force one month after receipt of the latter of these notifications and shall thereupon have effect:

(a) In the case of taxes withheld at source on dividends, interest, royalties and fees for technical services, in respect of amounts paid on or after the first day of January of the calendar year next following that in which the Agreement enters into force;
(b) In the case of other taxes, in respect of taxes levied for periods beginning on or after the first day of January of the calendar year next following that in which the Agreement enters into force.

Article 29 – Termination

This Agreement shall continue in effect indefinitely but either of the Contracting States may, on or before the thirtieth day of June in any calendar year beginning after the expiration of a period of five years from the date of its entry into force, give the other Contracting State, through diplomatic channels, written notice of termination and, in such event, the Agreement shall cease to have effect:

(a) In the case of taxes withheld at source on dividends, interest, royalties and fees for technical services, in respect of amounts paid on or after the first day of January of the calendar year next following that in which notice of termination is given;
(b) In the case of other taxes, in respect of taxes levied for periods beginning on or after the first day of January of the calendar year next following that in which notice of termination is given.

Done at Hanoi on 16 November 1995 in two originals, each in the German, Vietnamese and English languages, all three texts being authentic. In case of divergent interpretation of the German and the Vietnamese texts, the English text shall prevail.

Protocol

The Socialist Republic of Vietnam and the Federal Republic of Germany have agreed at the signing at Hanoi on 16 November 1995 of the Agreement between the two States for the avoidance of double taxation with respect to taxes on income and on capital upon the following provisions, which shall form an integral part of the said Agreement.

1. **With reference to Article 2**
   It is understood that the profit tax as mentioned in Article 2, paragraph 3, sub-paragraph (a), includes the foreign petroleum sub-contractor tax and the foreign contractor tax.

2. **With reference to Article 7**

   (a) In the Contracting State in which the permanent establishment is situated, no profits shall be attributed to a building site or construction or installation project except those, which are result of such activities themselves. Profits derived from the supply of machinery or equipments connected with such activities and effected by the principal permanent establishment or any other permanent establishment of the enterprise or by a third party shall not be attributed to the building site or construction or installation project.

   (b) Income derived from design, planning, engineering or research or from technical services which a resident of a Contracting State performs in that State and which are connected with a permanent establishment in the other Contracting State shall not be attributed to that permanent establishment.

   (c) In the absence of appropriate accounting or other data permitting the determination of the profits to be attributed to a permanent establishment, the tax may be assessed in the Contracting State in which the permanent establishment is situated in accordance with the laws of the Sate, in particular regard being had to the normal profits of similar enterprises engaged in the same or similar conditions, provided that, on the basis of the available information, the determination of the profits of the permanent establishment is consistent with the principles stated in this Article.

3. **With reference to Article 10**

   (a) The limitation provided in paragraph 2 of Article 10 includes in the case of Vietnam the profit remittance tax.

   (b) For the purpose of taxation in the Federal Republic of Germany the term "dividends" includes income derived by a sleeping partner ("stiller Gesellschafter") from his participation as such and distributions on certificates of an investment fund or investment trust.

4. **With reference to Article 10 and Article 11**
   Notwithstanding the provisions of these Articles, dividends and interest may be taxed in the contracting State in which they arise, and according to the law of that State, if they

   (a) Are derived from rights or debt-claims carrying a right to participate in profits (including income derived by a sleeping partner from his participation as such, from a "partiarisches Darlehen" and from "Gewinnobligationen" with the meaning of the tax law of the Federal Republic of Germany), and

   (b) Under the condition that they are deductible in the determination of profits of the debtor of such income.

5. **With reference to Article 11**
   Notwithstanding the provisions of paragraph 2 of Article 11, as long as, according to the German tax law, the Federal Republic of Germany does not levy a tax at source on interest paid to a resident of Vietnam, the percentage provided for in this paragraph shall be reduced to 5 per cent of the gross amount of the interest.
6. **With reference to Article 23**

    (a) Where a company being a resident of the Federal Republic of Germany distributes income derived from sources within Vietnam, paragraph 2 of Article 23 shall not preclude the compensatory imposition of corporation tax on such distributions in accordance with the provisions of German tax law.
    (b) The Federal Republic of Germany shall avoid double taxation by a tax credit as provided for in paragraph 2 sub-paragraph (b) of Article 23, and not by a tax exemption under paragraph 2 sub-paragraph (a) of Article 23,

    aa) if in the Contracting States income is placed under different provisions of the Agreement or attributed to different persons [other than under Article 9 (Associated Enterprises)] and this conflict cannot be settled by procedure pursuant to Article 25 and

    i) if as a result of such placement or attribution the relevant income would be subject to double taxation; or
    ii) if as a result of such placement or attribution the relevant income would remain untaxed or be subject only to inappropriately reduced taxation in Vietnam and would (but for the application of this paragraph) remain exempt from tax in the Federal Republic of Germany; or

    bb) if the Federal Republic of Germany has, after due consultation and subject to the limitations of its internal law, notified Vietnam through diplomatic channels of other items of income to which it intends to apply this paragraph in order to prevent the exemption of income from taxation in both Contracting States or other arrangements for the improper use of the Agreement.

    In the case of notification under sub-paragraph (bb) Vietnam may, subject to notification through diplomatic channels, characterize such income under the Agreement consistently with the characterization of that income by the Federal Republic of Germany. A notification made under this paragraph shall have effect only from the first day of the calendar year following the year in which it was transmitted and any legal prerequisites under the domestic law of the notifying State for giving it effect have been fulfilled.

7. **With reference to Article 24**
   If Vietnam has signed an Agreement for avoidance of double taxation with a member country of the OECD which contains a lower rate of the tax on remitted profits than that provided for in paragraph 2 of Article 24 then this lower rate shall also apply to residents of the Federal Republic of Germany.
8. **With reference to Article 26**
   If personal data is exchanged under this Article, the following additional provisions shall apply subject to the domestic laws of each Contracting State:

   (a) The data supplying Contracting States shall be responsible for the accuracy of the data they supply. If it emerges that inaccurate data or data, which should not have been supplied, have been communicated, the receiving State shall be notified of this without delay. That State shall be obliged to correct or destroy said data.
   (b) The Contracting States shall be obliged to keep official records of the transmission and receipt of personal data.

(c) The Contracting States shall be obliged to take effective measures to protect the personal data communicated against unauthorized access, unauthorized alteration and unauthorized disclosure.
(d) Upon application the person concerned shall be informed of the information stored about him and of the use planned to be made of it. There shall be no obligation to give this information if on balance it appears that the public interest in withholding it outweighs the interest of the person concerned in receiving it. Apart from that, the right of the person concerned to be informed of the data stored about him shall be a matter of the domestic law of the Contracting State in whose sovereign territory the application for the information is made.

Done at Hanoi on 16 November 1995 in two originals, each in the German, Vietnamese and English languages, all three texts being authentic. In case of divergent interpretation of the German and the Vietnamese texts, the English text shall prevail.

Bibliography

AA VV (2010) Global corporate tax handbook. IBFD, Amsterdam
Baker P (2001) Double taxation conventions: a manual on the OECD model tax convention on income and on capital, 3rd edn. Sweet & Maxwell, London
Cheng B (1953) General principles of law, as applied by international courts and tribunals. Stevens, London [reprinted (2006) Cambridge University Press, Cambridge, New York]
Consulate General of Canada in Ho Chi Minh City (2011) An investment guide to Vietnam. Government of Canada, Ho Chi Minh City
Cullen R, Van der Wolk J, Xu Y (2011) Green taxation in East Asia. Edward Elgar Pub, Cheltenham Glos
Delegation of the European Union to Vietnam (n.d.) Political and economic ties. European Union. http://eeas.europa.eu/delegations/vietnam/eu_vietnam/political_relations/index_en.htm. Accessed 5 Feb 2013
Doernberg RL (2009) International taxation in a Nutshell. Thomson/West, St. Paul
European Commission (2012) EU and Vietnam launch negotiations for a comprehensive Free Trade Agreement. Europa Press Releases RAPID. http://europa.eu/rapid/press-release_IP-12-689_en.htm. Accessed 1 Feb 2013
Feinschreiber R, Kent M (2012) Asia-Pacific transfer pricing handbook. Wiley, Singapore
Government of Canada (2012) Canada–Vietnam relations. Canada International (Government of Canada). http://www.canadainternational.gc.ca/vietnam/bilateral_relations_bilaterales/index.aspx?lang=eng&menu_id=7&view=d. Accessed 17 Jan 2013
Government of Singapore (n.d.) Singapore Vietnam relations. Embassy of Republic of Singapore, Hanoi. http://www.mfa.gov.sg/content/mfa/overseasmission/hanoi/foreign_policy.html. Accessed 21 Jan 2013
Gustafson CH, Peroni RJ, Pugh RC (2010) Taxation of international transactions: materials texts and problems. West Group, Eagan
Hiep LH (2011) Vietnam: under the weight of China. East Asia Forum. http://www.eastasiaforum.org/2011/08/27/vietnam-under-the-weight-of-china/. Accessed 22 Jan 2012
Holmes K (2007) International tax policy and double tax treaties: an introduction to principles and application. IBFD, Amsterdam
Indian Business Chamber in Vietnam (2012) India–Vietnam economic and commercial relations. Indian Business Chamber in Vietnam: http://www.incham.vn/resource-center/india-vietnam-economic-and-commercial-relations.html. Accessed 18 Jan 2013
International Monetary Fund (2013) World economic outlook databases. IMF, Vietnam. http://www.imf.org/external/country/VNM/index.htm
Isenbergh J (2006) International taxation: U.S. taxation of foreign persons and foreign income, 4th edn. CCH, Chicago
Isenbergh J (2010) International taxation. Foundation Press/Thomson Reuters, New York

Levey MM, Wrappe SC (2007) Transfer pricing: rules, compliance and controversy, 2nd edn. CCH, Chicago

Manyin ME (2013) U.S.–Vietnam relations in 2013: current issues and implications for U.S. policy. Congressional Research Service, Washington

McIntyre M (2002) International tax primer. Kluwer Law International, The Hague

Miller A, Oats L (2012) Principles of international taxation. Bloomsbury Professional, Haywards Heath

Ministry of External Affairs, India (n.d.) http://meaindia.nic.in/meaxpsite/foreignrelation/vietnam.pdf. Accessed 18 Jan 2013

Ministry of Foreign Affairs, Singapore (n.d.) Bilateral relations. Vietnam. http://www.mfa.gov.sg/content/mfa/countries_and_region/southeast_asia/vietnam.html. Accessed 21 Jan 2013

Ministry of Trade and Industry, Singapore (2011) Singapore–Vietnam economic ties strengthening as bilateral business linkages grow. The Treasury, Singapore

Park J-W (2012) Korea and Vietnam: the bilateral relations. Keynote speech at the 4th annual conference on Korea and Vietnam: the national experiences and foreign policies of middle powers: http://iis-db.stanford.edu/evnts/6954/Transcipt_Luncheon_Speech_WEB.pdf. Accessed 21 Jan 2013

Postlewaite PF, Hoffer S (2010) International taxation: corporate and individual, 5th edn. Carolina Academic Press, Durham

Reynolds T, Flores AA (2000) Foreign law guide: current sources of codes and basic legislation in jurisdictions of the world. University of California, Berkeley

The World Bank (2013) World development indicators. http://data.worldbank.org/country/vietnam

U.S. and Foreign Commercial Service and U.S. Department of State (2012) Doing business in Vietnam: 2012 country commercial guide for companies. United States of America Department of Commerce, Washington

Vietnam Chamber of Commerce and Industry (2011) Vietnam–Singapore investment cooperation: on steady rise. Investment: http://vccinews.com/news_detail.asp?news_id=24877. Retrieved 21 Jan 2013

Vietnam Ministry of Foreign Affairs (2007a) Vietnam–Japan relations. Embassy of the Socialist Republic of Vietnam in Japan: http://www.vietnamembassy-japan.org/en/nr070521165956/news_object_view?newsPath=/vnemb.vn/cn_vakv/ca_tbd/nr040818111106/ns070907111923. Accessed 21 Jan 2013

Vietnam Ministry of Foreign Affairs (2007b) Vietnam–Singapore relations. Embassy of the Socialist Republic of Vietnam in the Republic of Singapore: http://www.vietnamembassy-singapore.org/en/nr070521165956/news_object_view?newsPath=/vnemb.vn/cn_vakv/ca_tbd/nr040819104347/ns050131133257. Accessed 21 Jan 2013

Vietnam Ministry of Foreign Affairs (2012) Joint statement of the second Thailand–Viet Nam Joint Cabinet Retreat. Embassy of Vietnam in Thailand. http://biengioilanhtho.gov.vn/eng/jointstatementofthesecondthailand-nd-0d2a7255.aspx. Accessed 29 Jan 2013

Vietnam Trade Promotion Agency, Ministry of Industry and Trade (VIETRADE) (2012, May 23) Japanese market – trade opportunities for Vietnamese companies. VIETRADE, Hanoi

VietnamNet (2012) Vietnam–EU relations strengthened. VietnamNet bridge. http://english.vietnamnet.vn/fms/government/51586/vietnam-eu-relations-strengthened.html. Retrieved 5 Feb 2013

Ward D (2005) The interpretation of income tax treaties with particular reference to the commentaries on the OECD model. International Fiscal Association (Canadian Branch)/International Bureau of Fiscal Documentation, Kingston/Amsterdam

Zhang N (2012) Research on trading relations between China and Vietnam. J Eng 1(2):30–35

Printed by Publishers' Graphics LLC
DBT131018.15.15.20